Cakes & Pastries

by
THE EDITORS OF TIME-LIFE BOOKS

TIME-LIFE BOOKS
EUROPEAN EDITOR: Kit van Tulleken
Assistant European Editor: Gillian Moore
Design Director: Ed Skyner
Photography Director: Pamela Marke
Chief of Research: Vanessa Kramer
Chief Sub-Editor: Ilse Gray

THE GOOD COOK
Series Editor: Alan Lothian
Series Co-ordinator: Liz Timothy
Head Designer: Rick Bowring

Editorial Staff for *Cakes & Pastries*
Text Editor: Ann Tweedy
Anthology Editor: Markie Benet
Staff Writers: Alexandra Carlier, Jay Ferguson,
Mary Harron, Thom Henvey
Designer: Zaki Elia
Researchers: Ursula Beary, Nora Carey,
Eleanor Lines
Sub-Editors: Katie Lloyd, Sally Rowland
Permissions Researcher: Deborah Litton
Anthology Researcher: Margaret Hall
Design Assistant: Cherry Doyle
Proofreader: Brian Sambrook
Editorial Assistant: Molly Sutherland

EDITORIAL PRODUCTION FOR THE SERIES
Chief: Ellen Brush
Quality Control: Douglas Whitworth
Traffic Co-ordinators: Pat Boag, Helen Whitehorn
Picture Co-ordinator: Philip Garner
Art Department: Julia West
Editorial Department: Debra Dick, Beverley Doe

THE ENCHANTED WORLD
LIBRARY OF NATIONS
HOME REPAIR AND IMPROVEMENT
CLASSICS OF EXPLORATION
PLANET EARTH
PEOPLES OF THE WILD
THE EPIC OF FLIGHT
THE SEAFARERS
WORLD WAR II
THE GOOD COOK
THE TIME-LIFE ENCYCLOPAEDIA OF GARDENING
THE GREAT CITIES
THE OLD WEST
THE WORLD'S WILD PLACES
THE EMERGENCE OF MAN
LIFE LIBRARY OF PHOTOGRAPHY
TIME-LIFE LIBRARY OF ART
GREAT AGES OF MAN
LIFE SCIENCE LIBRARY
LIFE NATURE LIBRARY
THE TIME-LIFE BOOK OF BOATING
TECHNIQUES OF PHOTOGRAPHY
LIFE AT WAR
LIFE GOES TO THE MOVIES
BEST OF LIFE
LIFE IN SPACE

Cover: Fragile chocolate shavings and a piped garland of
sweetened whipped cream adorn a sumptuous three-tier
cocoa sponge cake (*page 28*). Hidden from view until the
cake is cut into wedges, the layers are sandwiched together
with poached, whole cherries and more whipped cream.

THE CHIEF CONSULTANT:
Richard Olney, an American, has lived and worked since 1951
in France, where he is a highly regarded authority on food and
wine. He is the author of *The French Menu Cookbook* and the
award-winning *Simple French Food,* and has contributed to
numerous gastronomic magazines in France and the United
States, including the influential journals *Cuisine et Vins de
France* and *La Revue du Vin de France.* He has directed
cooking courses in France and the United States and is a
member of several distinguished gastronomic and oenologi-
cal societies, including *L'Académie Internationale du Vin, La
Confrérie des Chevaliers du Tastevin* and *La Commanderie
du Bontemps de Médoc et des Graves.*

SPECIAL CONSULTANTS:
Pat Alburey is largely responsible for the step-by-step photographic sequences in this
volume. Her experience includes preparing foods for photography and teaching
cookery.
Alice Wooledge Salmon is a chef who has worked at both *Ma Cuisine* Restaurant and
The Connaught Hotel in London. She is a frequent contributor to many publications,
including the Journal of the International Wine and Food Society.

THE PHOTOGRAPHERS:
John Elliott, based in London, trained at the Regent Street Polytechnic. He has extensive
experience in photographing a wide range of subjects for advertising and magazine
assignments, as well as in his special interest, food photography.
Bob Komar is a Londoner who trained at both the Hornsey and Manchester Schools of
Art. He specializes in food photography and in portraiture.

THE INTERNATIONAL CONSULTANTS:
Great Britain: *Jane Grigson* was born in Gloucester and brought up in the north of
England. She is a graduate of Cambridge University. Her first book on food,
Charcuterie and French Pork Cookery, was published in 1967; since then, she has
published a number of cookery books, including *Good Things, English Food* and *Jane
Grigson's Fruit Book.* She became cookery correspondent for the colour magazine of
the London *Observer* in 1968. *Alan Davidson* is the author of *Fish and Fish Dishes of
Laos, Mediterranean Seafood* and *North Atlantic Seafood.* He is the founder of
Prospect Books, which specializes in scholarly publications on food and cookery, and
of the Oxford Symposia on food history. **France:** *Michel Lemonnier* was born in
Normandy. He began contributing to the magazine *Cuisine et Vins de France* in 1960,
and also writes for several other important French food and wine periodicals. The co-
founder and vice-president of the society *Les Amitiés Gastronomiques Internationales,*
he is a frequent lecturer on wine and a member of most of the vinicultural confraternities
and academies in France. **Germany:** *Jochen Kuchenbecker* trained as a chef, but
worked for 10 years as a food photographer in many European countries before
opening his own restaurant in Hamburg. *Anne Brakemeier,* who also lives in Hamburg,
has published articles on food and cooking in many German periodicals. She is the co-
author of three cookery books. **Italy:** *Massimo Alberini* divides his time between Milan
and Venice. He is a well-known food writer and journalist, with a particular interest in culinary history. Among his 18 books are *4000 Anni a Tavola, 100 Ricette Storiche* and *La
Tavola all'Italiana.* **The Netherlands:** *Hugh Jans,* a resident of Amsterdam, has been
translating cookery books and articles for more than 25 years. He has published
several books of his own, including *Bistro Koken, Koken in een Kasserol* and *Vrij
Nederlands Kookboek,* and his recipes are published in many Dutch magazines. **The
United States:** *Carol Cutler,* a resident of Washington, DC, is the author of *Haute
Cuisine for Your Heart's Delight* and the award-winning *The Six-Minute Soufflé and
Other Culinary Delights. Julie Dannenbaum* has directed a cooking school in
Philadelphia, Pa., for many years and is the author of two cookbooks and numerous
magazine articles. The late *José Wilson* was food editor of *House and Garden*
magazine for 15 years, and wrote many books on food and interior decoration.

Valuable help was given in the preparation of this volume by the following members of
TIME-LIFE Books: *Maria Vincenza Aloisi, Joséphine du Brusle* (Paris); *Janny Hovinga*
(Amsterdam); *Elisabeth Kraemer* (Bonn); *Ann Natanson* (Rome); *Bona Schmid*
(Milan).

CONTENTS

The Essence of Celebration

Cakes and pastries are to be enjoyed at any hour, whether outside the limits of a meal or as a graceful ending to a menu. At parties and celebrations, they are anticipated delights. At other times, they themselves create the occasion. Served with coffee or tea, a slice of gingerbread or pound cake or a tempting array of rich, cream and fruit-filled cakes and pastries breaks the day deliciously, and there are few better conclusions to a dinner than a freshly baked apple pie made from fruit spiced with cinnamon and nutmeg and pastry enriched with eggs and butter (*opposite*).

Cakes and pastries are based on mere flour, but cooks for centuries have been inspired by special events—a religious ceremony, a birth, an anniversary, a harvest festival or even a special market day—to transform that humble component into something unusual and celebratory. In the words of Urbain Dubois, a great Parisian chef of the 19th century, cake and pastry-making is a "prestigious science filled with memories and traditions". No shop-bought product can give you the satisfaction that a home-baked cake or pastry brings; ready-prepared mixtures may save a little time, but their dehydrated and artificially flavoured ingredients produce dull—if predictable—results.

This book addresses the entire field of cake and pastry-making. The following pages give some historical and practical information on the various ingredients—flour, butter and other fats, leavening agents, sugar and other sweeteners, seasonings, spices, nuts, fruit and chocolate. These pages also give advice on using ovens for baking, and on enjoying wines with cakes and pastries. Next, a series of practical demonstrations teaches you how to prepare and use sugar syrup, caramel and glazes, how to prepare chocolate in various ways for flavouring and decorating and how to make creams, butter creams and icings.

The book then presents a series of chapters demonstrating step-by-step the principal methods and techniques used to produce cakes and pastries. The first deals with the lightest and airiest of cakes—the whisked sponges, made by beating air into whole eggs or separated eggs. It also explains basic decoration techniques—with variations—which can be used for many other cakes. The second teaches methods of creaming, rubbing and melting ingredients, to produce cakes as varied as a chocolatey devil's food, a homely vinegar cake and a spicy gingerbread.

The focus then switches to pastry. This section begins with a step-by-step guide to the preparation of pastry doughs—from shortcrust and puff to strudel and choux. It is followed by chapters on pie and tart-making, and on the creation of such classic pastry confections as *mille-feuille* and éclairs. Used in conjunction with the international Anthology of cakes and pastries that constitutes the second half of the book, all these demonstrations will help you to become skilled and versatile in an important branch of cookery that Urbain Dubois characterized "*un art dans l'art*"—an art within the art.

Knowing your ingredients

The beginnings of this special art can be discerned at the misty edge of recorded history. A bas-relief in the tomb of the Egyptian Pharaoh Rameses III at Thebes, carved more than 30 centuries ago, shows a variety of cakes produced by the royal bakery—possibly made from a simple bread dough of coarsely ground wheat grain, enlivened with fruits, honey and spices. Six centuries later, the Greeks baked confections of almonds, poppy seeds, honey and black pepper enclosed in pastry made with flour, honey and sesame seeds—flavourings and methods still used in the Middle East and reflected in the French *pithiviers* (*recipe, page 149*). Aristophanes, a Greek playwright of the fifth century B.C., wrote in *The Knights* of two kinds of honey cake, and in *The Archarnians* of sesame cakes and fruit pastries. Similar ingredients appear in classical Roman recipes which survive in medieval transcriptions of the oldest surviving cookbook—the recipes of Apicius, a Roman epicure of the first century A.D.

In 327 B.C. the armies of Alexander the Great found sugar cane under cultivation in the valley of the Indus in Northern India. They carried it back to the lands of the eastern Mediterranean and, as a result, sugar began to supplement honey as a sweetening ingredient. From there, the use of sugar spread throughout North Africa and into Spain by the seventh century A.D., but was not introduced to Northern Europe until after the Crusaders' 11th-century conquest of Mediterranean lands.

The Crusaders also brought back with them the spices and nuts of the Orient: cinnamon, ginger, nutmeg and cloves, almonds and walnuts. As a result, the cooking of medieval Europe was greatly enriched: the Italians, for example, learned to make marzipan (*page 14*) with crushed almonds and sugar, and various religious orders in Italy, Germany and France became celebrated for their gingerbreads.

Chocolate, brought to Spain in the 16th century by the conquerors of Aztec Mexico, was the next significant contribution to cake and pastry-making. By the early 17th century, knowledge of the preparation of chocolate began to spread from Spain to other European countries brought via itinerant Spanish monks and royal marriages—notably that of Anne, daughter of Philip III of Spain, to King Louis XIII of France.

From the middle of the 18th century, the wealth of Europe encouraged refinement and display—in cookery as well as clothing, architecture and furnishing. Just as elegant round tables replaced the traditional long boards, now felt to be unfashionably crude, so delicate puff pastries such as *mille-feuille* supplanted the heavily spiced meat and fruit pies enjoyed by earlier generations. Cookery increased in status and came to be treated as a formal art. The new diversity of cakes and pastries was probably due to the lighter, finer flour which millers obtained by sieving flour through silk instead of the hemp, coarse linen or woollen cloth they had used formerly.

The unprecedented affluence of the period prompted thousands of pastrycooks in cities throughout Europe to establish shops where they could sell the products they had learned to make. Vienna and Budapest vied with Paris for supremacy in cake and pastry-making; the lasting influence of these cities is still reflected today in such classics as strudel (*page 84*) and *gâteau St. Honoré* (*page 88*).

The nature of flour

Of all the ingredients that may go into a cake or pastry, flour is the least understood. All flours are produced by grinding grains—wheat, rye or maize, for example—to varying degrees of fineness. Before grinding, the grain's white, starchy interior, called the endosperm, is partially or totally separated from its germ and its outer protective layers, known as bran. White wheat flours made from the pure endosperm are the most widely used for cakes and pastries. These flours are milled to a very fine powder that has a tendency to pack in storage but that produces a fine crumb when it is baked.

Wheat produces the best flour for cakes and pastries because it contains complex proteins—absent or of poor quality in other grains—which combine in the presence of water to produce gluten, a substance that helps doughs to rise and set firm. When water is mixed with the wheat flour, the resulting gluten forms an elastic network throughout the mixture. During baking, the water trapped in the strands of gluten turns to steam, while the air which has been incorporated into the dough expands. At the same time, the high heat of the oven also causes the gluten to set into a fairly rigid structure.

Different strains of wheat vary in the amount of gluten their flours yield. General-purpose flours combine soft and hard wheat in a proportion suitable for cakes and pastries as well as for breads. These flours yield 8 to 10 per cent gluten—the proportion needed to make the most tender but resilient pastry and the finest textured cakes. Hard wheats give a stronger flour that produces 11 to 13 per cent gluten. Flour made from hard wheat alone is best suited to bread-making, where greater strength is essential to support the risen dough.

Shortenings and leavenings

Fats, in addition to contributing their flavour to cakes and pastries, tenderize or "shorten" them; when fat is added to flour and water, the particles of fat are distributed throughout the mixture, and prevent the formation of long elastic strands of gluten. Depending on how much fat is added and on how well it is blended with the flour, the baked product can be tender enough to "melt in the mouth". In cake batters, the fat is usually well mixed with the flour to give a fine, even crumb. In some doughs, such as puff pastry, thorough blending of fat and flour is purposely avoided in order to produce paper-thin layers of pastry separated by microscopic layers of fat.

Of the fats used in pastry-making, butter adds the most luxurious flavour. Lard, used on its own or with butter, has a blander taste but is economical and produces a more tender and crumbly result than butter does, a quality admired by many people. In Mediterranean countries, olive oil is sometimes used to make cakes and pastries; it yields a very soft and distinctively flavoured crumb. Other fats suitable for general use include flavourless vegetable shortenings and rendered beef fat—dripping. Until the 19th century, dripping was a commonplace substitute for butter, and dripping is still used today in some versions of traditional British farmhouse cakes.

Any cake batter or pastry dough is an intricate structure of flour, fat and moisture interlaced with myriads of tiny air bubbles. The moisture—in the form of steam—and the air, expanding in the oven's heat, are natural leavening agents. The presence of such leavenings may not always be obvious: anyone can see their effect in an airy puff pastry or a sponge cake, but it is less apparent—although no less important—in contributing lightness to a shortcrust or gingerbread.

In cakes, the chief natural leavening is the air trapped in whole eggs and sugar, or egg whites alone, when they are beaten to many times their original volume. Folded immediately into

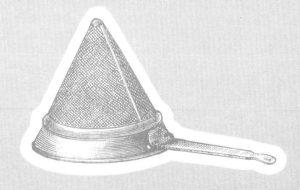

the other ingredients and baked straightaway, these foams produce sponge cakes that seem light enough to float.

When cakes do not contain enough eggs to leaven them, some form of chemical assistance is often necessary. All chemical leavenings produce carbon dioxide, a colourless, odourless gas that expands during the baking in the same way that steam does. A common source of carbon dioxide is the combination of baking soda—sodium bicarbonate—and an acid. When mixed together, a chemical reaction occurs and produces carbon dioxide. The necessary acids are supplied by familiar kitchen staples. Vinegar, soured cream, soured milk or buttermilk all contain enough acid to trigger the carbon dioxide reactions—as demonstrated by the vinegar cake on page 44, for example. Natural acids in honey, treacle or molasses will also react with baking soda; these acids are exploited in the gingerbread demonstrated on page 46. In commercial baking powders, as distinct from baking soda, the acids are present in dehydrated form. When the powder is added to a moist cake batter, the gas is released.

Once you add a chemical leavening, you must work quickly, or the gas will bubble out of the batter before the cake reaches the oven. Some baking powders are more sophisticated; only a fraction of the gas is released on contact with moisture. In these so-called double acting powders, heat is necessary to complete the chemical reaction, and most of the carbon dioxide is not freed until the batter is placed in a preheated oven. Thus the gas is put to work raising the cake, instead of escaping into the kitchen air.

Unfortunately, chemicals can impart a more or less unpleasant aftertaste to a cake. However, if only small quantities of the leavening are used, the spices and other flavouring in the cake mixture will mask these unwanted residues.

Flavourings

Salt, spices, nuts, fruit—fresh and dried—and chocolate are the prime sources of flavour for cakes and pastries. Salt, which brings out other flavours, is as indispensable to sweet things as it is to tart ones. Of the spices, pepper too has savoury connotations; it has appeared in cakes and pastries since ancient times. Pepper often counterbalances blends of the sweet spices—nutmeg, cinnamon and ginger—which are such a feature of so many cakes and pie fillings. Along with cloves, these are the spices of the Far East, brought westward during the Crusades. The spices of the ancient world—coriander, sesame, cumin, anise and saffron—have been largely supplanted, in Europe at least, by these relative newcomers. However, in the Anthology you will find a sampling of recipes that exploit these older flavours.

Nuts making appearances in cake mixtures, in pastries, and as decorations, provide some fat in the form of aromatic oils, and moisture as well as flavour. Walnuts and hazelnuts are important, but almonds are by far the most ubiquitous—whole or chopped, cut into flakes or ground.

Fresh fruit gives an unparalleled lusciousness. In addition to its obvious role as a filling for pies or tarts (*pages 64-70*) fruit is layered in sponges or presented in mouth-watering cases of puff pastry (*page 82*). Some vegetables, too, make useful flavourings; the spinach tart demonstrated on page 71 is an example of how vegetables produce a delicious sweet. Dried fruits, full of natural sugar, have a concentrated perfume that pervades anything they are cooked with. A fruit cake (*page 40*) depends on dried fruit for its full-bodied flavour; but a handful of raisins or sultanas can be an important part of a pie or pastry filling as well.

Chocolate is made from cocoa beans—the podded, fat-bearing seeds of the cocoa tree, which is cultivated mainly in Central and South America and in West Africa. The method by which the beans are transformed into chocolate is complex. The beans are scraped from the pods, along with the pulp that adheres to them, then left to ferment for a few days. During fermentation the beans lose some of their natural bitterness and change in colour from their original pale violet to dark brown; the fermented beans are sun-dried, then exported for further processing.

Chocolate manufacturers roast the beans to develop their flavour, then husk and grind them. Grinding produces heat, which melts out the fat—cocoa butter—from the ground beans. The resulting sticky mixture—about half ground-up solids and half cocoa butter—is a sort of crude, bitter chocolate, from which cocoa powder and more refined chocolates are prepared.

The simplest form of chocolate for cooking is unsweetened, and is little more than the original crude mass, shaped into blocks. Most chocolate used in cakes and pastries is a more complex mixture, however. Sugar is added to counter the chocolate's bitterness, and varying proportions of cocoa butter and cocoa solids are mixed to produce either a soft chocolate that melts easily or a harder chocolate for chopping and grating.

Knowing your oven

Of all the equipment you will use to prepare cakes and pastries, your oven is the most important. All ovens vary, and thermostats are not always accurate. Obviously, you should follow the manufacturers' instructions for operation. Even so, you must be ready to make slight adjustments, in the light of your own experience, to both heat settings and cooking times. Some modern ovens are fan-assisted: their constantly circulating air ensures uniform heating. But most older ovens have hotter and cooler areas. Generally speaking, the top and back parts of the oven are hotter than the bottom, depending on the heat source, and it is best to cook cakes and pastries on the middle shelves, turning them round as necessary for even baking. In any case do not bake more than two or three large articles at a time; no oven can generate enough heat to compensate for overloading. For crisp pastry and for perfect cakes, dry heat is essential; avoid baking these items along with a steam-producing dish, such as a stew, which might in any case contaminate their flavour.

Wines with cakes and pastries

When cakes and pastries are served at the end of the meal, wine is a natural accompaniment. But the enjoyment of cakes and pastries is not restricted to mealtimes, and there is no reason why they cannot be matched with a fine wine at other times of day.

The best wines for the purpose are the white, naturally sweet dessert wines—the French Sauternes, the German Beerenauslese and Trockenbeerenauslese, the sweet Hungarian Tokay. All these wines are made from grapes that have been touched by the fungus Botrytis—the so-called "noble rot". The effect of the fungus is to shrivel the grapes, giving them a withered appearance. But within the wrinkled grapes, the juices are concentrated into a fragrant essence, and wine made from them has a depth and a richness that can be duplicated by no other means. These wines are served well chilled, cooled quickly in an ice bucket or freezer: overlong chilling would mute their taste.

Cakes and pastries served with wine should always be less sweet than the wine that accompanies them; otherwise the wine's subtlety will be masked. Some ingredients are best enjoyed without wine; chocolate, for example, overwhelms a wine, and very creamy fillings may prevent full appreciation of an accompanying wine. Acid fruits such as strawberries or redcurrants may undercut the richness of a sweet wine, but apples and pears, peaches—or anything made with almonds—make excellent companions. A *pithiviers* with a great Sauternes is magnificent, and pound cake (*page 38*) or a lightly iced sponge will also balance the qualities of a great wine. There are many other such marriages, and in search for new partnerships, ample scope for pleasurable experiment.

Transforming Sugar into Syrups and Caramels

As an embellishment for cakes and pastries, sugar appears in many guises: lustrous glazes and icings, brittle threads of sugar and hard coatings of caramel. All of these transformations are based on a sugar and water syrup that also serves as a poaching liquid for fruit, as a sweetener for butter creams (*page 12*) or glacé icings (*page 15*), or boiled down, as a glaze for cakes or tarts.

For preparations such as the apricot glaze shown here (*box, opposite page*), you will need a syrup with a high water content so that the mixture remains liquid when it cools. Here, the syrup combines 500 g (1 lb) of granulated sugar and 30 cl (½ pint) of water. To minimize evaporation the syrup is heated to not more than 102°C (215°F). The mixture is a useful stock syrup that can be made in advance and kept for several months in an airtight jar.

For thick fondant icings, sugar threads and caramel, you need denser sugar syrups that will harden as they cool. Because most of the water must evaporate during boiling to produce the required concentration, such syrups are made with a minimum of water—about 4 tablespoons to every 500 g (1 lb) of sugar.

If a sugar crystal drops into the syrup during cooking, the whole syrup may crystallize as it cools. To prevent this, dissolve the sugar thoroughly, avoid splashing the syrup against the sides of the cooking pan, stop stirring the syrup once the sugar has dissolved, and use a wet pastry brush to wipe away any crystals (*Step 1, right*).

The demonstrations here include practical tests to determine the stages of syrup boiling known as small thread, soft ball, hard crack and caramel—each stage denoting a density suitable for a particular use. For maximum accuracy, use a sugar thermometer. Small thread syrup is stock syrup—the first stage of sugar cooking. Syrup heated to soft ball stage remains pliable until cold; it is used to make fondant or boiled icings (*pages 16-17*). The hard crack stage provides pale, brittle, sugar threads for decorating cakes and pastries, while syrup heated to caramel can be brushed or poured over pastry to make hard, smooth coverings or spun into a fine amber veil (*page 90*).

1 **Dissolving sugar.** Place sugar and water in a heavy pan. Stir gently over low heat to dissolve the sugar. With a pastry brush dipped in hot water, dissolve any sugar crystals on the side of the pan (*above*); left undissolved, such crystals act as seeds that will cause all of the syrup to crystallize around them.

2 **Boiling the syrup.** When the sugar has dissolved, stop stirring and increase the heat a little to bring the syrup to the boil. If you plan to test the boiling temperature of the syrup with a thermometer, place it in the pan as soon as the sugar dissolves.

3 **The small thread stage.** After about 20 seconds boiling, start testing for the small thread stage. Allow some of the syrup to dribble from a spoon. If it falls in a fine, short thread, it has reached the small thread stage (*above*). This stage gives a thermometer reading of 102°C (215°F).

4 **The soft ball stage.** For the soft ball stage, boil the syrup for 2 to 3 minutes; drop a little into a bowl of iced water. Lift out the solidified lump; if you can roll the syrup into a soft ball between your fingers (*above*), it has reached the soft ball stage—a thermometer reading of 115°C (238°F). To arrest the cooking, stand the pan in cold water.

A Fruit-Flavoured Glaze

1 **Poaching fruit in syrup.** Bring a stock syrup to the boil. Lower the heat and add fruit—here apricots, halved and stoned. Gently simmer the apricots until tender—about 8 to 10 minutes. Remove them with a slotted spoon, and allow them to cool before use in tarts or cakes.

2 **Adding jam to the syrup.** Reduce the syrup by boiling it for a few minutes. To add more colour and flavour, stir in several spoonfuls of jam. Apricot jam is used here to complement the flavour of the fruit. Continue to boil for about 1 minute; stirring constantly.

3 **Finishing the glaze.** Remove the glaze from the heat and let it cool until tepid. Strain the glaze through a nylon sieve to remove any solids (*above*). Use the glaze to add sheen to fruit in tarts, or to provide a smooth coating for cakes.

5 **The hard crack stage.** For the hard crack stage, boil the syrup for about 4 minutes. To test it, remove the pan from the heat and drop a little syrup into a bowl of iced water. With your fingers, remove the solid lump and bend it. If the lump snaps apart (*above*), the syrup has reached the hard crack stage—a thermometer reading of 157°C (315°F).

6 **The caramel stage.** Boil the syrup until it begins to turn a pale amber colour, and reaches the caramel stage—a thermometer reading of 173°C (345°F). Caramel grows darker rapidly and soon burns. When the caramel is still slightly lighter then the colou you want, place the pan in cold water to arrest the cooking. Use the caramel immediately, before it sets (*above*). To keep caramel liquid for a short time, put the pan in warm water. □

Chocolate's Many Guises

The dark block chocolate used throughout this book is both a flavouring and a delicious decoration for cakes and pastries. A mixture of cocoa and cocoa butter, chocolate ranges from unsweetened or bitter to semi-sweet and sweet, depending on the proportion of sugar used.

Block chocolate also varies in texture from soft to hard according to the amount of cocoa butter it contains. A hard chocolate is easier to chop or grate (*box, far right, above*) than a soft chocolate which is high in cocoa butter and tends to clog knives and graters. But for shaping delicate curls and scrolls, a soft, more pliable chocolate gives the best results (*box, far right, centre*). The high fat content of soft chocolate also enables you to melt it quickly. Any type of chocolate melted alone over direct heat—even very low heat—may scorch and stiffen as the non-fat solids in the cocoa powder overheat and become hard: it is safer to melt the chocolate gently on a plate or in a bowl over a pan of hot water (*box, right, above*).

By melting either hard or soft chocolate with a little water and butter (*box, right, centre*) you can produce a rich, smooth cream that is easier to spread than chocolate melted on its own. Melted with double cream, the chocolate becomes richer still (*box, right, below*), and if the mixture is cooled and then whisked it will double in volume to provide a thick light icing (*recipe, page 93*).

While the chocolate is still warm and fluid, you can make unusual moulded decorations, such as the chocolate leaves shown here (*box, opposite page, below*) from soft or hard chocolate, or hard chocolate enriched with butter. Once the chocolate has cooled and hardened it can be made into decorative scrolls and cut outs (*boxes, opposite page, above and centre*). You can use these chocolate decorations immediately, or store them for 1 to 2 weeks in an airtight container in a cool, dry place. If the chocolate is not kept cool, the decorations will soften and lose their shape. And in time, the cocoa butter could rise to the surface of the chocolate and dry, causing white spots.

Melting Safely over Water

Heating chocolate gently. Put hard or soft chocolate pieces into a bowl that will fit snugly over a saucepan. Fill the pan a quarter full of water and heat it almost to the boil. Remove the pan and place the bowl of chocolate over it. Use a metal spatula to break up the chocolate (*above, left*). Stir until smooth.

Enriching with Butter

Combining the ingredients. Put pieces of hard or soft chocolate, butter, and a little water into a heavy saucepan. Set the pan over a low heat and stir constantly with a wooden spoon until the mixture is smooth and evenly blended; the chocolate should form a thin coat on the back of the spoon.

A Smooth Amalgam with Cream

Heating the mixture. Pour the double cream into a heavy saucepan. Place the pan over a low heat and bring the cream just to the boil. Add pieces of hard or soft chocolate and stir the ingredients with a wooden spoon until the chocolate melts and the mixture thickly coats the back of the spoon.

Forming Neat Scrolls

1 **Cooling chocolate.** Brush a work surface with oil to prevent sticking. Pour melted soft chocolate on to it. Use a flexible metal spatula to spread the chocolate 3 mm (⅛ inch) thick.

2 **Forming scrolls.** Let the chocolate cool and harden. Push a stiff, wide-bladed tool—such as the scraper here—under the chocolate. Use a continuous motion to roll the chocolate.

Cutting Decorative Shapes

1 **Making a chocolate slab.** Line a tray with greaseproof paper. Pour in melted chocolate to a depth of about 5 mm (¼ inch). Allow the chocolate to set, then turn it out gently (*above*).

2 **Cutting shapes.** Peel off the paper. Using a small, sharp knife or biscuit cutters, cut the slab of chocolate into many different shapes such as circles, triangles and crescents (*above*).

Fashioning Perfect Leaves

1 **Coating a leaf.** Melt pieces of hard or soft chocolate on a plate set over hot water. Wash and dry some leaves— here, rose leaves. Hold a leaf by the stem and draw it through the chocolate.

2 **Peeling the leaf.** Dry the leaves, either flat on greaseproof paper or curved, chocolate side up, over a rolling pin. When the chocolate is firm, peel off each leaf, starting from the stem.

Chopping, Peeling and Grating

Chopping chocolate. Break some hard chocolate into small pieces and put them on a chopping board. Hold a large, sharp knife by the handle and tip of the blade and chop the chocolate into coarse or fine bits (*above*).

Making curls of chocolate. Hold a block of chocolate over a plate. Draw the blade of a vegetable peeler towards you along the thin edge of the block. Soft chocolate, as used here, yields longer shavings than hard chocolate.

Grating chocolate. Chill a block of chocolate—preferably hard—in the refrigerator; warm chocolate would clog the grater. Rest one side of the grater on a plate (*above*) to catch the chocolate as you grate the block.

A Trio of Icings and Fillings

A seemingly endless variety of fillings and icings for cakes and pastries can be produced from the three bases called creams—although only one, whipped cream, contains that ingredient. Butter cream is largely butter, egg yolks and sugar syrup; pastry cream is a custard-like mixture thickened with egg yolks and a small amount of flour. Any of the three may be flavoured with everything from melted chocolate and liqueurs to chopped nuts, praline and orange or lemon zest. With whipped cream, the heavier flavourings are most easily incorporated by folding them in after whisking, while liquids, sugar and lighter flavourings can be added at any stage. For pastry cream and butter cream, stir in any flavouring after the creams have been made.

Sweetened whipped cream (*box, opposite page, above*) is the lightest mixture and the easiest to make: simply whisk fresh double cream and castor sugar together. As air is whisked into the cream the mixture will approximately double in volume. Before you begin, chill the cream, the whisk and the bowl; if they are warm, the cream will whip to a lesser volume. Whip the mixture only until it thickens and forms soft peaks; overwhipping would cause the cream to separate.

Butter cream (*box, right; recipe, page 92*) is a richer mixture. It is made by whisking hot sugar syrup and beaten egg yolks together until they are cool and pale in colour, then beating them into softened butter. The hot syrup cooks the eggs slightly to thicken the consistency of the mixture; the butter adds flavour and gives the cream a silky texture.

Pastry cream (*box, opposite page, below; recipe, page 166*) is thicker still. Egg yolks and sugar are beaten together, a little flour is added, then scalded milk is incorporated. The hot mixture is cooked gently for about 2 minutes to set the egg yolks and produce a smooth, thick mixture. To prevent a skin from forming on the mixture as it cools, stir the cream occasionally with a wooden spoon or rub the surface with a small lump of butter.

Basic Butter Cream

1 **Mixing egg yolks and syrup.** Cut butter into cubes and leave it in a bowl to soften. In a saucepan, boil water and sugar to the small thread stage (*page 8*). Separate eggs and whisk the yolks until they are thick and creamy—about 5 to 7 minutes if whisked by hand. Slowly pour the hot syrup over the yolks (*above, left*), and continue to whisk until the mixture is cool and fluffy (*above, right*)—about another 15 minutes.

2 **Creaming the butter.** Using the back of a wooden spoon, mash the butter against the sides of the bowl then beat it until it is smooth and creamy—about 10 minutes. Make sure that no more lumps remain: they would spoil the texture of the butter cream.

3 **Blending the ingredients.** Add the egg mixture in a stream to the beaten butter, beating it in with the wooden spoon (*above*). To make sure that the ingredients are evenly mixed, scrape the sides of the bowl occasionally.

4 **Finishing the cream.** Continue adding and beating in the egg mixture until all of it is thoroughly incorporated into the butter; the finished butter cream will be smooth, firm and shiny. Use the butter cream immediately, or store it in a refrigerator, covered with plastic film or aluminium foil, for several days.

Sweetened Whipped Cream

1 **Adding sugar.** Pour double cream into a bowl and add sugar to taste—here, vanilla sugar; 30 cl (½ pint) of double cream will yield enough whipped cream to fill and ice a 20 cm (8 inch) cake.

2 **Whipping the cream.** Steady the bowl with one hand and use a circular motion to whisk the ingredients, until the mixture begins to thicken and form soft peaks (*above, right*). The cream is best used immediately; however, if covered with plastic film or aluminium foil and refrigerated, it will keep for an hour or so.

Classic Pastry Cream

1 **Mixing the ingredients.** In a large bowl, beat egg yolks and sugar with a wooden spoon until thick and light (*above, left*). Add sieved flour and stir until blended. Put milk and a vanilla pod in a pan and bring to the boil. Remove the pod. Pour the milk into the flour and egg mixture, stirring constantly (*above, right*).

2 **Transferring the mixture.** Continue stirring the mixture with the wooden spoon until all of the ingredients are thoroughly combined. Pour the contents of the bowl back into the pan.

3 **Cooking the cream.** Set the pan over a medium heat and bring the mixture to the boil. Stir constantly, to prevent the pastry cream from sticking to the pan. Turn down the heat and continue to stir for a further 2 minutes; the mixture will thicken and become very smooth in texture.

4 **Straining the cream.** To ensure a smooth cream, strain it into a bowl. Cool the cream before use. To store the finished cream, press a piece of plastic film against its surface; it will keep for up to 2 days in a refrigerator.

A Choice of Sweet Toppings

A finishing touch of icing not only contributes generously to a cake's appeal, it also serves a practical purpose: cakes that have been filled and iced will stay moist for a longer period of time. The icings demonstrated here and on the following pages range from a simple blend of sugar and water, to more elaborate mixtures that include sugar syrups and egg whites. Add flavourings and colouring (*recipes, pages 92-94 and 109*) to suit the cake you are decorating: coffee or chocolate, for example, or citrus juice or zest.

The least complex and easiest icing is glacé, made by combining finely powdered sugar—icing sugar—with enough warm water to make a fluid mixture (*box, opposite page, below*). While still warm, the liquid is poured over cakes or pastries to form a smooth, glossy covering. Fondant, another pouring icing, is softer than glacé and can be prepared in large quantities and stored in an airtight container for several months. Fondant is made by cooking granulated sugar and water together to create a syrup. The syrup is then worked into a smooth, creamy mass (*overleaf*) which is reheated and thinned to a pouring consistency before it is used.

Royal icing, prepared by beating egg whites with a high proportion of icing sugar, becomes very hard as it sets. A little lemon juice is often added to offset the sweetness of the sugar. For pouring, thin the mixture with unbeaten egg whites; for piping, thicken the mixture, if you like, with more sugar.

The ingredients of meringue (*opposite page, above*), are similar to those of royal icing but meringue is usually made with castor sugar and contains a lower proportion of sugar to egg whites. It can be baked briefly in a hot oven to set the whites and to give the topping a pale-brown colour.

In a boiled icing (*overleaf*), the egg whites are cooked by whisking them with a hot sugar syrup. While still warm, the mixture can be swirled with a spatula over a cake to form several peaks. As the icing cools, the surface becomes slightly firm, contrasting with the soft interior.

When making any icing with beaten egg whites, be sure that the whites are completely free of yolk. Egg yolk contains fat, and the slightest trace will prevent the whites from mounting fully. A plastic bowl can harbour grease; use a bowl made of glass, porcelain or metal. Copper is ideal: a chemical reaction between the metal and the egg whites ensures an especially stable foam. However, do not leave egg whites in a copper bowl for more than about 5 minutes, or the copper will begin to turn the egg whites green.

Unwhisked egg whites can be combined with a rich mixture of sweet, ground almonds, castor and icing sugar and lemon juice to make marzipan. Egg yolks or whole eggs will produce a richer, yellow paste (*box, below*). The ingredients are stirred together into a thick mixture that is rolled out and cut to fit the cake. It can be used either on its own, or to create a smooth underlay for other icings.

Marzipan: an Almond-Flavoured Paste

1 Mixing nuts and sugar. Squeeze half a lemon and set the juice aside. In a small bowl, lightly whisk a whole egg. Blanch sweet almonds, then grind them in a food processor. In a large bowl, mix together the ground nuts, the castor sugar and the icing sugar (*above*).

2 Adding lemon juice and egg. Use a knife to stir the lemon juice into the almonds and sugar; the mixture would stick to the bowl of a spoon. Add just enough beaten egg—a little at a time—to make a stiff paste. If the mixture is very sticky, add a little more icing sugar.

3 Completing the mixture. Steady the bowl with one hand and use the other to gather the ingredients gently together. Handle the paste lightly—overworking will draw out the oil from the almonds and make the paste greasy.

Meringue: Whisked Egg Whites and Sugar

1 Separating the eggs. Crack each egg shell on the side of a small bowl and pass the yolk from one half of the shell to the other (*above*), allowing the white to drop into the bowl. Pour each white into a copper bowl. Reserve the yolks for fillings and butter creams (*page 12*).

2 Whisking the whites. Using a scrupulously clean wire whisk, beat the whites with a regular figure-of-eight motion. When the whites begin to form soft peaks, gradually add the castor sugar (*above, left*)—about 60g (2 oz) for each egg white used. Continue to whisk until the meringue forms stiff peaks and becomes smooth and glossy (*above, right*). Use immediately.

4 Kneading the marzipan. Sprinkle a work surface with icing sugar to prevent sticking. Knead the marzipan lightly until smooth and pliable, then shape it into a ball (*above*). Use immediately or store, wrapped in plastic film or foil in a refrigerator for up to 2 weeks.

Glacé: Icing Sugar Blended with Water

Adding water. Sieve icing sugar into a mixing bowl to eliminate any lumps. Use a spoon to make a well in the centre of the sugar. In a saucepan, heat some water until it is warm to the touch. Pour the water—a spoonful at a time—into the well (*above, left*), stirring the mixture continuously. Add only enough water to give the mixture a thin, coating consistency. Use the icing immediately.

Royal Icing: Egg Whites Beaten with Icing Sugar

1 **Adding lemon juice.** Sieve icing sugar into a bowl. Squeeze and reserve the juice of half a lemon. Separate eggs (*page 14*) and put the whites in a mixing bowl; with a wooden spoon stir half to three quarters of the sugar into the whites, then add the lemon juice.

2 **Adding the remaining sugar.** With the spoon, or an electric mixer, beat the mixture vigorously until it is light and smooth. Add the remaining sugar, a little at a time (*above*), beating well after each addition to mix thoroughly.

3 **Completing the icing.** Continue beating the mixture until it is stiff—a total of about 15 minutes by hand. Use the icing immediately or keep it for up to 30 minutes, covered with a damp cloth to prevent it from drying out. Beat the icing again before using it.

Fondant: Syrup Kneaded to Smoothness

 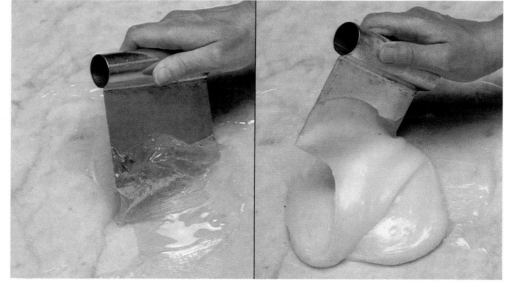

1 **Pouring the syrup.** Cook a sugar syrup to the soft ball stage—115°C (238°F) (*page 8*). Sprinkle a little cold water on to a cool work surface—here, a marble slab—and pour the hot syrup on to it (*above*). The water will prevent the syrup from sticking to the slab.

2 **Working the syrup.** Leave the syrup to cool slightly. With a palette knife or, as in this demonstration, a sugar scraper, work the syrup by repeatedly scooping it up from the edges and folding it into the centre (*above, left*). Continue to work the syrup until it becomes thick and opaque (*above, right*).

Boiled Icing: Whisked Egg Whites and Syrup

Adding sugar syrup. Cook a sugar syrup to the soft ball stage—115°C (238°F) (*page 8*). Whisk egg whites until they form soft peaks. Gradually whisk the hot syrup into the whites (*above, left*). Continue to whisk until the icing thickens (*above, right*) and loses its sheen. Use the icing immediately.

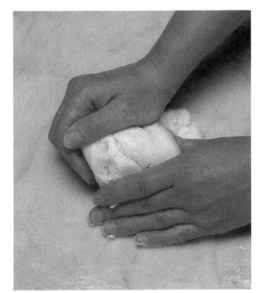

3 **Kneading the fondant.** Knead the cooled syrup with your hands for about 10 minutes, repeatedly folding it and pressing it until it is smooth, white and firm. For a smoother texture, wrap it in plastic film or foil and allow it to mellow for at least 1 hour before use. Stored in an airtight container in a cool place, the icing will keep for several months.

4 **Preparing fondant for use.** Half fill a saucepan with water. Put as much fondant as you need into a small, heatproof bowl and set the bowl over the water. Place the pan over a low heat. When the fondant begins to melt, stir in cool water or, for a glossier icing, sugar syrup (*above, left*). Continue to stir the fondant mixture over a gentle heat until it has the consistency of thick cream (*above, right*). Use the icing immediately.

1
Whisked Cakes
Airy Sponges for all Occasions

Feather-light and delicately flavoured, whisked sponge cakes have always been favourites of cake-makers. Their exceptional lightness is due to the myriad air cells created in the batter by the whisking process, and to moisture in the butter and eggs which converts to steam and expands in the oven. No chemical leaveners are necessary.

You can make whisked cakes in two basic ways. Beating whole eggs with the sugar over heat and then adding the flour will produce a slightly sticky, soft-textured cake (*page 22*). Or, by first beating the egg yolks alone with the sugar, then adding the separately beaten whites and the flour (*page 24*), you can create a firmer cake with a more pronounced crust. The addition of butter to either mixture will yield a richer cake that keeps longer without drying out. In all cases, however, the resulting cake is airy and springy in texture and both types of cake can be flavoured, decorated and served in the same fashions.

The lightness and resilience of sponge cakes make them remarkably versatile; for example, a shallow sponge baked in a rectangular cake tin can be rolled into a cylindrical shape—a feat not possible with other types of cake mixture. More often, however, deeper sponge cakes are baked and set one on top of the other or split into several thin layers, and sandwiched with almost any kind of filling you like. In the demonstration on page 30, for example, four layers of sponge are filled and covered with generous helpings of sweetened whipped cream and poached orange segments. On page 34, layers of sponge alternate with baked rounds of almond-flavoured meringue to produce an interplay of textures. And in the illustration opposite, a sponge with a hollowed-out centre provides a foil for the contrasting flavours of whipped cream, unsweetened raspberries and a covering of glacé icing (*page 30*).

Whisked sponges do not clamour for ornate decoration. The cakes themselves are delicious enough to be enjoyed plain or with a simple filling of jam and a light dusting of icing sugar (*page 25*). At the same time, sponge cake is a perfect canvas for decorations—as this chapter indicates. An attractive finish of piped, plain butter cream and chopped hazelnuts completes a triple-layer sponge on page 26. And on page 32 a combination of plain, chocolate-flavoured butter cream and small meringue mushrooms give a rolled sponge a festive appearance.

A surprise filling of whipped cream and raspberries appears as a slice of sponge cake is lifted from a serving stand. After the filling was piled into a hollow cut from the top of the cake, the cream mixture was covered with a lid of sponge cake and a smooth topping of glacé icing and decorative rings of berries were applied to conceal the cut surface.

Tailor-Made Linings for Baking

To prevent a cake from sticking to its tin as it bakes, the tin should, at the very least, be greased—preferably with butter, for its flavour—and dusted with flour. This is sufficient precaution for any simple cake intended to be cut in and served informally from its tin; it will also allow most cakes to be turned out easily.

When a cake includes fruits or other ingredients that may stick to the tin, it is wise to take the additional step of lining the tin with greaseproof paper. Shown here are three common tins each of which requires a different lining technique.

The shallow, circular tins used for sponge and layered creamed cakes (*box, right*) are buttered and a disc of greaseproof paper is fitted into the bottom; the tin itself serves as a template for the paper disc. Cakes baked in deeper tins are often rich, thick mixtures—fruit cakes (*page 40*), for example. Because of their depth and density, such cakes require a longer cooking time, which increases the risk of sticking. To protect these cakes, both the sides and the bottoms of their baking tins are lined with greaseproof paper (*boxes, right below, and opposite page*). If the cooking time is less than $1\frac{1}{2}$ hours, a single layer of paper is sufficient, but cakes with longer cooking times are better protected by a double thickness.

Once a tin's lining is in place, brush it with butter to ensure that the paper will peel off easily. A dusting of flour over the butter will produce a light crust. After baking, most cakes are left in the tin to settle—sponges and plain creamed cakes for 5 to 10 minutes, richer mixtures for up to 2 hours. The cake shrinks a little and becomes slightly firmer as it cools, which makes it easier to turn it out of its tin and to transfer it intact to a serving dish.

Any cake can be left to cool with its greaseproof paper still in place; the paper will minimize loss of moisture, but when peeled away, some of the cake's surface may adhere, leaving it rough and patchy. For cakes such as sponges or creamed cakes that are often turned upside-down to give a flat surface for simple icings, smoothness is essential for an attractive result. To ensure this, remove the cake from its tin and gently peel away the paper while the cake is still warm.

Covering the Base of a Shallow Tin

1 **Cutting out the paper.** Place one tin on a sheet of greaseproof paper. Hold the tin firmly down with one hand and draw its outline on to the paper with a pencil (*above*); remove the tin. With a pair of scissors, cut round the paper just inside the pencil line to produce a shape that will fit the bottom of the tin neatly.

A Double Thickness for Longer Cooking

1 **Cutting the paper.** Cut two paper discs to fit inside the tin; place one on the buttered base. Cut four strips, slightly longer than half the tin's circumference and 2 cm (1 inch) wider than its height. Fold over the excess width and snip it diagonally at 2 cm (1 inch) intervals.

2 **Lining the sides.** Butter the inside wall. Place two paper strips in the tin to line the wall half-way round, with the snipped edges on the bottom. Position the remaining two strips to complete lining the wall. Put the second paper disc on top of the first. Butter the lining.

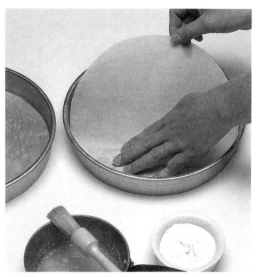

2 **Greasing the tins.** In a small saucepan, melt a little butter. With a pastry brush, paint a thin layer of butter on to the inner sides and the base of each tin (*above*). Have some flour at hand to complete the lining process.

3 **Fitting the paper.** Lay the shaped greaseproof paper on the base of each buttered tin (*above*): smooth it down with your hand. Brush the paper with a little more melted butter.

4 **Dusting with flour.** Put 1 tablespoon of flour into one buttered tin. Lift the tin and swirl the flour around until the inside of the tin is lightly coated. Tip the excess flour into the next buttered tin (*above*): repeat the procedure for each remaining tin, adding flour as needed.

A Neat Fit for a Rectangular Shape

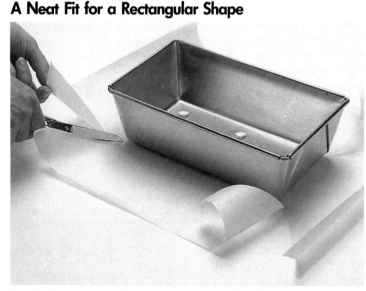

1 **Cutting corners.** On a working surface, lay down a sheet of greaseproof paper large enough to cover the base and the sides of the tin. Set the tin at its centre. With scissors, cut the paper from each corner to the nearest corner of the tin (*above*).

2 **Fitting the paper.** Brush the bottom and sides of the tin with melted butter. Lay the paper in the tin (*above*) and press it securely against the sides and the base, overlapping the corner flaps neatly. Then brush the paper with more melted butter and—if you like—dust the butter with a little flour.

The Classic Method: Whole Eggs Whisked over Heat

Two methods of making light, delicate sponge cakes are shown here and on the following page (*recipes, page 167*). In this demonstration, whole eggs and sugar are initially whisked together over a gentle heat then sieved flour and melted butter are folded in. On page 24, the yolks are whisked separately with the sugar—not over heat—then the whites are whisked to firm peaks and folded into the yolk and sugar mixture with the flour. Although cakes made by either method can be cut and decorated in exactly the same way, whisking whole eggs produces a cake with a soft, springy texture; sponges made with separated eggs are slightly firmer. Butter can be used or not, as you prefer— its addition results in a richer cake that will stay moist for 2 or 3 days.

Whichever method you use, the secret is to whisk as much air as possible into the eggs and sugar and to bake the cake immediately to prevent the mixture from deflating. In the oven, the air expands and causes the cake to rise.

Warming the eggs and sugar is a time-saving technique: heat coagulates the protein in the eggs, enabling them to trap and hold large quantities of air and thus increase quickly in volume. The sugar dissolves into the warm eggs to form a homogenous mixture (*Step 1*). You can speed up the whisking process still further by using a hand-held, electric mixer.

To heat the eggs and sugar gently, put them in a bowl that will fit snugly over a saucepan of hot water. Be sure that the base of the bowl does not touch the water and that the water does not boil, otherwise, the eggs would cook. As you whisk, the air beaten into the eggs turns the mixture a pale cream colour and causes it to treble in volume. Fold in the sifted flour gently, a little at a time (*Step 2*). If the flour were added all at once or the mixture folded too strenuously at this stage, much of the air beaten into the eggs would be lost and the cake would be heavy.

1 Whisking eggs and sugar. Whisk eggs and sugar lightly in a large bowl. Put a little hot water into a saucepan, set it over a low heat and place the bowl on top. Heat the mixture until lukewarm, whisking constantly for 5 to 10 minutes. Remove the saucepan and bowl from the heat and continue to whisk until the mixture has tripled in bulk and falls from the whisk in a thick ribbon (*above, right*)—about 20 minutes by hand or 10 by electric mixer.

3 Filling the tin. Pour the batter into a prepared cake tin (*page 20*)—here, a 7.5 cm (3 inch) deep spring-form tin is used to help unmould the cake easily. Bake the cake in an oven preheated to 180°C (350°F or Mark 4) for about 35 to 40 minutes (20 to 25 minutes for a shallow tin) until it feels springy and begins to shrink from the sides of the tin.

4 Unmoulding the cake. Using a cloth to protect your hands, remove the cake tin from the oven, and place it on a wire rack to cool for 5 minutes. Run a knife around the inner edge of the tin to loosen the cake. Pull back the clip of the spring-form to release the ring from the base and lift away the ring.

2 **Adding flour.** Put some butter in a saucepan and melt it over a low heat: allow to cool. Sieve flour into the egg and sugar mixture in two or three stages, adding it alternately with the cooled butter. Use a metal spoon or a whisk to fold in the ingredients gently after each addition; starting from the centre of the mixture, draw the spoon along the bottom of the bowl and bring it up around the sides (*above, centre*). Continue until the ingredients are blended.

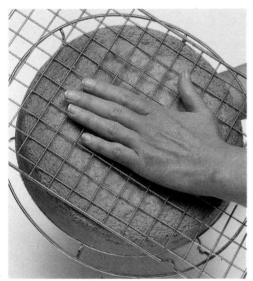

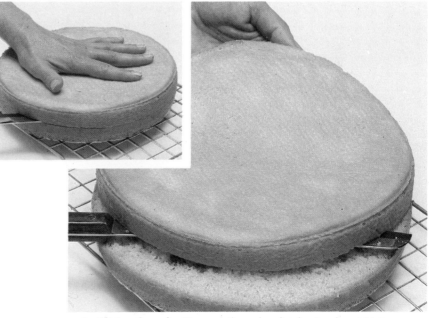

5 **Cooling the cake.** Place a wire rack over the top of the cake. Place one hand under the bottom rack and lift up the cake (*above*), reversing it on to the top rack. Lift off the base of the spring-form tin and peel away the greaseproof lining paper. Leave the cake to cool.

6 **Slicing the cake.** To serve the cake plainly, simply cut it into wedges. For a layered cake, either assemble two cakes (*page 24*) or slice one cake into two, three or four layers, depending on its depth. Cut the cake by using a long serrated knife to score a guide-line round the sides (*inset*) then slicing through the cake, carefully following the guide-line (*above*). □

Separating Eggs for Extra Lightness

In the separated egg sponge demonstrated here (*recipe, page 167*), the batter is leavened in two stages: some air is incorporated by whisking egg yolks and sugar together, and more by whisking the egg whites into soft peaks. Altogether it will take about 40 minutes to whisk the ingredients sufficiently for the cake to rise to its full height in the oven; an electric mixer will shorten the time by about 15 minutes. To prevent breaking down the air bubbles, combine the ingredients by folding the egg whites and flour alternately into the yolks and sugar mixture with a whisk or metal spoon (*Step 2*).

If you like, you can flavour a sponge cake with cocoa, chopped nuts, or the grated zest of orange and lemon. To allow the citrus oils to permeate the batter, add the zest with the yolks and sugar. Cocoa powder should be sifted in with the flour; but heavier flavourings, such as chopped almonds or pistachio nuts, are best folded into the batter at the last moment.

Like the whole egg sponge on page 22, a separated egg cake can be served plain, or decorated as shown on pages 25-35.

1 **Whisking yolks and sugar.** Prepare two cake tins (*page 20*). Separate the eggs, dropping the whites into one bowl—not copper in case they discolour (*page 15*)—and the yolks into another. Add sugar to the yolks, reserving 2 tablespoons, and whisk until the mixture falls in a thick ribbon—about 20 minutes by hand or 10 by electric mixer.

2 **Adding egg whites and flour.** Tip the whites into a large bowl—here copper, to help stabilize the whites (*page 15*) and whisk until they form soft peaks. Add the reserved sugar and continue to whisk until the whites are firm. Sieve half the flour into the yolk mixture and fold it in. Fold in half of the whites and repeat until all the ingredients are combined.

3 **Filling the tins.** Pour the batter into the cake tins (*above*), smoothing it with the back of the spoon. Bake the cakes in an oven preheated to 180°C (350°F or Mark 4) for 20 to 25 minutes (35 to 40 minutes for a deeper tin) or until they are golden and firm to the touch.

4 **Cooling and slicing.** Cool the sponges for 5 minutes—they will shrink slightly and be easier to turn out. Run a knife round the inner edge of each tin and unmould the cakes on to a cooling rack. When cool, serve the cakes in wedges, or assemble them, whole or sliced in half, with a filling, such as jam or butter cream. □

Simple Fillings and Finishes

Quick and simple fillings and decorations can produce results that rival more elaborate cakes bedizened with icings, nuts and butter creams.

Sweetened whipped cream, for example (*page 13*), makes an admirable filling for any cake, especially if you include fresh fruit, such as pineapple slices, orange segments or berries. A thick layer of fruit jam is even more basic and no less delicious. In this demonstration, two sponge cakes (*page 22 or 24*) sandwich a layer of raspberry jam (*Step 1*).

The cake's topping is equally simple—a dusting of icing sugar. You can achieve a striking effect, as here, by sieving the sugar over thin strips of greaseproof paper. The paper acts as a stencil, and when it is removed a pattern of strips is revealed. By cutting the paper into different shapes—circles, spirals or diamonds, for instance—you can create a variety of designs. If you like, use attractively shaped leaves as stencils; it may be necessary to press the leaves flat under a heavy weight for a day or two first.

1 Spreading jam. Bake and cool two sponge cakes—here, made with butter and whole eggs. Using a knife or a metal spatula, spread the surface of one of the cakes with jam—here, raspberry. Set the second cake on top. To make a thick jam easier to spread, warm it gently in a saucepan set over a low heat.

2 Sifting icing sugar. Cut eight strips of greaseproof paper, each about 1 cm ($\frac{1}{2}$ inch) wide and slightly longer than the diameter of the cake. Lay the strips on top of the cake. Spoon icing sugar into a small sieve and tap it gently to sprinkle an even layer of sugar over the surface.

3 Removing the paper. Hold one strip of paper at each end and carefully lift it vertically from the cake to leave a clear pattern (*below*). Lift away the other strips. Cut the cake in wedges and serve.□

Spreading and Piping: Decorative Basics

The contrasting colours and textures of butter cream and chopped nuts make them classic partners for decorating sponge cakes. In this demonstration, the butter cream is used to layer and cover the cake, and provides an adhesive surface for the nuts. Hazelnuts are used here, but almonds, pistachios or walnuts are good alternatives. To remove the skins from the hazelnuts—and to bring out their full flavour—toast the shelled nuts in an oven 180°C (350°F or Mark 4) until the skins split, then rub them briskly in a towel.

Decorating the cake will be easier if you set it on a disc cut from firm cardboard, then hold the cake in one hand and turn and tilt it as you apply an icing. You need not remove the disc for serving; to prevent it from showing, cut it slightly smaller than the cake.

To ice a cake, you can use a flexible, metal spatula or even a wooden spoon (*box, opposite page, above*). For finer work use a greaseproof paper piping bag (*box, opposite page, below*). Home-made piping bags save time and washing up, especially if you use small quantities of several different icings, or melted chocolate, or butter cream, for example. Make as many bags as you need and discard them after use. The bags can be made in any size; as a rough guide, a bag made from a 28 by 38 cm (11 by 15 inch) rectangle of paper will hold enough icing to pipe the decorations shown here.

To pipe lines and dots, fill the bag about two-thirds full, close the top firmly and cut off the tip; the smaller the opening, the finer the decorating point will be. For more elaborate shapes, cut about 1 cm ($\frac{1}{2}$ inch) from the tip of the empty bag and insert a metal nozzle; a star nozzle will produce both star and shell shapes. To make a star, hold the nozzle steady, at right angles to the surface of the cake. Squeeze out the icing with a firm pressure and then lift away the bag. To make a shell, hold the nozzle at an oblique angle. Then squeeze out a dab of icing, lift the bag slightly and move the nozzle to one side, bringing it back down to the surface. Practise on a piece of greaseproof paper or an over-turned cake tin. Egg whites and icing sugar whisked to stiff peaks make a good, basic material to practise with.

1 Layering the cake. Make butter cream (*page 12*)—you will need about 350 g (12 oz)—and chop hazelnuts. Bake a 20 cm (8 inch) sponge in a 7.5 cm (3 inch) deep tin; cut it into three layers. Set the bottom layer on a cardboard disc. Assemble the cake, using a spatula to spread each layer and the top with butter cream, reserving some cream for piping.

2 Covering the sides. Slide a spatula under the cardboard disc and raise it so that you can lift the cake up with your hand. With the spatula, spread butter cream round the sides of the cake, using long, even strokes so that the surface of the icing is smooth.

5 Finishing and serving. Place a circular, open-ended biscuit cutter on the centre of the cake. Spoon in a layer of chopped hazelnuts (*inset*) and then carefully lift away the cutter. Pipe a border of butter cream—here of shells—around the circle of chopped nuts. Cut the cake into wedges (*above*) and serve.□

3 **Decorating with nuts.** Still holding the cake, scoop up some of the chopped hazelnuts in the palm of your free hand. Press them on to the side of the cake, cupping your palm so that they adhere in an arc shape. Continue round the cake to create a scalloped effect.

4 **Piping a shell border.** Set the cake on a serving plate. Fit a piping bag with a star nozzle, fill it two-thirds full of butter cream and fold over the top. Hold it at an oblique angle to the edge of the cake. With an even pressure, squeeze the bag between fingers and thumb (*above*) to make a chain of shells.

A Raised Rim for Poured Icing

Covering the top. To cover the top of a butter cream decorated cake with a poured icing, pipe a border of butter cream—here, of stars—round the cake's edge. Pour fondant (*page 16*)—or the glacé icing (*page 15*) shown above—on the cake, smoothing it with the back of a spoon. The piped border will prevent the icing from overflowing.

How to Improvise a Piping Bag

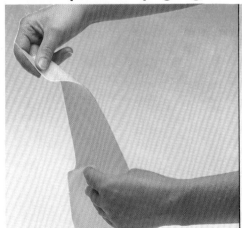

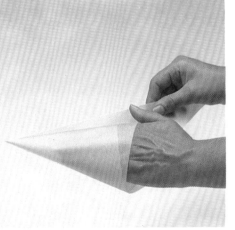

1 **Shaping the bag.** Cut a rectangle of greaseproof paper diagonally into two triangles; only one is needed to make the bag. Hold the triangle by both corners of its longest side. Loop one corner inside the other (*above, left*) to form a loose cone with its point facing away from you. Hold the cone together with one hand and put your other hand into the cone, then pull on the loose, outside end to close up the point (*above, right*). To strengthen the bag and prevent it from uncoiling, fold the top ends down inside the cone.

2 **Completing the bag.** Cut about 1 cm (½ in) from the tip of the bag and fit it with a metal nozzle. Fill the bag two-thirds full with icing. To close the bag, flatten the cone above the filling and fold over both corners (*above*). Fold the end of the bag over twice. As you pipe, press the icing towards the nozzle by folding over the end of the bag.

A Cocoa Sponge Enrobed in Chocolate

A satin-smooth coat of poured icing provides an immaculate surface for decoration and gives extra elegance to a whisked sponge cake. The icing is poured quickly over the top of the cake and allowed to flow down the sides—a technique so simple that the cake almost ices itself.

Glacé and fondant icing (*pages 15 and 16*) or the luxurious cream and chocolate mixture shown here (*page 10*), all have a fluid consistency which makes them ideal for pouring. To ensure that the poured icing sets smoothly, first brush the loose crumbs from the cake and cut away any rough edges, then apply an undercoat of fruit glaze (*page 9*) or butter cream (*page 12*) before pouring on the icing. In the cake shown here, the filling, the undercoat and the icing are made from the same mixture of chocolate and double cream, providing a harmonious blend of flavours on a single theme (*recipe, page 93*). Ropes of piped chocolate cream, poached cherries and chocolate leaves (*page 11*) complete the decoration.

To make a chocolate sponge, use either of the methods shown on pages 22 and 24 (*recipes, page 167*) and simply replace between a quarter and a half of the flour with unsweetened cocoa powder. Sift the flour and cocoa together first to combine them thoroughly before folding them into the batter. Here, the cake is sliced into three layers—necessitating a baking tin at least 5 cm (2 inches) deep—then cooled completely and decorated.

The basic icing and filling mixture is made by bringing cream to the boil in a saucepan, then adding chocolate (*page 10*). The portion to be used for the filling and the undercoat is chilled and whisked until it is light and fluffy (*Step 1*). It is then spread over the cake, and allowed to set. The rest of the chocolate mixture, reheated if necessary, is poured over the whisked chocolate cream (*Step 3*).

If you like, you can add a tablespoon of brandy or dark rum to the chocolate cream. Here, additional flavouring is provided by adding a cherry-flavoured liqueur to the syrup used to poach the cherries and brushing the liquid over each cake layer. This technique has a practical advantage: the liqueur helps to keep the cake moist.

1 **Beating chocolate and cream.** Make a chocolate sponge—in this case, baked in a tin 25 cm (10 inches) square, and cool it on a rack. Melt chocolate in double cream (*page 10*); for a 25 cm (10 inch) cake, you will need 1.25 litres (2 pints) cream and 1.25 kg (2½ lb) chocolate. Put a little less than half the mixture into a bowl and chill for at least 1 hour; reserve the remainder in the melting pan. Prepare chocolate leaves (*page 11*). When the chilled chocolate mixture is firm, break it up with a wooden spoon (*above, left*), then vigorously whisk until light and fluffy (*above, right*).

4 **Lifting the cake.** Leave the cake for about 15 minutes until the icing has set completely. Slide two firm metal spatulas under opposite sides of the cake, slightly away from its centre (*above*). Lift the cake gently and place it on a large plate or, as shown here, on an inverted baking sheet.

5 **Piping and decorating.** Fit a piping bag (*page 27*), with a star nozzle and fill the bag with the remaining whisked chocolate cream. Close the bag and pipe a border of cream around the base of the cake. Pipe a dab of cream at each corner, set a poached cherry and two chocolate leaves on the cream.

2 **Covering the cake.** Poach stoned cherries in stock syrup (*page 8*) for 5 to 7 minutes. Remove the fruit and add cherry-flavoured liqueur. Cut the cake into three; brush each layer with syrup. With a spatula, spread the first and second layers and the top and sides of the cake with whisked chocolate cream (*above*), saving some for piping.

3 **Pouring the icing.** Make sure the chocolate and cream covering is completely smooth, then chill the cake on its rack to firm the mixture. If the reserved chocolate and cream in the pan has hardened, place it over a low heat until it is melted and lukewarm. Set the cake on a tray to catch drips, then pour the tepid icing in a continuous stream over the cake (*above*). If necessary, use the spatula to spread the icing over any uncovered areas. The icing will begin to set quickly; work rapidly to avoid leaving marks.

6 **Completing the decoration.** Arrange the remaining chocolate leaves on top of the cake. If you like, you can prop them up on a dab of chocolate cream. Lightly sieve a little icing sugar over the leaves and carefully set the remaining poached cherries among them (*right*).☐

Two Strategies with Fruit and Cream

In combination, whipped cream and brightly coloured fruit offer sumptuous ways to fill and decorate cakes. The cream may be sweetened or not, flavoured with brandy or liqueur as you like. In the demonstration on the right, raspberries and sweetened whipped cream (*page 13*) are ingeniously concealed inside a deep one-layer sponge cake (*pages 22 or 24*). In the lower demonstration, orange segments and cream yield filling and garnish for a four-layer sponge cake. Any kind of whole fresh berry or cut up, soft-textured fruit, raw or poached, such as peaches or even pineapple, is suitable. Whether to use a whole egg or separated egg sponge (*recipes, page 167*) and where to put the cream and fruit is, of course, the cook's choice.

To hold the filling inside the raspberry cake, a hollow is formed by cutting a thin lid from the top and then scooping out the cake's centre (*Step 1, right*). Do not waste the scooped-out crumbs; scatter them over strudel dough (*page 84*) or pre-baked tart shells before adding a filling (*page 72*). Stored in an airtight jar, cake crumbs will keep for several weeks. After the filling is piled into the hollow, the lid is replaced and the cut surface hidden by a coating of icing (*page 16*) or more whipped cream and embellished with more fruit.

If a poured icing is used, such as the glacé in this demonstration, you can achieve an interesting effect by letting it flow only partly down the sides (*Step 3*).

A four-layer orange cake (*right*) is created most easily by baking two sponge layers and slicing each one horizontally. Poached orange segments and whipped cream provide both a filling and a simple yet stylish decoration. To permeate the whole cake with an orange taste, the poaching liquid can be reduced, flavoured with orange liqueur, and brushed over the cut surfaces of the sponge before they are coated with cream.

Any cake decorated or filled with cream and fruit should be served on the day it is made, preferably within minutes of its completion. If it is kept for more than 3 to 4 hours—even in a refrigerator—the moisture from the cream and fruit will soak into the sponge and make it soggy.

A Hidden Filling

1 **Cutting the lid.** Bake a sponge in a round, deep cake tin—here 22 by 7.5 cm (9 by 3 inches). Prepare about 500 g (1 lb) of fruit—in this case, raspberries. Add sugar to 60 cl (1 pint) of double cream. With a serrated knife, cut a circle 4 cm (1½ inches) deep, 2.5 cm (1 inch) from the edge of the top of the cake. Then, keeping the blade almost horizontal, cut to the centre of the circle 5 mm (¼ inch) beneath the cake's surface. Rotate the cake until the lid is free (*above, left*). Remove the lid (*above, right*) and set it aside.

A Tiered Assemblage

1 **Preparing the oranges.** Working over a bowl to collect juices, cut the rind and pith from about eight oranges with a sharp knife. Make segments by cutting down each side of the dividing membrane (*above*). Add the segments and the juice to a simmering syrup (*page 9*). Poach the fruit for 3 to 5 minutes.

2 **Reducing the poaching syrup.** Strain the syrup into another pan (*above*), and bring it to the boil, adjust the heat and let the syrup simmer until it has reduced by half. With a slotted spoon transfer the poached orange segments to paper towels to drain. Leave the syrup to cool; if you like, add some orange-flavoured liqueur to the syrup.

2 **Filling the cake.** Using a metal spoon, scoop out the interior of the cake to the depth of the circular cut—4 cm (1½ inches). Whip the cream until it forms soft peaks. Spoon a little whipped cream into the cake. Pile about two-thirds of the raspberries on top of the cream; reserve the remaining fruit. Spoon the rest of the cream over the fruit (*above*).

3 **Pouring the icing.** Place the cake on a serving stand or plate. Replace the cut-out lid on top of the cake. Make a glacé icing (*page 15*) and pour it on to the centre of the cake. For an informal effect, stop pouring when the icing begins to run over the edge of the cake; let the icing trickle down the sides of the cake, setting as it falls.

4 **Serving the cake.** While the icing is still sticky, decorate the top of the cake with the reserved raspberries. Form a large circle of raspberries around the edge of the cake; then make a smaller circle of fruit inside it. Cut the cake into wedges (*above*) and serve.□

3 **Layering the cake.** Bake two 22 cm (9 inch) round sponges and cut each into two layers. Whip 1.25 litres (2 pints) of double cream until soft peaks form; if you like, add castor sugar. Set a layer of cake, cut side up, on a cake stand; brush on some syrup. Use a spatula to spread it with cream. Add another layer; coat it with syrup (*above*) and cream.

4 **Arranging the filling.** To make a fruit-filled middle section, arrange about half of the orange segments in one layer of concentric circles on top of the whipped cream. Stack the last two layers of cake, spreading each one with syrup and whipped cream, as before.

5 **Decorating the cake.** With a spatula, spread the remaining whipped cream over the top and sides of the cake, using circular strokes to produce a rippled finish. Decorate the top of the cake with more circles of orange segments (*above*). Serve as soon as possible, cutting the cake into wedges.□

A Masterpiece of Illusion

To make a simple rolled cake, a sheet of baked sponge is spread with jam, rolled up into a neat cylinder and sprinkled with sugar. For festive occasions, you can decorate a rolled cake as fancifully as you like. For the yule log demonstrated on the right (*recipe, page 95*), plain and chocolate-flavoured butter cream (*page 12*) is piped over the cake to resemble the bark of a tree, and small meringue mushrooms (*box, opposite page*) are scattered on the top to complete the whimsical effect.

To make the sponge batter, you can use either of the techniques shown on pages 22 and 24, and bake the mixture in a wide, shallow tin. Here, a whole egg butter sponge is used (*recipe, page 167*).

The method of rolling the cake depends on the type of filling you use. If you plan to spread the cake with jam, warm the filling first in a saucepan set over a low heat so that it will be easier to spread. Cover the sponge with the jam while both are still warm, and roll up the cake; a cool cake would crack as you roll it.

Fillings with a high fat content, however, such as whipped cream or the butter cream used here, become oily if they are spread over a warm cake. Before adding the filling, shape the warm sponge by rolling it around a sheet of greaseproof paper then leave it to cool under a damp cloth. The paper prevents the cake from sticking to itself and enables you to unroll it easily; the cloth will keep the cake moist and flexible while it cools.

1 Baking the sponge. Butter and line a shallow, rectangular baking tin (*page 20*). Make a sponge mixture (*pages 22-24*). Pour it into the tin, smoothing it so that it will cook evenly. Bake the sponge in an oven preheated to 230°C (450°F or Mark 8) for about 12 minutes, or until it is springy and golden-brown.

2 Turning out the cake. Spread a kitchen towel on a work surface. Cover it with greaseproof paper, and sprinkle the paper with castor sugar. Reverse the tin, protecting your hand with a towel, and ease the cake on to the sugared paper. Peel off the paper used to line the tin.

4 Rolling the filled sponge. In a large bowl, prepare plain butter cream (*page 12*); put about one-fifth of it in a smaller bowl. Melt some chocolate (*page 10*) and stir it into the large bowl of butter cream. Unroll the sponge, remove the top layer of paper, and brush some sugar syrup (*page 8*)—here flavoured with orange liqueur—over it. With a spatula, cover the sponge with some of the chocolate butter cream and roll it up (*above*).

Mushrooms from Meringue

Dusting with cocoa. Spread a sheet of greaseproof paper on a baking sheet. Pipe meringue mixture (*page 15*) into various sized circles for caps and strips for stalks. Dust them with sifted cocoa powder. Bake the meringue at 100°C (200°F or Mark ¼) for about 3 hours or until the meringue is crisp and dry.

3 **Rolling the cake.** Trim the crusty edges of the sponge with a knife. To make the sponge easier to roll at the start, cut a shallow groove along a short side of the cake about 2.5 cm (1 inch) from the edge (*inset*). Cover the sponge with greaseproof paper. Fold the sponge over at the groove. Grasp the ends of the towel and roll up the sponge around the top layer of paper (*above*). Cover the rolled sponge with a damp cloth until it is cool.

5 **Applying butter cream.** Set the roll on a plate, with the seam underneath the cake. With a spatula, cover both ends with plain butter cream and use the rest to make a mound (*above*). When completely decorated, the mound will resemble a sawn-off branch.

6 **Making the branch.** Fit an icing bag with a star nozzle and pipe chocolate butter cream along the cake. Use a small, plain nozzle to pipe spirals at each end. Chill the cake to firm the icing— about 30 minutes. With a warm knife, slice off the top of the mound (*above*).

7 **Decorating the log.** Make mushroom stems and caps from meringue (*box, above*); assemble them by pressing them together with a little butter cream. Place the mushrooms on top of the log. Slice the cake into rounds and serve. □

A Counterpoint of Texture and Flavour

Rounds of baked meringue alone make a delicious case for a filling of fresh or poached fruit and cream. But by alternating the crisp meringue with layers of moist, tender sponge (*pages 22 and 24*), you can create an unusual contrast of flavour and texture, and build an assembly of impressive height.

In the demonstration on the right, layers of sponge cake are combined with rounds of baked meringue flavoured with ground almonds (*recipe, page 97*), and each layer is spread with a mixture of praline—crushed caramelized almonds—and butter cream (*recipes, pages 92 and 94*). The cake is then decorated with yet more butter cream and praline and finally topped with an informal arrangement of chocolate scrolls (*page 11*).

For an interesting variation, flavour both the sponge and the meringue with chocolate, and spread each layer with whipped cream. If you prefer a simpler decoration than butter cream and praline, you could dust the cake with icing sugar. To make a pattern, use a stencil made from paper or leaves (*page 25*).

For a neat presentation, the layers of meringue and sponge should be of equal circumference. To ensure that the layers of meringue are the right size, trace the outline of the tin used to bake the sponge on a sheet of greaseproof paper and pipe the meringue to fill this shape (*Step 3, right*). The meringue may spread out slightly during baking; use a knife to trim any excess before assembling the cake.

1 Preparing meringue. Bake a sponge cake. Line two baking trays with greaseproof paper, securing each corner with a dot of butter. Combine castor sugar with ground almonds. Whisk egg whites until they form soft peaks. Add castor sugar a little at a time, and whisk until very stiff. Gently fold in the sugar and almond mixture (*above*).

2 Filling a piping bag. Insert a plain nozzle, approximately 1 cm (½ inch) wide into a piping bag. To fill the bag easily, fold the top third back over your wrist and spoon in the meringue mixture (*above*) until the bag is about two-thirds full. Close the bag by twisting the top.

4 Removing the paper. Allow the meringues to cool. Remove the greaseproof paper from each tray with each meringue still attached. To separate each meringue from its paper, place the paper on a table so that one side of the meringue projects over the edge. Gently peel away the paper, turning the spiral until it is free.

5 Preparing butter cream. Make praline, using equal amounts of almonds and sugar. Sift the fine praline powder into a bowl; the coarser pieces into a separate bowl. Make a butter cream using about 500 g (1 lb) of butter, and set aside one-third. Mix the praline powder to the remaining two-thirds.

3 **Piping the meringue.** Using the sponge cake tin as a guide, pencil a circle on each paper-covered baking tray. On each tray, pipe a spiral of meringue from the inside of the circle to the outer edge, or from the outer edge inwards; here, the baking tray is placed on a cake-stand which can be turned as you work to facilitate piping. Bake the meringue spirals at 170°C (325°F or Mark 3) for about 1 hour, until crisp and lightly coloured.

6 **Assembling the cake.** If the meringue has spread out during baking, use a knife to trim it to the size of the cake. Cut the sponge into two layers. Set a layer of meringue on a cardboard disc, so that you will be able to lift it freely to decorate the sides. Spread the meringue with the praline-flavoured butter cream. Cover with alternate layers of sponge, flavoured butter cream and meringue, ending with a layer of sponge.

7 **Decorating and serving.** Lift the cake in one hand, supporting it by the cardboard disc at its base. With a metal spatula, spread the reserved, unflavoured butter cream over the top and sides of the cake. Use your free hand to scoop up the coarser pieces of praline and press them on to the sides of the cake. Stand the cake on a serving platter. Make chocolate scrolls, and arrange them on top of the cake. Sift a little icing sugar over the scrolls. Cut the cake in wedges and serve (*above*). □

2
Creamed, Rubbed and Melted Cakes
A Matter of Method

A wedge of vinegar cake (*page 44*), studded with raisins and currants, is lifted from a serving plate. Despite the cake's name, the fruit is the main flavouring ingredient. A small amount of vinegar reacts with bicarbonate of soda to form a leavening that makes the cake rise but does not affect its flavour.

Cakes are often described simply in terms of their flavouring—chocolate or ginger cake, for example. Many cooks, however, prefer to classify cakes by the methods used to make them. The following pages show cakes made by creaming, rubbing and melting the ingredients.

The proportions of a cake's various ingredients determine the method used. For example, cakes that contain a large amount of butter—such as pound cake or rich fruit cake (*pages 38 and 40*) are made by the creaming method, which permits the butter to be easily combined with the other ingredients. Economical cakes, such as the vinegar cake on page 44, are made with a low proportion of butter to flour. These ingredients are combined by rubbing them together to distribute the butter evenly through the flour—a technique similar to that used in making rich or plain shortcrust dough (*pages 50 and 52*).

The third method—the melting method—is used to make particularly sweet and moist cakes such as gingerbread (*page 46*) or honey cake (*recipe, page 118*). These cakes are usually sweetened completely, or in part, with treacle, honey or molasses. To incorporate the sweet ingredients easily, they are melted with the butter before the flour is folded in.

All of these cakes vary in texture and flavour, but the batter must rise in the oven or the result will be heavy and unpleasant. When a high proportion of eggs is used, they are capable of trapping enough air to provide a natural leavening. Moisture from both the eggs and butter converts to steam in the oven and also helps to raise the cake. However, cakes with a low proportion of these ingredients need a boost in the form of chemical leavening; bicarbonate of soda mixed with an acid—such as lemon juice, buttermilk, treacle or vinegar—or baking powder, a ready-made blend of bicarbonate and an acid.

When it comes to decoration, the richness of creamed cakes makes them good candidates for embellishments of fillings and icings; some ideas are shown in the previous chapter. On the other hand, the economy of the ingredients used in rubbed or melted cakes is usually reflected in simple decorations, or none at all

Beating in Air for a Natural Lift

Cakes that contain a high proportion of butter—half, or more than half of the weight of the flour used—are especially rich and moist. To ensure that the large amount of butter is smoothly incorporated, such cakes are usually made by the so-called "creaming method". In the demonstration here, butter is first beaten to a creamy consistency so that it will combine easily with sugar, then egg yolks are beaten in. Lastly, flour and whisked egg whites are gently folded into the mixture. Not all recipes for creamed cakes call for separating the eggs. However, this technique permits you to incorporate a large amount of air into the batter—some when the butter, sugar and egg yolks are beaten, much more when the whisked egg whites are added. The natural leavening of air lifts the batter and results in a firm, close-textured cake; a chemical leavening agent is sometimes required when the eggs are added whole (*page 43*).

You can use the creaming method to make fruit cakes, layered cakes to fill with butter cream or jam, or a simple loaf cake like the pound cake shown on the right (*recipe, page 100*). And, if you like, you can flavour the cake with lemon or other citrus rind (*recipe, page 100*), caraway seeds, chocolate or chopped nuts such as almonds, pistachios or walnuts.

The pound cake's name is virtually a recipe in itself: traditionally a pound—500 g—of each ingredient was used. Here, the amounts are reduced, but the proportions remain equal. Use the eggs as your measuring standard: by placing them on one side of a kitchen balance you can weigh out the right amount of sugar, butter and flour on the other side (*Step 1*).

Whatever the cake's size, its success will depend on trapping the maximum amount of air in the batter and on using a light touch to combine the batter with the flour and beaten egg whites. If the mixture is beaten too much after the flour is added, the gluten in the flour will become elastic and produce a tough cake. The whisked egg whites must be mixed very gently with the batter, or their air will be lost and the cakes will not rise.

1 Creaming the butter. Butter a loaf tin and line it with buttered greaseproof paper (*page 21*). Weigh butter, castor sugar and flour against eggs, so that you will have an equal weight of each ingredient. Place the butter in a large mixing bowl; using a wooden spoon or an electric mixer, beat the butter until it becomes pale and soft. Pour in the castor sugar (*above*).

4 Adding flour and egg whites. Sieve the flour into the mixture and fold it in with a metal spoon (*above*)—just enough to combine the ingredients. Transfer the egg whites into a copper bowl. Whisk the whites until stiff. To incorporate the whites easily, blend a little into the mixture, then lightly fold in the rest.

5 Filling the cake tin. Spoon the finished mixture evenly into the prepared cake tin (*above*). Bake the cake in an oven preheated to 180°C (350°F or Mark 4) for about 1¼ hours or until it is well risen and golden-brown. The cake is cooked when a skewer or toothpick inserted into its centre comes out clean.

2 **Blending the butter and sugar.** Beat the butter and the sugar together by hand or by electric mixer until all of the sugar has been incorporated into the butter—the butter will become creamy and almost white in colour as more and more air is beaten in. To make sure the sugar is completely blended with the butter, scrape the sides of the bowl occasionally with a rubber spatula.

3 **Adding egg yolks.** Separate an egg, dropping the white into a bowl and the yolk into the butter and sugar mixture. Use a wooden spoon to beat in the yolk (*above*). Continue separating the eggs, reserving the whites and beating each yolk into the mixture thoroughly before you add the next yolk.

6 **Cooling and serving.** Leave the cake to cool in the tin for about 10 minutes; it will shrink slightly from the sides. Turn it out on to your hands and place it, right side up, on a wire rack (*above*). Allow it to cool completely, then remove the lining paper. Place the cake on a serving dish, cut it into slices (*right*) and serve.☐

An Extravaganza Packed with Fruits

A traditional, rich fruit cake (*right; recipe, page 102*), decorated with garlands of icing (*page 42*), provides a centrepiece for a special occasion. Even unadorned, the cake's dense crumb and robust flavour make it a handsome offering.

Because rich fruit cakes have a high fat content, they are prepared by the creaming method (*page 38*). They always contain eggs and are usually made with equal amounts of flour, butter and brown sugar. The stiff batter of these cakes is thickly studded with chopped nuts, citrus zest, candied fruit and peel and dried fruits—here, sultanas, currants and seedless raisins. Treacle, spices and brandy provide additional flavouring.

Before adding the dried fruits to the batter, pick them over carefully and rinse them if necessary. Candied fruit and peel should be brought to the boil and drained in order to make them easier to chop, then dried on paper towels.

The density of a rich fruit cake batter means that the cake requires a long baking time. To prevent the cake's surface from burning, the oven temperature must be kept low. Put the cake into a fairly warm oven to begin with, to heat the batter through and start the cooking. After about 20 minutes, you should reduce the heat slightly. After a further 40 minutes, reduce it once more, to a low temperature that will not scorch the cake during the rest of the cooking period.

Because of the fruit and brandy it contains, as well as its high proportion of butter, the finished fruit cake will be a moist one that matures and improves with keeping. It may be kept, un-iced, for up to a year. Indeed the un-iced cake should be stored for a minimum of 2 weeks to let its flavour develop properly.

The matured cake can be served simply sprinkled with icing sugar or decorated more elaborately with icing—royal icing (*page 16*) is used here. For a smooth finish and a rich flavour, you can cover the cake with marzipan (*page 14*) before you ice it, as shown here. Apply the marzipan about a week before you plan to ice the cake: then store the cake, loosely covered with foil, so that the marzipan dries somewhat. Otherwise, oil from the almond paste will discolour the icing.

1 Combining the ingredients. In a large bowl, cream butter and sugar with a wooden spoon until light and fluffy. Add grated orange and lemon zest. Stir in treacle (*above*). Beat in eggs one at a time, then fold in sifted flour and spices—here, grated nutmeg and mixed spices. Pour in brandy. Add fruit, nuts and chopped peel, and mix thoroughly.

2 Filling the tin. Prepare a deep cake tin (*page 20*). Mix the batter with your hand to make sure that the fruit is evenly distributed, then put the batter into the tin and smooth it flat. Tie a band of brown paper around the tin, about 2.5 cm (1 inch) higher than the sides of the tin, to shield the sides and top of the cake from the direct heat of the oven.

6 Preparing to decorate. Unwrap the cake, turn it over for a smooth icing surface and measure its circumference with string. Roll out two long strips of marzipan about 5 mm (¼ inch) thick. Using the string as a guide (*above*), trim the strips so that each is almost as long as half the cake's circumference to prevent a bulge when the strips meet.

7 Brushing with egg whites. Trim both strips to the height of the cake. To help bond the marzipan to the cake, brush each strip with apricot glaze (*page 9*) or lightly beaten egg white (*above*). Press their coated surface against the cake; the strips should just meet on one side, leaving a 2.5 cm (1 inch) gap between them on the other side.

3 **Cooking the cake.** Bake it in an oven preheated to 170°C (325°F or Mark 3) for 20 minutes; then reduce the heat to 150°C (300°F or Mark 2). After 40 minutes, reduce the heat again to 140°C (275°F or Mark 1) and continue baking the cake—here for about 4 hours. When done, a skewer inserted into the cake (*above*) will come out clean.

4 **Storing the cake.** Cool the cake in its tin—about 2 hours—then remove the cake from the tin. To store the cake, place it on a large piece of plastic film. Cover the cake tightly with the plastic, then wrap it in aluminium foil and place it in an airtight container.

5 **Adding brandy.** If you are storing the fruit cake for a long period of time, refresh its flavours and keep the cake moist by adding brandy: unwrap the cake and use a small skewer to pierce the cake deeply several times (*above*). Dribble brandy over the cake and let it fill the pierced holes. Repeat at least every 3 to 4 months.

8 **Ensuring a snug fit.** To close the gap between the strips smoothly, steady the cake with one hand and roll a bottle or a drinking glass round the sides of the cake (*above*). Use a firm, even pressure so that the marzipan flattens out and stretches to close the gap.

9 **Cutting a marzipan top.** Roll out a circle of marzipan that is slightly larger than the diameter of the cake and about 5 mm (¼ inch) thick. Use the baking tin as a template to cut the marzipan circle to the exact size (*above*).

10 **Sealing the marzipan.** Brush a little beaten egg white or glaze on the top of the cake to help the marzipan adhere. Lift the marzipan on to the cake. Run a rolling pin across to smooth the marzipan and press it into place. With a spatula, seal the top and sides (*above*). Wrap loosely in foil and store for 1 week before icing.▶

11 **Icing the top.** Prepare royal icing (*page 16*). Spoon icing on to the top of the marzipan covered cake. Use a metal spatula to spread the icing about 2 mm (¹/₁₀ inch) thick. To smooth the icing, hold the spatula— or, as here, an icing ruler—flat against the top and draw it firmly towards you (*above*).

12 **Icing the sides.** Cover the sides of the cake with icing about 2 mm (¹/₁₀ inch) thick. Rotate the cake as you work; a jagged edge will form round the rim. Leave the cake uncovered for a day to allow the icing to harden, then scrape the rough edge with a knife. Repeat Steps 11 and 12 two or three times.

13 **Making a stencil.** Cut a strip of greaseproof paper to fit round the cake. To make a pattern with repeated loops use a ruler to mark off equal lengths and fold the paper over at each mark. Draw a semi-circle between two corners of the paper, from the fold to the opposite edge; cut it out (*above*).

14 **Tracing the loops.** Open the paper and place its straight edge along the base of the cake. Fasten each peak to the cake with a pin (*above*). To outline the pattern, use a pin to prick a series of small marks in the icing just above the looped edge of paper. Unpin the paper.

15 **Completing the decoration.** If necessary, thicken the royal icing by beating more icing sugar into it. Fit a small icing bag (*page 27*) with a star nozzle, and fill it two-thirds full with the icing. Pipe garlands of shells following the pattern markings on the cake's sides, then pipe rows of pendant stars from the peaks of the garlands (*page 26*). Finally pipe borders of shells along the bottom and top edge of the cake (*above*). □

Flavouring with Melted Chocolate

Adding melted chocolate to a batter gives cakes a dark, tempting colour as well as a rich flavour. However, the heaviness of chocolate means that such cakes require a good deal of leavening to make them rise.

In the devil's food cake shown on this page (*recipe, page 109*), air is incorporated into the batter by creaming the butter and sugar—here, brown sugar—and by beating in the eggs (*Step 1*). This natural leavening is supplemented with bicarbonate of soda and an acid, such as lemon juice, buttermilk or the soured cream used here. The bicarbonate reacts with the acid to produce bubbles of carbon dioxide. In the oven, the air and the carbon dioxide expand to lift the chocolate batter.

After the devil's food cake has been cooked and cooled, chocolate lovers can fill and cover it with yet more chocolate. Use chocolate-flavoured icing, whipped cream or butter cream (*pages 10-13*), and garnish the cake, if you like, with fresh or poached cherries or with orange segments. For a contrast of flavour and colour, as in this demonstration, you can use a white boiled icing.

1 Adding eggs. Prepare three shallow 20 cm (8 inch) cake tins (*page 20*). Sift flour and bicarbonate of soda into a small bowl and assemble eggs, soured cream and slightly cooled, melted chocolate (*page 10*). In a large bowl, cream butter and sugar with a whisk or wooden spoon. One at a time, beat in the eggs, then stir in the chocolate.

2 Adding soured cream. Add the flour and bicarbonate in two or three stages, folding it into the chocolate mixture alternately with the soured cream (*above*). Continue until the flour and cream are used up and the batter is smooth. Pour the batter into the tins and bake in an oven preheated to 190°C (375°F or Mark 5) for about 25 minutes.

3 Layering the cake. Test the cakes for doneness with a toothpick or a skewer (*page 38*). When they are ready, remove them from the oven. Cool the cakes in the tins for about 10 minutes, then turn them out on to wire racks to cool. Make boiled icing (*page 17*). Sandwich the cooled cakes together with about one-third of the icing.

4 Decorating the cake. Spoon the remaining icing on to the cake. Spread it over the top and sides of the cake with a metal spatula, swirling the icing to create an attractively rough finish (*inset*). You can serve the devil's food cake immediately, or store it for up to three days, loosely wrapped in plastic film or aluminium foil so as to avoid damaging the icing. Serve the cake cut into wedges. □

Leavening with Vinegar and Soda

Economical cakes containing a relatively low proportion of butter—often less than half the weight of their flour content—are made by the rubbing method, demonstrated here for a vinegar cake (*recipe, page 114*). Instead of being creamed (*pages 38-43*), the butter is rubbed into the flour to distribute it thoroughly, and milk is used to moisten and bind the ingredients smoothly together. The rubbing process (*Step 1, right*) must be accomplished quickly and with a light touch. Overworking the butter would make it oily, resulting in a tough cake.

Rubbed cakes often contain no eggs, and only a little air is incorporated into the cake batter by the rubbing method itself. As with the devil's food cake on page 43, a chemical leavening agent is needed to make the cake rise—here, bicarbonate of soda activated by vinegar.

Although the vinegar gives the cake its name, it does not contribute to its flavour. The acid in the vinegar reacts with the soda, causing it to release bubbles of carbon dioxide that leaven the cake. If the soda were added directly to the vinegar, the mixture would froth up very quickly and much gas would be lost. To prevent this, the soda is dissolved in a little warm milk. The vinegar is added to the remaining milk and the two mixtures combined. The large volume of milk slows the reaction, and less gas is wasted before the liquid is added to the rubbed ingredients.

The consistency of the cake batter is important: if it is too liquid, the cake will be heavy and damp; if it is too stiff, the cake will be dry and crumbly. Use just enough of the foaming milk to make a mixture that will drop off a spoon when the spoon is gently shaken. The leavening of the cake will not be noticeably affected if you do not use every last drop of milk.

1 **Preparing the ingredients.** Line a deep cake tin (*page 20*); in this case, a raised base tin with a removable base is used to allow the cake to be unmoulded easily. The tin is lined with a double thickness of greaseproof paper to protect the cake during its long cooking time. Prepare some fruit—here raisins and currants—and put them in a bowl with sugar. Sieve flour into another bowl, add cold butter cut into cubes, and lightly rub them together with your fingertips (*above*) until the mixture resembles breadcrumbs.

4 **Baking the cake.** Spoon the mixture into the tin and smooth the surface. Bake the cake in an oven preheated to 190°C (375°F or Mark 5) for about 20 minutes to let the mixture rise and set. Then reduce the heat slightly and bake the cake for about 40 to 50 minutes, or until a skewer or wooden toothpick inserted into the centre comes out clean.

5 **Unmoulding the cake.** Allow the cake to cool for 10 minutes. Put the tin on an upturned bowl and push the sides of the tin down (*above*), leaving the cake on the base. Remove the side paper. Place a wire rack on top of the cake and invert base, cake and rack. Lift off the base and peel away the paper. Turn the cake over on to a serving platter.

2 **Preparing the leavening.** Mix the fruit and sugar into the flour and butter. Measure some milk into a jug and pour a little of the milk into a small saucepan. Gently warm the milk over a low heat. Stir vinegar into the remaining cold milk. Remove the saucepan from the heat, add bicarbonate of soda (*above*), stirring the milk until the soda dissolves.

3 **Adding the leavening.** Pour the contents of the saucepan into the cold milk and vinegar. The vinegar will react with the bicarbonate of soda and cause the milk to foam. Quickly pour some of the liquid on to the dry ingredients (*above*). Stir with a spoon, and continue adding liquid until the mixture is just thick enough to drop off the spoon.

6 **Serving and storing.** Let the cake cool completely before serving it or it will crumble as you cut it. Because a cake made with a low proportion of butter loses its moisture more quickly than a richer cake, it is best eaten soon after it is cool. Wrapped in plastic film or foil, however, vinegar cake will keep fresh in an airtight container for a few days.□

A Molten Mixture of Sugar and Spice

The rich brown colour and moist texture of such cakes as honey cake, molasses cake or gingerbread—sometimes called ginger cake—(*recipes, pages 116 and 117*) are primarily due to the fact that they are highly sweetened—with honey, molasses or treacle as well as with sugar.

Sugar and butter are first melted together with the treacle over a low heat (*Step 1, right*). Once blended, they are easy to incorporate into the other ingredients: flour, spices and a little milk and egg to give the batter a liquid consistency.

Because these economical cakes are usually made with a very low proportion of eggs—sometimes none at all—a chemical leavening agent, bicarbonate of soda, is added to ensure their lightness. Natural acids in honey, molasses or treacle react with the bicarbonate to produce bubbles of carbon dioxide.

In this demonstration (*recipe, page 116*), the flavour of the treacle is enhanced by brown sugar, ground ginger and chopped candied lemon, orange and citron peel. Other flavourings, such as chopped almonds, ground cinnamon or raisins can be added to the gingerbread (*recipes, page 117*).

Because of the cake's high proportion of sugar, it will burn easily. Bake the gingerbread at a moderate heat—here, 180°C (350°F or Mark 4)—until it is firm and springy to the touch. Cakes that are baked at low or moderate oven temperatures cook and rise slowly. Do not open the oven door during the early stages of baking or the rush of cool air will reduce the temperature in the oven and cause the cake to sink.

1 **Melting butter and sugar with treacle.** To make the treacle easier to pour, place its container in hot water for a few minutes. Set a saucepan on kitchen scales, weigh it, then pour in treacle until the extra weight equals the amount required. Add butter and sugar and place over a low heat. Stir the mixture with a wooden spoon until the butter has melted and thoroughly combined with the treacle. Remove the saucepan and let the mixture cool.

3 **Combining the ingredients.** Pour the eggs into the flour mixture and add the peel. Use your fingertip to test the temperature of the butter and treacle mixture—it should be cool; if the syrup is too hot it will cook the flour on contact and produce a hard, tough cake. Pour in the treacle mixture (*above*).

4 **Adding milk to the batter.** Lightly stir the ingredients with a wooden spoon. Add milk to the mixing bowl, stirring as you do so (*above*). Continue stirring until the batter is smooth and thick, and all of the ingredients are evenly mixed.

2 **Sifting the dry ingredients.** With a fork, beat eggs lightly in a small bowl. Place a mixture of candied peels in cold water and bring to the boil to soften them and remove excess sugar; drain the peels and chop them. Sieve the flour, ground ginger and bicarbonate of soda into a large mixing bowl (*above*).

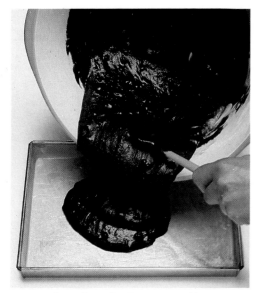

5 **Baking the cake.** Prepare and line a shallow cake tin (*page 20*). Pour the batter into the tin, using the rubber spatula to scrape all of the batter from the mixing bowl. Place the cake in an oven preheated to 180°C (350°F or Mark 4) for about an hour—until the gingerbread is firm and springy to the touch.

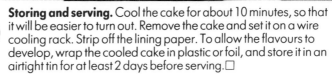

6 **Storing and serving.** Cool the cake for about 10 minutes, so that it will be easier to turn out. Remove the cake and set it on a wire cooling rack. Strip off the lining paper. To allow the flavours to develop, wrap the cooled cake in plastic or foil, and store it in an airtight tin for at least 2 days before serving. □

3
A Repertoire of Pastry Doughs
Beginning with the Basics

Rubbing and cutting in butter

Mixing dough on a work surface

Egg and sugar enrichment

Layering with butter

Tactics for stretching a dough

A dough made over heat

There is no mystery to the making of a good pastry dough. The only requirement is an understanding of the function of a few simple ingredients and the methods of handling them. Flour provides body, fat gives tenderness. Although it is possible to make good pastry with lard or vegetable shortening, butter produces pastry of surpassing flavour and richness, qualities reinforced in some doughs by the addition of eggs and sugar. These ingredients, combined in different ways, yield the full range of doughs demonstrated in this chapter: shortcrust, rich shortcrust, flaky, rough puff, puff, choux and strudel. One or more of these doughs will serve for almost any pie, tart or pastry. Occasionally, two doughs are used together, combined with fillings to make marvellous pastry assemblies.

Shortcrust and puff doughs demand light handling and cool ingredients. Work the dough as little as possible and use chilled butter and cold water to prevent the gluten in the dough from developing too much elasticity, which would result in a paste that is difficult to roll out. Shortcrust, which bakes to a crisp, firm pastry, is made by cutting or rubbing butter into flour and moistening the ingredients with a little water (*page 50*). The addition of eggs and sugar transforms plain shortcrust into rich shortcrust dough (*opposite and page 52*) that results in a sweeter, more crumbly pastry. The preparation of flaky, rough puff and puff doughs (*pages 54 and 56*) begins in much the same way as shortcrust. Subsequently however, these doughs are rolled and folded to create a multiplicity of layers. As they bake in the oven, the doughs rise and the layers separate: the cooked pastries are light, crisp and meltingly tender.

Very different techniques are used for strudel and choux. Strudel (*page 58*) is made with warm water and melted butter and the dough is kneaded vigorously. As a result, the gluten develops enough strength for the dough to be stretched into a thin but resilient sheet that is spread with a filling and rolled up—resulting in a layered effect very like puff pastry. Choux (*page 60*) differs even more widely in its preparation. The ingredients, which include a high proportion of water and eggs, are beaten together over heat until they form a well aerated paste. The dough is too soft to be rolled: it must be piped or spooned on to a baking tray. In the oven, the choux's moisture turns to steam, puffing up the dough and leaving a hollow interior for a filling such as whipped or pastry cream (*page 13*).

As the first step in producing a rich shortcrust dough, flour and icing sugar are sieved on to a work surface, where they will be combined with the other ingredients—butter and eggs. Sieving ensures that the dry ingredients are free from lumps, making for a light, even-textured pastry. The marble work surface shown here is ideal for keeping the butter cool and helps to produce a firm yet tender result.

Shortcrust: Simple and Versatile

Crisp, light and easy to prepare, short-crust is the most frequently used of all pie and tart pastries (*recipe, page 165*). Its firm texture complements most fillings such as custard, apple or rhubarb, while a base of baked shortcrust can provide the foundation for elaborate assemblies (*recipes, pages 155-156 and 159*).

Shortcrust dough is made from flour, butter, water and a little salt—usually, half the amount of butter to flour. The dough takes very little time to make. Indeed, to achieve perfect, tender shortcrust pastry, speed is essential; overworking would only strengthen the gluten in the dough and make the butter oily—resulting in a mixture that will become hard and tough on baking.

To help keep the dough cool, chill the water and butter and use your fingertips to rub the butter lightly together with the flour. Lift the mixture well out of the bowl and let it fall back through your fingers (*Step 2*), shaking the bowl occasionally to bring the larger crumbs to the surface. Some cooks minimize handling even further by using an electric food processor which can combine the ingredients in sec-onds. Another method of making short-crust dough is to cut the butter into the flour with two knives (*box, opposite page, below*)—a technique that produces a crumbly, less uniform mixture that bakes to a flakier pastry.

Whichever method of incorporating the butter you use, finish the dough by adding just enough water to make the dough cohere (*Step 4, below*). Too much water will produce a sticky dough that is difficult to roll out, too little water leaves it unmanageably dry. In either case, the resulting pastry will be hard. Start with less water than you think you need and supplement it—if necessary—by adding more water a drop or two at a time.

Chilling any dough before use relaxes the gluten, making the dough less elastic and thus softer and easier to roll out. To prevent air from drying out the resting dough and forming hard, crusty streaks on its surface, wrap the dough in plastic film, greaseproof paper or aluminium foil before placing it in a refrigerator or other cool place. If it is not required immediately, the dough can be stored in this way for up to three days.

1 **Preparing the ingredients.** Cut cold butter into pieces. Assemble flour, salt and iced water. Add a pinch of salt to the flour and sift them together into a large mixing bowl (*above*).

4 **Finishing the dough.** Quickly stir in the water with a knife to distribute the water evenly without overworking the dough (*above, left*). Gather the mixture together with one hand; if it feels too crumbly, add a little more water until the dough begins to cohere (*above, centre*). Press the dough into a ball (*above, right*). To make the dough easier to roll out, wrap it in plastic film, greaseproof paper or foil and chill for 15 minutes before using. □

2 **Rubbing the butter into the flour and salt.** Add all of the cubes of butter to the flour. Using the tips of your fingers and thumbs, pick up a small amount of butter and flour, lightly rub them together and let the mixture fall back into the bowl (*above, left*). Continue for about 2 to 3 minutes, until all of the butter is incorporated and the mixture resembles very coarse breadcrumbs (*above, right*).

3 **Adding water.** Use a spoon to make a shallow well in the mixture; spoon in a little iced water (*above*). Because some flours absorb more water than others, the quantity of water you need may vary; always start with a minimum amount in order to avoid soggy results.

An Alternative Approach: Working with Knives

1 **Cutting in the butter.** Chill water and butter. Cut the butter into cubes and put them into a mixing bowl with sifted flour and salt. With two knives, cut the butter into the flour using a rapid criss-cross movement until the lumps of butter are about the size of peas.

2 **Adding the water.** Sprinkle a little cold water over the mixture and blend it in lightly with a knife. Then, use your hands to lightly gather the dough together. Add a little more water if necessary; the mixture should cling together without being damp (*above*).

3 **Finishing the dough.** Lightly press the dough together and form it into a ball. Wrap the dough in plastic film, greaseproof paper or aluminium foil to prevent drying out, and chill the dough for about 15 minutes before use.

Rich Shortcrust: Adding Sugar and Eggs

By adding sugar to flour, butter and a pinch of salt, and by moistening the mixture with eggs instead of water, you can transform plain shortcrust (*page 50*) into a rich shortcrust dough (*recipe, page 165*). The sugar—castor sugar, or as here, icing sugar—adds flavour and helps the dough to bake to a golden-brown pastry with a crumbly, biscuit-like texture. The eggs bind the other ingredients to produce a slightly firmer, richer pastry than plain shortcrust. Although any pastry will gradually absorb moisture from a soft filling and become soggy, a pie or tart made with rich shortcrust will stay crisp longer—up to 2 days in a cool, dry, place.

One way of ensuring that the eggs are evenly distributed is to blend them first with the butter in a well or hollow made within the flour mixture (*Step 3*). Use butter that is malleable enough to work but not oily. If the butter is too cold, it will be difficult to combine with eggs; if it is too warm, it will cause the flour to clump together and result in pastry which is interspersed with hard, dry patches.

This technique of dough-making called the "well" method permits you to gradually gather in the dry ingredients so that the flour mixture is evenly and thoroughly coated with the butter and egg paste. If the flour were to be added all at once, it would be hard to blend it in evenly without overworking the dough. In the demonstration here, the ingredients are mixed directly on a work surface—this is a particularly useful way of handling a large volume of ingredients. Small quantities of dough, however, can be prepared just as easily in a mixing bowl.

Making rich shortcrust by hand takes about 5 minutes, but an electric food processor will produce a slightly less crumbly version in seconds. If you use softened butter, you can process all the ingredients into dough in one operation; hard butter should first be cut up by hand and blended with the dry ingredients before adding the eggs and blending again.

However you make the dough, the addition of the sugar will make the dough crumbly and more difficult to handle than plain shortcrust. The dough will be easier to roll if you first chill it in a refrigerator for at least half an hour.

1 **Assembling the ingredients.** Soften unsalted butter by leaving it at room temperature for 1 to 2 hours. Assemble the eggs, and dry ingredients: flour, sugar—here, icing sugar—and a pinch of salt. Sieve the dry ingredients into a mound on a cool work surface (*above*).

2 **Adding the butter and eggs.** With your hand, make a deep well in the centre of the mound of dry ingredients. Place the softened butter into the centre of the well; break the eggs over the butter (*above*).

5 **Blending the ingredients.** Continue to chop in the flour (*above, left*), flipping the bottom of the mixture to the top, until the dough forms large crumbs about the size of a pea—about 2 minutes. The dough should be rough and crumbly (*above, right*). If the mixture is too dry to incorporate all the flour, add a little water— a drop or two at a time—until the dough begins to cling together.

3 **Mixing the moist ingredients.** Using the fingers of one hand, pinch the butter and eggs together repeatedly until they are lightly blended (*above, left*). Work quickly, so that the butter does not become oily; after about a minute, the mixture will have the consistency of a slippery paste (*above, right*).

4 **Incorporating the flour and sugar.** Use a metal spatula to gather in the dry ingredients. Flip the flour mixture, little by little, over the butter and egg mixture (*above*), and then chop the ingredients with the edge of the spatula, using quick, light movements.

6 **Finishing the dough.** Use your hands to push the crumbly dough mixture together, pressing gently so that the crumbs adhere and form a loose mass (*inset*). Form the dough into a ball (*left*), wrap it in wax paper, plastic film or foil, and chill it in the refrigerator for at least half an hour before rolling it out. □

Rough-Puff: Quick and Flaky

Pastry that rises in crisp, light flakes is made by incorporating air and butter between layers of dough. As the dough bakes, heat from the oven transforms moisture in the dough and butter to steam, which expands and, along with the trapped air, lifts the pastry. Such doughs are described as rough-puff or puff, depending on how they are made and on the resultant height and texture of the baked pastry (*recipe, page 166*).

The technique of making classic puff, the lightest and highest rising of all pastry doughs, is demonstrated on page 56. The rough-puff doughs shown here are quicker to prepare. You can use them to make pastries, such as fruit turnovers and cream horns (*recipes, pages 150 and 163*), that do not depend upon the exceptional rising properties of classic puff.

The simplest rough-puff is a shortcrust dough—made with between half and equal quantities of butter to flour—rolled out three or four times to create extra layers (*box, opposite page*). Another method of making rough-puff, sometimes called "flaky" dough (*right*), takes longer since the butter—usually two-thirds butter to flour—is added in stages, to give particularly flaky results.

To make flaky dough, malleable butter is divided into four portions. One portion is rubbed into flour, and water is added to make a preliminary dough. After the dough has rested for about 30 minutes, it is rolled into a rectangle, dotted with a second portion of butter, then folded into a parcel (*Step 4*). The butter should be soft but fairly cool. If the butter is too hard, it tears the dough; if it is too soft, it melts as you roll the dough, and runs out at the sides of the parcel.

The sequence of rolling, buttering and folding is repeated twice more until all the butter has been incorporated. After each folding, rest the dough in the refrigerator to relax the gluten in the flour and make the dough easier to roll. To keep the layers uniform and to ensure that the butter is evenly distributed, always turn the dough before rolling it so that the folded seams are at the side, and the two open ends at top and bottom.

1 Preparing the dough. Sift the flour and salt into a mixing bowl. Divide the softened butter into four equal portions. Using your fingertips, lightly rub one portion into the flour for about a minute or until the mixture looks like breadcrumbs. Gradually add cold water and work the dough until it comes cleanly away from the sides of the bowl (*inset*). Cover the ball of dough with plastic film and let it rest in a refrigerator for about 30 minutes.

4 Folding the dough. Fold the unbuttered third of the rectangle of dough over the centre. Bring the buttered top third down (*above, left*). To keep the layers uniform, and the butter from squeezing out, press the open sides of the package together with your hands (*above, right*); complete the sealing process by pressing gently on the sides of the dough with a rolling pin.

2 **Rolling out the dough.** Sprinkle a little flour on to a work surface to prevent the dough from sticking. Roll the dough into a rectangle about 5 to 10 mm ($\frac{1}{4}$ to $\frac{1}{2}$ inch) thick and about three times as long as it is wide. Pat the sides of the rectangle into straight lines so that the rolled out dough can be folded neatly.

3 **Adding butter.** With a brush remove any surplus flour from the dough. Use a palette knife to dot another portion of butter over two-thirds of the dough (*above*), leaving a border of about 1 cm ($\frac{1}{2}$ inch) around the edge of the dough to prevent the butter from being squeezed out as the dough is rolled.

1 **Making three layers.** Lightly sprinkle the work surface with flour. Roll the dough into a rectangle (*Step 2, left*), then fold it into three. Turn the dough out so that the folds are on the sides and roll it into a rectangle again.

5 **Resting the dough.** Line a small tray with plastic film—as here—or with kitchen foil. Place the dough on the tray and cover the dough with more plastic or foil to prevent it from drying out. Rest the dough in the refrigerator for about 30 minutes, then unwrap the dough and put it on a lightly floured work surface.

6 **Completing the dough.** Repeat Steps 2 to 5 twice more until all of the butter has been incorporated. To distribute the butter evenly, roll the dough at an angle of 90° to the folds (*above*). Roll, fold and chill it before rolling it out for use. □

2 **Completing the dough.** Fold the ends of the rectangle so that they meet in the centre, then fold the dough in half to make four layers; chill for 30 minutes. Roll, fold—into four layers—and chill twice more before rolling out for use.

Puff: Myriad Layers of Dough and Butter

Puff dough rises to the lightest and highest of all pastries (*recipe, page 167*), it can be baked with a light filling of jam or pastry cream, or pre-baked and filled with fresh fruit or almost any type of flavoured cream (*recipes, pages 149-150*).

The ingredients for puff—flour, butter and water—are the same as for shortcrust or rough-puff doughs (*pages 50 and 54*). Only proportions differ. Whereas rough-puff is usually made with more flour than butter, puff dough is made with equal amounts of these ingredients. Some cooks add a little lemon juice or vinegar to strengthen the strands of gluten and allow the puff dough to retain its layered structure during baking. But their use has no effect on the lightness of the dough and excellent puff can be made, as in this demonstration, without them.

The technique for making puff dough is essentially the same as for flaky; the dough and butter are repeatedly rolled and folded to create multiple layers. However, the method of incorporating the butter is very different. For puff, a small amount of the butter—about one eighth of the total amount—is used to make the basic mixture; the remainder is pounded into a sheet and the rolled out dough is folded over it (*Step 5*). To give the pastry its characteristic height and leafy layers, the parcel of dough and butter is rolled and folded six times, instead of the usual four times for rough-puff. Between each rolling sequence the dough is chilled in order to firm the butter and relax the gluten in the dough.

You can use a food processor to make the basic mixture, as you can for shortcrust and rough-puff dough. The food processor will save very little time, however, since the rolling out must be done by hand. Because puff dough takes so much time to make—about 3 hours in all—it is well worth making a large quantity and storing it. Wrapped in plastic or foil to prevent it from drying out, puff dough will keep in a refrigerator for up to 4 days or for several months in a freezer.

1 **Preparing the dough.** Sift flour and salt into a bowl, add a little cold butter and rub the ingredients together with your fingertips. Gradually add enough cold water to bind, working the dough lightly. Sprinkle a little flour into a plastic bag to prevent the dough from sticking (*above*); put the dough mixture inside and chill for about 30 minutes.

4 **Placing the butter.** Peel the top sheet of greaseproof paper from the butter. Invert the butter over the rolled-out dough, placing it diagonally on the dough (*above*). Then peel the second sheet of paper from the butter.

5 **Enclosing the butter.** Draw up the four corners of the dough and fold each one over the butter to make an envelope, (*above*) leaving about 1 cm (½ inch) all round the butter. Press the edges and seams of the envelope gently together with your fingers or the rolling pin.

6 **Rolling the folded dough.** Pressing evenly but lightly, so as not to squeeze out the butter, roll the dough into a rectangle three times as long as it is wide. Pat the edges of the dough with the sides of your hands to keep the edges neat. Brush off any surplus flour, lest the pastry becomes tough and dry.

2 Flattening the butter. Take the dough out of the refrigerator. Put a sheet of greaseproof paper on a work surface, place some cold butter on top and cover it with another sheet of greaseproof paper. The paper will prevent the butter from sticking to both the rolling pin and the work surface. With a rolling pin, beat the butter into a square about 2 cm (¾ inch) thick.

3 Rolling the dough. Remove the dough from the plastic bag and place it on a lightly floured work surface. Roll the dough into a square about 1 cm (½ inch) thick, and large enough for its corners to fold over and envelope the butter. Use light, quick strokes to roll the dough, turning it so that it is rolled evenly.

7 Folding the dough. Fold the top third of the dough over the centre, then fold the bottom third over, to make three layers of dough (*above*). Seal the air inside the layers by pressing the edges of the dough down lightly with the rolling pin.

8 Completing the sequence. Repeat Steps 6 and 7—always rolling with the folded edges at the sides (*above*). Mark the dough with two fingers (*right*) to show you have rolled it twice. Wrap and chill the dough for about 30 minutes. Repeat Steps 6, 7 and 8 twice, imprinting the dough each time. □

Strudel: a Flexible Wrapper

Strudel dough has a unique quality: an extraordinary strength that allows it to be stretched extremely thin. Rolled repeatedly around a filling, then baked (*page 84*), the dough emerges as a crisp, golden cylinder of fragile pastry layers.

In most pastry-making, elasticity is something to be avoided; in order to give strudel its exceptional qualities, the rules which govern the making of most other doughs are turned upside down. The ingredients—flour, butter, eggs, water— are warm, not cool, the butter is melted, not chilled, and the dough is thoroughly kneaded and beaten, not handled lightly. The result is a strong, elastic dough (*recipe, page 166*). When left to relax under a warm bowl (*Step 4*) the dough loses its springy quality but retains its strength— making it easy to roll and stretch.

Because so-called strong bread flour yields more gluten than ordinary soft flour—and thus produces a more elastic dough—some cooks use only strong flour for making strudel, or a combination of strong and soft flour for a dough that is slightly easier to handle. When a soft flour is used, the presence of an acid will help to develop the flour's gluten; a dash of vinegar or lemon juice is often added to the ingredients.

Vigorous kneading is vital to develop the gluten in the dough. As you knead, you will feel the dough becoming less sticky, increasingly resilient, and finally, smooth and silky.

After it has been rolled out, the dough is stretched by hand on a floured cloth (*Step 7*). The cloth makes it easier to lift and handle the dough.

As the dough is stretched more and more, it will gradually become so thin that it is translucent. If you have long fingernails, use clenched fists to stretch the dough, so as not to puncture it. But do not be too concerned if you make a small tear. Such a mishap is not disastrous: once the dough has been rolled repeatedly around its filling, the accumulating layers will prevent any leakage.

1 Assembling the ingredients. Sieve flour and salt into a large mixing bowl, and break eggs into a smaller bowl. Melt butter in a small saucepan and let it cool. Add lukewarm water and the melted butter to the eggs (*above*) and beat them together with a fork until smooth. Add a dash of vinegar to the mixture.

2 Combining the ingredients. Make a well in the middle of the sieved flour and fill the hollow with the egg and butter mixture. Use your hands to combine the ingredients, gradually drawing the flour into the centre: the mixture will be soft and sticky (*above*). If necessary, add more lukewarm water.

5 Preparing to roll the dough. Cover a large table with a clean cloth. To prevent the dough from sticking, sprinkle the cloth lightly with flour. Place the rested dough in the centre of the table. To keep the dough moist, brush it with a little melted butter (*above*).

6 Rolling out the dough. Roll the dough in a lengthwise direction (*above*) until it is about 6 mm ($\frac{1}{4}$ inch) thick; then move round the table and roll the dough crosswise until it is about 3 mm ($\frac{1}{8}$ inch) thick. If the dough starts to dry out, brush it with melted butter.

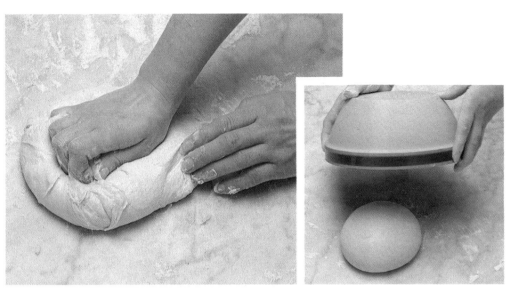

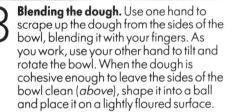

3 **Blending the dough.** Use one hand to scrape up the dough from the sides of the bowl, blending it with your fingers. As you work, use your other hand to tilt and rotate the bowl. When the dough is cohesive enough to leave the sides of the bowl clean (*above*), shape it into a ball and place it on a lightly floured surface.

4 **Kneading the dough.** Press the dough with the heel of your hand and push forward (*above*) then turn the dough slightly and repeat the process. Continue kneading until the dough no longer sticks to your hand—about 15 minutes. Shape the dough into a smooth ball: rinse a bowl in hot water; dry the warmed bowl and invert it over the dough (*inset*). Leave the dough for about 30 minutes.

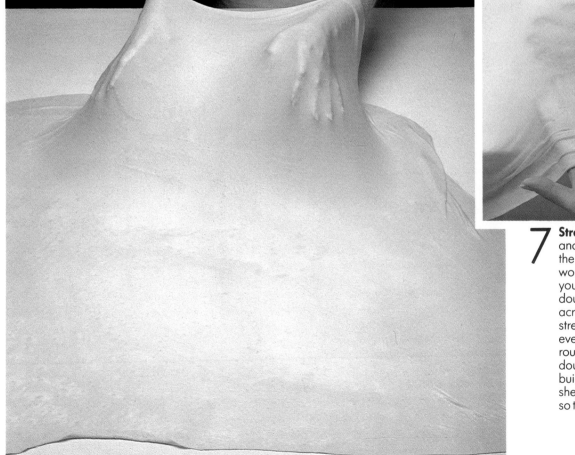

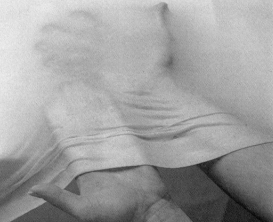

7 **Stretching the dough.** Flour your hands and slip them—palms down—beneath the dough. Starting at the centre, and working towards the nearest edge, move your hands apart repeatedly until the dough stretches to a translucent sheet across your knuckles. As the dough stretches, it will take up more room and, eventually, drape over the table. Move round the table stretching a section of dough at a time. A thick border will build up round the edge of the stretched sheet. Use scissors to trim off the border so that the dough will roll up evenly. □

Choux: a Twice-Cooked Formulation

Choux dough consists of flour, butter, water and a generous complement of eggs (*recipe, page 166*). Whereas most other pastry doughs require cold butter and water, choux is made by bringing butter and water to the boil together and then stirring in the flour, off the heat. When the flour comes in contact with the hot liquid the mixture thickens. Finally, eggs are beaten into the hot paste to produce a soft, light dough. Choux is too sticky to be rolled out like other doughs; it must be piped or spooned on to a tray for baking.

In the oven, the moisture in the dough becomes steam, which expands along with the air beaten into the dough during the mixing process and causes the choux to swell up to about three times its unbaked size, leaving a hollow interior. The feather-light result is delicious served simply dusted with icing sugar, or topped with a rich combination of chocolate and cream (*page 10*). Filled with ice cream or sweetened creams, baked choux balls or strips can be used to make the pastries demonstrated on pages 86-90.

1 Preparing the ingredients. Put the water into a heavy saucepan and place it over a low heat. Add butter (*above*). Sift the flour and salt on to a piece of greaseproof paper.

2 Boiling the water. Once the butter has melted, increase the heat to bring the water to the boil. Turn off the heat immediately: prolonged boiling would evaporate enough water to alter the proportions of the ingredients.

5 Adding eggs. Cool the dough briefly to prevent the eggs from setting as they are added. Break an egg into a bowl and add it to the pan (*above, left*). Beat the dough to incorporate the egg thoroughly. Beat in the remaining eggs one by one. Flours vary in their absorbent qualities; as a precaution against too liquid a dough, some cooks beat the last egg lightly and add only enough to make a firm dough that will slowly drop off a spoon.

3 **Adding the flour.** Pick up the piece of greaseproof paper and slide the flour and salt into the hot liquid (*above*). Add all the flour mixture at once: added in stages, it would form lumps.

4 **Stirring in the flour.** Stir the mixture as soon as the flour is added (*above, left*), and continue until the ingredients are thoroughly combined. Turn on the heat—a moderate heat will eliminate any extra moisture in the dough. Continue stirring the mixture vigorously, until the dough forms a solid mass that comes away cleanly from the sides of the pan (*above, right*). This should take about one minute. Remove the pan from the heat.

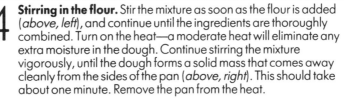

6 **Filling a piping bag.** Continue beating until the ingredients are thoroughly blended (*left*). Use a piping bag to shape the choux for cooking. To fill the bag easily, fold the top third back over your wrist. Spoon the mixture into the folded bag (*above*) until it is about two-thirds full. Unfold the bag and twist the top to secure its contents. □

4
Pies and Tarts
Crisp Cases
for all Manner of Fillings

Any of the shortcrust and puff doughs demonstrated in the previous chapter can be used to make pastry cases for a myriad of sweet fillings; the different flavours and textures combine to produce a dazzling array of pies and tarts. Although the words pie and tart have various meanings in different countries, a pie usually consists of a pastry case with a deep filling that is covered with pastry, whipped cream or meringue—as in the lemon meringue pie shown opposite (*page 76*). In a tart, the pastry case and filling are shallower and the filling is rarely completely covered.

Pies are made either with a single top crust—as in the rhubarb pie on page 64 where a deep dish of sugared fruit is covered with a pastry lid—or with a double crust, where the filling is enclosed between two layers of pastry (*page 66*). Tarts may be left open to reveal a filling of fruit, custard or flavoured creams, or partly covered with a decorative lattice of pastry strips, as in the spinach custard tart on page 71. An upside-down tart is an intriguing variation; on page 68, a filling of pears and red wine is covered with plain shortcrust and reversed on to a plate before serving.

The pies and tarts demonstrated on the following pages are made with shortcrust dough; in many cases, puff dough could be used in its place. Although the weight of a pie or tart filling will inevitably prevent a puff dough from baking to its maximum height, puff makes a superb pastry lid that will rise to a golden, flaky dome.

Fillings may be added either before or after the dough is baked. However, when the dough is covered with a filling and then cooked, the moisture of the filling may prevent the base from baking crisply; thus, a filling with a high liquid content can result in a soggy base. In this chapter, some hints are given on how to minimize this risk; you can scatter bread or cake crumbs over the dough to absorb some moisture from a filling, or brush a film of egg whites on the base, but the most effective method is to pre-bake the case before it is filled (*page 72*).

Glazes provide a finishing touch by giving a glossy sheen to pastry and to open fruit fillings. A clear glaze for pastry is made by brushing lightly whisked egg whites over uncooked dough (*page 64*), while egg yolks beaten with a little water or milk yield a deep golden colour (*page 71*). To highlight the bright colours of fresh or cooked fruit, brush on a glaze of apricot or redcurrant syrup (*pages 70 and 73*).

A wedge of pie is lifted from its serving dish to reveal a smooth lemon filling. The filling—a cooked mixture of eggs, butter, sugar and lemon—was spooned into a pre-baked pastry case of shortcrust flavoured with sugar and lemon. A thick topping of meringue was swirled into peaks that coloured delicately in the oven.

A Deep Dish of Fruit with a Golden Dome

Fresh fruit sweetened with sugar and covered with a lid of dough makes the simplest of all pies. Since there is no bottom crust, you can use any fruit—juicy or firm-fleshed—with no risk of the pastry becoming soggy. In this demonstration (*recipe, page 136*), the pie is filled with tender, young rhubarb—a deliciously tart but lavishly moist vegetable that most cooks consider to be a fruit. Plums, berries and apples are other good choices for fillings: use them alone or combine two or three complementary fruits.

Any filling will lose volume as the juices are drawn out during cooking. For an ample pie filling, heap the fruit into a deep baking dish, moulding it slightly to give the baked pie an attractive shape.

Whatever dough you choose for the pie lid—a plain shortcrust (*page 50*) has been used to cover the rhubarb—the pastry will contract slightly during baking because the oven heat will evaporate its moisture. To prevent the crust from shrinking from the lip of the dish and falling into the filling, anchor it firmly to a collar of dough placed round the rim (*Step 2*). Steam rising from the fruit will raise the lid, leaving a firm, domed crust.

1 **Cutting the pastry.** Wash and chop the rhubarb and assemble bowls of sugar and water, and the dough—here shortcrust. Roll the dough until it is about 5 mm (¼ inch) thick and about 5 cm (2 inches) larger all round than the pie dish. Make the lid by cutting round the inverted dish, leaving a margin of about 1 cm (½ inch) to allow for the mound of filling. Make a second cut about 2.5 cm (1 inch) outside the first to form a pastry collar (*above*).

4 **Trimming the dough.** With your fingers, press the lid firmly on to the collar of dough. Trim off the excess dough by holding the knife so that the blade angles up and outwards (*above*) to leave a slightly overhanging edge that will allow for shrinkage during baking.

5 **Sealing the edges.** To prevent the lid and the collar from separating as the pie bakes in the oven, hold the knife horizontally and tap the blade against the edge of the pie all round. As you tap, press the lid down firmly with the back of your index finger (*above*).

6 **Decorating the edge.** Using the dull edge of the knife blade, make several indentations round the rim of the pie to create a scalloped edge (*above*). If you like, you can cut leaves or other decorative shapes from any leftover dough; dampen them with a little water and arrange them on the lid.

2 **Fitting the collar.** Turn the dish over. Using a pastry brush, moisten the rim of the pie dish with water to help the collar of dough adhere. Press the collar firmly on to the rim (*above*), overlapping the ends. Fill the dish with alternating layers of rhubarb and sugar.

3 **Covering the filling.** Again using the pastry brush, moisten the collar of dough lightly (*above*) so that the lid of the pie will stick to it. Then fold the lid loosely in two, and place it over one half of the filled pie dish. Unfold the lid to cover the dish completely (*right*).

7 **Glazing the pie.** For a glossy pie crust, lightly whisk an egg white and brush it over the top of the pie. Dust the pie with castor sugar and bake it in an oven preheated to 190°C (375°F or Mark 5) for about 45 minutes or until golden.

8 **Serving the pie.** Remove the pie from the oven and sprinkle it with a little more sugar. Serve the pie warm or cold, with double cream or ice cream. Using the knife, carefully cut a wedge of crust, and put it on an individual serving plate. Spoon out some of the rhubarb and liquid and place it next to the crust.□

A Two-Crust Favourite

The trick in making a two-crust pie is to keep the base from getting soggy, a disaster you can prevent with simple precautions. In the first place, you should choose a filling that will not render much liquid as it cooks—the firm apples used in the demonstration on the right, for example (*recipe, page 129*), or a thick cream filling or a mincemeat.

For extra insurance, you can brush the bottom layer of pastry dough lightly with whisked egg white before adding the filling. In the oven, the egg white will cook to a thin glaze that will prevent the filling's moisture from seeping into the dough. A little flour added to a fruit filling will absorb some of the juices that are exuded during cooking. A few slits cut into the upper pastry crust will allow much of the remaining moisture to escape as steam.

To make the pie base and top, you can use any shortcrust, rough-puff or puff dough (*recipes, pages 165, 166 and 167*). A plain, simple-to-make shortcrust dough is well-suited to the traditional apple pie illustrated on these pages.

Although the pie can be baked and served without adornment, you can, if you like, glaze it before baking by brushing the top with a lightly whisked egg white and sprinkling on some castor sugar. For an attractive matt finish, sift a little icing sugar over the surface of the baked pie.

1 Mixing the apple filling. Place flour, salt, sugar and ground spices—nutmeg and cinnamon are used here—in a mixing bowl. Peel, core and slice the apples, and add them to the bowl. With your hands, toss the apples until they are evenly coated with the dry ingredients.

2 Preparing the dough. Divide the dough—here, plain shortcrust—into halves, one for the top of the pie and one for the base. Wrap one half of the dough in plastic film (*above*) or aluminium foil to prevent it from drying out.

5 Fitting the pastry base. Use your fingers to mould the dough firmly to the shape of the tin. Try not to stretch or tear it; if necessary, patch any damaged area with a bit of extra dough.

6 Filling and covering the pie. Fill the base with the apples and dot them with butter. If the apples are sweet, sprinkle them with lemon juice and grated lemon rind. Using a pastry brush, moisten the dough round the edge of the tin with water. Roll the remaining dough to a thickness of about 5 mm ($\frac{1}{4}$ inch) and place it over the filling (*above*).

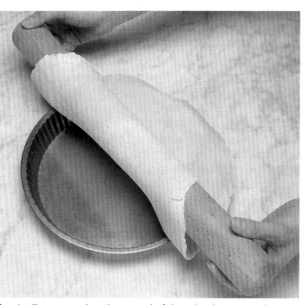

3 **Rolling into a circle.** Sprinkle a little flour on to the work surface to prevent the dough from sticking. To make the base, roll the dough forwards only, using firm, light strokes; then, for an even surface, give the dough a quarter turn and roll it again. Roll and turn the dough until it forms a round about 5 mm ($\frac{1}{4}$ inch) thick.

4 **Lining the tin.** To ensure that the round of dough is big enough to cover the base and overlap the sides of the tin, hold the tin over the dough as a guide; the pastry should be slightly wider than the tin all round (*inset*). To lift the dough, roll it loosely round the rolling pin and then unroll it over the pie (*above*).

7 **Finishing the edges.** Use a knife to trim away the excess dough, angling the blade up and outwards so as to leave a slightly overhanging margin of dough. Using your thumb and index finger (*above*), pinch the dough firmly to seal the base and top. With the knife, pierce the top in several places to allow steam to escape as the pie bakes.

8 **Serving the pie.** Bake the pie in a preheated, 220°C (425°F or Mark 7) oven for 10 to 15 minutes, then at 180°C (350°F or Mark 4) for 40 to 45 minutes, or until the pastry is firm and golden-brown. Hot pastry crumbles easily: let the pie cool for a few minutes before cutting it. Serve the pie warm or cold.□

An Upside-Down Tart of Wine-Drenched Fruit

A tart can be made upside-down by baking a lid of pastry dough over a filling of cooked fruit and reversing the assembly on to a plate. Any pastry, except choux or strudel, is suitable, and you can make the tart with most fruits—apples (*recipe, page 132*), peaches, apricots or pears, for example. To complement the crisp texture of the pastry, the cooked fruit should remain fairly firm. Apples are usually just sliced and sautéed with a little butter and sugar. Apricots or peaches can be cooked in the same way, or poached in a sugar syrup (*page 8*).

In this demonstration (*recipe, page 132*), pears are poached in sweetened red wine for about 1 hour and then baked with a lid of shortcrust (*page 50*). The wine adds flavour and gives the pale fruit a reddish-purple colour. In addition, its natural acidity slows the breakdown of the fruit's cell structure and helps to keep the pears intact during the lengthy cooking necessary for a full exchange of flavours. Even so, you should use firm-fleshed pears: over-ripe fruit might well break up despite the wine's effect.

Choose a good wine, deeply coloured, young and full-bodied: cooking concentrates the flavour, and the quality of the wine will be reflected in the finished tart.

To prevent the filling from being too liquid, pour the poaching wine for the pears into a saucepan and reduce it over high heat to a thick syrup—about a quarter of its original volume (*Step 5, right*). Then return the thickened syrup to the pears, cover them with pastry and bake the tart. If possible, use the same pan for poaching and baking: if you have to transfer the poached pears to a baking dish, you will risk breaking them.

To prevent juices from the filling seeping into the pastry and making it soggy, unmould the tart at the last possible moment; serve it warm or cold, accompanied, if you like, by fresh, thick cream.

1 **Preparing the pears.** Assemble firm, slightly under-ripe pears, red wine, sugar and spice—ground cinnamon is used here. Using a small, sharp knife, halve, peel and core the pears. Arrange the halves, cored surface up, in a heavy-bottomed pan so that the wide ends of the pears fit snugly against the edge.

2 **Covering the pears with wine.** Fill the centre of the pan with more pear halves. Arrange them with the narrow ends pointing outwards so that the fruit will form an attractively symmetrical design when the dessert is unmoulded. Sprinkle the ground cinnamon and sugar over the pears. Pour enough red wine into the pan to cover the fruit.

6 **Preparing the pastry lid.** Roll the dough—here, plain shortcrust—into a circle slightly larger than the pan and about 5 mm (¼ inch) thick. Pierce the dough circle with a fork to create holes through which steam can escape. Make a pastry border by folding over the edge of the dough; press the edge flat, crimping it with a fork (*above*).

7 **Covering the pears.** Carefully lift the dough and place it over the pears with the folded side down. Bake the tart in a preheated, 190°C (375°F, Mark 5) oven for about 40 minutes, until the pastry is golden-brown and crisp.

3 **Poaching the pears.** Place the pan of pears and wine over a high heat. Bring the wine to the boil, then cover the pan, reduce the heat, and simmer the pears for about 1 hour, or until tender. Test the fruit by gently inserting the tip of a knife into one of the pears (*above*).

4 **Making the syrup.** Holding the lid of the poaching pan firmly against the pears to keep them in place, pour off the liquid into a small saucepan (*above*). Set the pan of pears aside. Put the saucepan over a high heat and boil the liquid, stirring it occasionally with a wooden spoon. Reduce the heat, if necessary, to prevent the liquid from boiling over.

5 **Reducing the syrup.** Continue to cook the syrup until it is thick and has reduced in volume by between two-thirds and three-quarters—about 10 minutes. Pour the syrup evenly over the pears.

8 **Serving the tart.** Remove the tart from the oven and leave it to cool slightly. To unmould the tart, invert a serving dish over the pan (*inset*) and turn the dish and pan over together. If the pan's handle prevents you from unmoulding the tart into the centre of the dish, slide it into place with your hand. Serve at once. □

A Free-Standing Fruit Case with an Amber Glaze

The size of a fruit tart need not be limited by the size of the baking tins you have. By using the technique shown on this page, you can create a free-form tart as small as you wish or as large as your oven will hold.

Roll the dough out to the size and shape you want—a square, a rectangle, or a circle. Transfer the dough to a baking tray or a metal oven shelf and fold up the edges of the dough to contain the filling (*Step 1*). A rich shortcrust dough is used here, but plain shortcrust, rough puff or leftover trimmings of puff dough are equally good choices (*pages 50-57*). Sliced apples with an apricot glaze provide the filling in this demonstration (*recipe, page 129*). Almost any other fruit—fresh or poached cherries, plums or pears for example—will yield a delicious and tempting result.

If you like, spread the dough with almond cream (*recipe, page 93*), jam or cooked, puréed fruit before you arrange the top layer of fruit and bake the tart.

1 Shaping the pastry shell. Roll out dough—here, rich shortcrust—into a large circle about 3 to 5 mm ($\frac{1}{8}$ to $\frac{1}{4}$ inch) thick. Transfer the dough to a buttered baking tray and turn up the edges to a height of about 2.5 cm (1 inch). Fold the raised edge over to make a border 1 cm ($\frac{1}{2}$ inch) high; pinch folded dough together firmly (*above*).

2 Arranging apple slices. With a sharp knife, halve, core and peel apples and cut them into slices 3 to 5 mm ($\frac{1}{8}$ to $\frac{1}{4}$ inch) thick. Starting at the border of the pastry, arrange the slices in concentric rings until the base is covered. Because the fruit will shrink slightly during baking, overlap the apple slices and the rings they form.

3 Adding sugar. Sprinkle the apple slices with sugar (*above*) to sweeten them and give them an attractive golden colour when baked. Cook in an oven preheated to 180°C (350°F or Mark 4) for about 50 minutes, or until the pastry is golden and the surface of the apples is caramelized.

4 Glazing the tart. To give the surface of the tart a glossy finish, make a fruit glaze—here, apricot. Brush the glaze generously over the fruit while it is still warm to cover the apples completely.

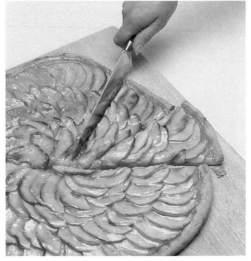

5 Serving the tart. Gently slide a long, wide metal spatula under the tart. Tip the baking surface slightly and use the spatula to help ease the tart on to a cutting board or serving platter. Cut the tart into wedges (*above*) and serve it either hot, warm or cold. □

Flavoured Custard with a Lattice Top

A deliciously smooth tart is made by baking a basic custard mixture of sugar, eggs and cream in a pastry case. You can flavour the custard simply with vanilla, or combine it with a wide variety of ingredients—spices, fruit or even vegetables such as carrots, pumpkin or spinach.

The sweet spinach tart shown here, for example (*recipe, page 138*), includes parboiled spinach that has been chopped and cooked lightly in butter, then added to the custard and mixed with raisins, pinenuts, lemon rind and spices.

When preparing an open custard tart, you can ensure a crisp pastry case by pre-baking the shell either partially or completely (*page 72*). Tarts covered with a decorative lattice top, however, such as the one here, are baked as an assembly because the raw strips of dough will not adhere to the crusty edges of a pre-baked pastry shell. Here, the shell and lattice are made of shortcrust dough, but rich shortcrust and rough-puff doughs are other possibilities (*pages 52-55*).

1 Preparing the spinach. Remove the stalks and wash the spinach in several changes of water. Parboil the leaves for 1 to 2 minutes to reduce the bundle to a manageable size. Drain, pour over cold water and squeeze out excess water with your hands. Chop the spinach finely (*above*) and, for added flavour, sauté it briefly in unsalted butter.

2 Making the filling. Line a pie tin with dough—here, shortcrust. Reserve some dough for the lattice top. Assemble the other ingredients—raisins macerated in brandy, pine-nuts, allspice, nutmeg, grated lemon rind and sugar. For the custard, whisk eggs and cream together in a large bowl (*above*).

3 Flavouring the custard. Add the spinach to the custard. Add the other ingredients, whisking them into the spinach mixture (*above*). Continue to stir the mixture, scraping down the sides of the bowl occasionally, until all the ingredients are evenly distributed. Pour the filling into the pastry case.

4 Making a lattice. Roll out the reserved dough to a thickness of 3 mm ($\frac{1}{8}$ inch). Cut it into strips 1 to 2 cm ($\frac{1}{2}$ to $\frac{3}{4}$ inch) wide and lay them across the filling in a simple lattice pattern. Trim off the excess and moisten the ends with water to help them adhere. Glaze the lattice top and the exposed pastry border with egg yolk beaten with a little water.

5 Baking and serving the tart. Bake the tart at 170°C (325°F or Mark 3) for 50 minutes to 1 hour—until the lattice is golden-brown. Test the tart for doneness by inserting the tip of a knife into the custard; it is cooked when the knife comes out clean. Allow the tart to cool slightly and serve it while it is still warm.□

Pre-Baking for Crispness

By pre-baking a pastry case—a process sometimes called "baking blind"—you can guarantee crisp pastry for any filling, cooked or raw. Cases of rich or plain shortcrust or rough-puff dough (*recipes, pages 165 and 166*) can all be baked blind. Whether they are completely or partially pre-baked depends on the filling you use. If the filling has already been cooked separately, as in a lemon meringue pie (*page 76*), or if you use a filling of raw fruit that needs no cooking as demonstrated on the opposite page, you can pre-bake the pastry completely and then fill it.

Partial pre-baking is called for when an especially moist filling is to be baked in the case; a cheesecake (*page 74*) for example. A fully baked pastry case will darken too much, and may burn, as the filling cooks; partially baked pastry will brown nicely while providing a firm case that does not absorb too much moisture from the filling. If, however, the pastry begins to turn too brown before the filling is completely cooked, protect it with a strip of foil folded over the edges.

When an empty pastry case is placed in a hot oven, air trapped in the dough and between the dough and the baking tin pushes up the dough. Unless it is weighted down, or pricked all over with a fork to allow the air to escape (*opposite page, Step 2*), the pastry will buckle as it cooks. Aluminium foil or, as in this demonstration, a piece of greaseproof paper, is fitted inside the case and weighted down with a layer of dried peas (*Step 2*). Dried beans or rice also make convenient weights; kept specifically for this purpose, they can all be re-used indefinitely. Alternatively, if you have flan tins of several sizes, you can weight the dough down by placing a smaller tin on top of it before baking. As a guide, pre-heat the oven to 180°C (350°F or Mark 4) for shortcrust, 190°C (375°F or Mark 5) for rich shortcrust and 220°C (425°F or Mark 7) for puff doughs.

1 **Lining dough with paper.** Line a flan tin or dish (*above*) with dough—here, rich shortcrust rolled out to a thickness of 3 to 6 mm (⅛ to ¼ inch). Cut a square of greaseproof paper slightly larger than the tin. Press the paper against the base and pleat it against the sides.

2 **Weighting the dough.** Pour enough dried peas (*above*), beans or rice on to the paper liner to fill to a depth of at least 1 cm (½ inch). With your hand, spread the peas evenly around the base and against the side of the dish.

3 **Partial pre-baking.** Bake the pastry case for about 15 minutes or until the sides are pale gold. To use the case partially baked, lift out the paper and peas (*above*) and bake the shell empty for about 5 more minutes to cook and colour the base. Remove it from the oven, add the filling and bake the tart until the filling is cooked.

4 **Total pre-baking.** Bake the weighted case for about 15 minutes until the edges are a light brown colour and firm to the touch. Remove the paper and peas and bake the empty case for about 15 minutes to dry out and colour the pastry base. Remove the case from the oven and allow it to cool before filling it.

Small Containers for Fresh Fruit

The method used to pre-bake large pastry cases shown in the box on the opposite page is less practical for small cases, such as those used in the fruit tartlets here (*recipe, page 132*). You can achieve similar results, however, by pricking the dough with a series of tiny holes (*Step 2*) that allow trapped air to escape. During baking, the holes will close up so that the filling will not seep through when it is added. Alternatively, you can weight the dough down by stacking four or five small dough-lined moulds with sloping sides, one inside the other, in the oven. Use an empty tartlet mould to cover the top case and bake them for about 10 minutes. Then separate the moulds and bake the cases spread out for a few minutes to allow them to dry out and colour.

Whatever size the pre-baked case is, you can prevent the pastry from absorbing moisture from the filling and becoming soggy by covering the base with jam or lining it with a breadcrumb mixture before adding the filling. Here, fresh, whole fruit are brushed with a glaze (*page 9*) to give them a shiny finish.

1 Lining tartlet moulds. Roll the dough—here, rich shortcrust—to a thickness of about 3 mm ($\frac{1}{8}$ inch). With a pastry cutter or the rim of a tin, cut circles of dough to fit your tartlet moulds. Gently press the dough into each mould with your thumbs, starting in the middle and working to the sides to eliminate any air trapped under the pastry (*above*).

2 Pricking for pre-baking. Place the tartlets on a baking sheet and prick the base and sides of the shells thoroughly with the prongs of a fork. Bake the tartlets in an oven preheated to 190°C (375°F or Mark 5) for about 15 minutes or until the pastry is golden-brown.

3 Adding spiced breadcrumbs. Take the baking sheet from the oven and allow the tartlets to cool. To unmould the tartlets, pick up each mould and turn it over, gently shaking the case out on to your other hand. Put the cases on a wire rack and sprinkle each tartlet base with breadcrumbs—here, flavoured with cardamom, grated nutmeg and sugar.

4 Filling the cases. Fill the cases with fresh, whole or cut up fruit—here, raspberries, strawberries and green grapes that have been peeled and seeded. Using a pastry brush, paint the fruit with glazes of complementary colour and flavour (*above*).□

A Two-Step Case for a Smooth Cheese Mixture

Cheesecake—here a combination of crusty pastry with a filling of velvety creaminess—can be made with almost any soft white cheese. The filling for the cheesecake in this demonstration (*recipe, page 138*) is made with cream cheese, but cottage cheese, *ricotta* or a combination of these cheeses would be equally delicious. The cheese is enriched with eggs and double cream, flavoured with vanilla sugar and citrus zest, and bound with a small amount of flour. For a slightly sharper taste, soured cream, yogurt or buttermilk might be substituted for the double cream. Additional flavours can be introduced by including other ingredients such as raisins or candied fruits, spices, nuts or honey to the cheese mixture (*recipes, pages 139 and 144*).

Some cheesecakes are made in an open pastry case, others on a pastry base. In the demonstration here, the pastry case is made of rich shortcrust (*recipe, page 165*) enlivened with grated lemon rind to complement the filling. You might substitute a plain shortcrust or simply line the baking tin with crushed biscuit crumbs bound with butter and sugar.

If you use a shortcrust for the case, the dense filling of cheesecake will prevent the base of the dough from cooking through. On the other hand, if the whole case is pre-baked, the edges will burn when next exposed to oven heat before the filling is cooked. To ensure that both the crust and the filling are fully cooked at the same time, you can pre-bake the base (*page 72*) in a cake tin or, as here, on the bottom of a spring-form tin (*page 22*). When the base is cool, complete the case by adding a strip of raw dough for the sides (*Step 2*).

After the cheesecake is baked, allow it to cool before unmoulding and refrigerating it. Serve the cake on its own, as in the demonstration here, or topped with a fruit glaze (*page 9*), or fresh fruit such as strawberries or pineapple.

1 **Pre-baking the pastry base.** Prepare the dough—here rich shortcrust. Divide the dough in half. Put one piece on top of the buttered base of a spring-form tin. Roll the dough to cover the base, about 3 mm to 6 mm ($\frac{1}{8}$ to $\frac{1}{4}$ inch) thick. Using a fork, prick the dough all over to prevent air bubbles from forming and to ensure that the base bakes evenly. Place in an oven pre-heated to 200°C (400°F or Mark 6) for 15 minutes or until pale golden.

4 **Beating in the eggs.** To ensure that the eggs and extra yolks are thoroughly incorporated in the mixture, beat them in one at a time using the wooden spoon or mixer (*above*). When all of the eggs have been added, stir in the double cream. Continue stirring until the mixture becomes smooth and satiny.

5 **Filling the shell.** Pour the filling into the prepared shell (*above*). Place the cheesecake in a hot oven, preheated to 230°C (450°F or Mark 8), for about 15 minutes to give the top of the filling a light golden colour. Reduce the heat to 100°C (200°F or Mark $\frac{1}{4}$) and bake for 1 hour, or until the pastry is brown and the filling is firm to the touch.

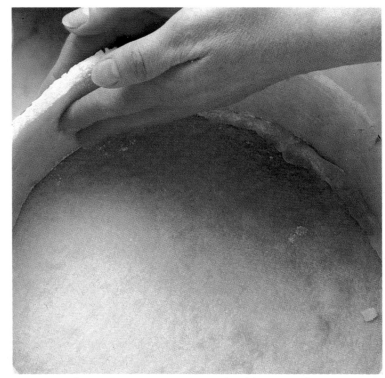

2 **Completing the case.** Butter the inside of the spring-form ring so that it will be easy to remove after the cake is baked; lock the ring on to the pastry-covered base. Because a single strip might break when you lift it, roll out the remaining dough into two strips about the depth of the ring—here, about 8 cm (3 inches) wide. Fit the strips inside the ring and press the bottom of the dough on to the baked pastry to seal it to the base (*above*). Trim the edges.

3 **Preparing the filling.** Refrigerate the case to firm up the pastry. For the filling, assemble whole eggs, egg yolks and cream. In a large bowl, combine vanilla-flavoured sugar, flour and the grated rind of a lemon and an orange. Place cream cheese in another bowl, and, using an electric mixer, or, as here, a wooden spoon, beat the cream cheese until it is fluffy. Add the sugar and flour mixture to the cheese (*above*) and mix well.

6 **Removing the ring.** To cool and set the cheesecake, leave it in the mould for at least 2 hours. Unlock the spring and gently lift off the ring (*above*). To remove the cake from the base, slide a wide spatula under the pastry, and ease the cheesecake on to a serving dish. Chill the cheesecake thoroughly in the refrigerator before serving in wedges. □

A Citrus Filling Embellished with Meringue

A mountainous topping of meringue (*page 15*), cooked briefly so that it browns on the outside but remains soft on the inside, makes a delicious and decorative covering for many pies.

The meringue can be used on top of fillings that are assembled with a pre-baked pie shell (*page 72*)—as in the lemon meringue pie demonstrated here (*recipe, page 144*)—or it can cover cooled fillings of custard or fruit baked with the shell.

In each case, you should whisk the egg whites and sugar for the meringue at the last possible moment, and spread the meringue over the pie after the filling has cooled. If you make the meringue too far in advance, the egg whites will lose their volume and become watery; if you apply it to a hot filling, the meringue will not adhere firmly.

The filling for a lemon meringue pie is made from a mixture of lemon rind and juice, eggs, sugar and butter cooked in a bain-marie until thick (*Step 2*). After the filling has cooled and set, it is spooned into a pre-baked pastry shell—here made of shortcrust dough (*page 50*) flavoured with sugar and lemon juice and rind. A layer of spiced breadcrumbs is sprinkled over the baked pastry before the filling is added to give extra flavour and to help keep the pastry crisp by absorbing some of the filling's moisture.

You can use the same techniques to make lime, orange or even grapefruit meringue pies. Or you could fill the pie shell with a combination of flavoured cream and poached fruit—such as apricots or cherries—before adding the meringue.

To cook the meringue, place the pie in an oven preheated to 190°C (375°F or Mark 5) until the top is lightly browned—about 10 to 15 minutes. Check the pie frequently and take care not to overcook the meringue: too high a heat or too long a cooking time causes the egg whites to shrink, toughen and finally burn.

To give the meringue a darker colour, sprinkle it with a little castor or granulated sugar before baking it. For a contrast in textures, scatter a handful of finely sliced almonds over the top of the meringue before or after baking.

1 Preparing the pie. Assemble lightly whisked eggs, butter, grated lemons and sugar. In a separate bowl, combine breadcrumbs, sugar and spices—here, ground cardamom. Place a flan ring on a baking sheet and line it with dough. Pinch the edges to make a border. Pre-bake the shell (*page 72*) and sprinkle the base with the breadcrumbs mixture.

2 Cooking the filling. Put a trivet in a large pan. Fill the pan with water to cover the trivet by about 2.5 cm (1 inch). Bring the water to a gentle simmer. Squeeze the lemons, add the juice to the grated rind, sugar, eggs and butter in a small saucepan and set it on the trivet. Cook the mixture for about 30 minutes, stirring constantly until thick and creamy.

5 Decorating and baking. Using a palette knife, spread the meringue over the filling so that it slightly overlaps the edge of the pie shell. It will shrink slightly as it cooks in the oven. Roughen the surface of the meringue by swirling the knife over the topping and lifting it quickly; the resulting peaks will brown attractively in the oven. Sprinkle the meringue with sugar and set the pie in an oven preheated to 190°C (375°F or Mark 5) for 10 to 15 minutes, until the topping begins to colour.

3 **Setting the lemon filling.** Remove the saucepan from the heat and pour the filling into a large bowl to cool to room temperature. Cover the bowl with plastic film, and refrigerate the filling for about 30 minutes until it has set firmly.

4 **Filling and covering the pie.** Loosen the pastry from the flan ring by sliding the blade of a knife between the case and the tin. Remove the ring. Slide the case from the baking sheet on to a large plate. With a spoon, fill the shell evenly with the lemon mixture, leaving a small rim of crust to help anchor the meringue topping. Whisk the egg whites and sugar together until they form stiff peaks and pile the meringue thickly over the filling (*inset*).

6 **Cutting and serving the pie.** Serve the lemon meringue pie warm from the oven or chill it by placing the pie in a refrigerator for about 1 hour. Serve the pie, cut into wedges; it is best eaten on the same day as it has been baked.□

A Meringue Flourish

Piping the meringue. To make a more elaborate topping, place a wide star nozzle inside a piping bag and fill the bag two-thirds full of meringue. Starting at the outside edge, pipe a ring of scallops along the pie crust, overlapping the edge slightly. Work inwards until the filling is covered. Pipe a second layer of rings slightly inside the first and continue until the pie is covered with three tiers of meringue. Sprinkle the top with sugar and return the pie to the oven to brown the meringue.

5
Classic Pastries
Creating Splendid Assemblies

Forming unusual cases
Piped fillings
Dealing with puff doughs
Handling sheets of strudel
Baking and frying choux
Combining different doughs
Decorating with caramel

The unique qualities of the various pastry doughs prepared on pages 49 to 61 provide the inspiration for the classic assemblies demonstrated in this chapter. Simple shortcrust doughs are often restricted to a supporting role, providing a stable base on which more complex pastries can be constructed. But doughs that rise as they bake—puff doughs, strudel and choux—can be artfully combined with creams, fruit, nuts and meringue to create vivid contrasts of colour, flavour and texture.

Among these, the puff doughs—rough-puff, flaky and classic puff—are often used interchangeably to produce a host of imaginative and delicious pastries. They can either be baked with a filling such as fruit, jam or almond cream (*recipes, pages 149 and 160-163*) or shaped into rectangles, circles or horns, then pre-baked and filled. Because pre-baking allows puff doughs to attain their full height and airiness unencumbered by a filling, they can be fashioned into a variety of delicate and attractive cases. A rectangle of puff, divided by strips of the same dough and baked, forms a many-sectioned container that can be filled with a selection of fruits and creams in striking patchwork design. Rings of baked puff dough, spread with meringue, make a capacious basket for a mixture of fruit such as cut-up apples, oranges and bananas, or for a tempting mound of lightly sugared strawberries (*page 82*).

Strudel dough is more specialized. Stretched to a thin, transparent sheet, strudel is always baked with a filling, either rolled round the filling or interleaved with it to form a multi-layered stack. The fillings for strudel can, however, provide endless variety. Spicy, cooked apples or a mixture of raisins and poppy seeds are traditional; in the picture on the opposite page, strudel pastry is wrapped round a delicious combination of cottage cheese, soured cream and raisins (*page 84*).

Whipped cream, ice cream or flavoured pastry creams are the most frequently used fillings for the hollow interiors of baked choux pastries. Once you have learnt how to fill strips and rounds of baked choux (*page 86*), you can make simple arrangements of choux balls topped with icing and butter cream (*box, page 89*), or a towering *croquembouche* bound in a web of caramel (*page 90*). Like a *gâteau St. Honoré* (*page 88*), in which a ring of choux encloses a rich cream, the fanciful *croquembouche* is constructed on a crisp base of shortcrust.

A rolled strudel, still warm from the oven, is cut into slices for serving. Paper-thin layers of crisp pastry enclose a soft cheese filling, flavoured with raisins and lemon. To give the pastry its rich golden colour, it is brushed with melted butter before it cooks. A light dusting of icing sugar sets off the flaky contours of the strudel.

Shaping and Layering Puff Doughs

Pre-baked to ensure their crispness, then filled with flavoured cream, the puff doughs (*pages 54-57*) produce some of the most delicate of all pastries. The doughs may be formed into different shaped containers for filling or baked in flat sheets and layered with fruit, pastry cream, whipped cream or almond cream (*recipes, pages 149-150*).

To make the cream-filled horns demonstrated here (*right; recipe, page 150*), thin strips of dough are wound round a conical mould in an overlapping coil. Before baking, the strips are moistened on one of the edges, so that the strips stick together to form a rigid cone. Flaky or rough-puff doughs are good choices for such shapes: they are light and rich but will not expand as much as puff on cooking, to make the horns cumbersome.

Puff dough is best for *mille-feuille*—here an assembly of three thin sheets of pastry interleaved with pastry cream and whipped cream and topped with icing sugar (*right, below; recipe, page 149*). Only puff could produce sufficient layers to merit the pastry's extravagant name, which translates as "thousand leaves". Nevertheless, the sheets of dough must not rise too much lest the assembled *mille-feuille* becomes too bulky to eat easily. To ensure that the dough rises evenly without buckling, prick the rolled-out dough all over with a fork before you bake it. The tiny holes allow some of the dough's moisture to escape as steam during cooking; the pastry will retain its characteristic flaky texture without puffing up to its full height. To keep the dough's butter firm and to permit the pastry to bake crisply, refrigerate the dough before you bake it.

Any cooked pastry must be left to cool completely before the filling is added. Warm pastry would melt most kinds of fillings, and absorb enough filling to become soft. Even cool, a filled pastry will soften in time; do not fill them until shortly before they are to be served.

Spiral Horns for Cream and Nuts

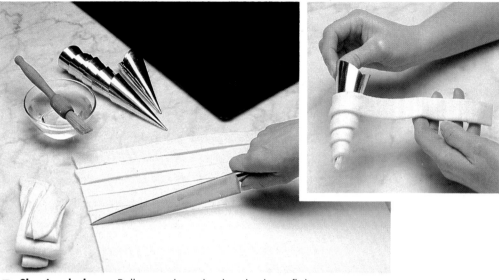

1 **Shaping the horns.** Roll out and trim the dough—here, flaky—into a rectangle 3 mm ($\frac{1}{8}$ inch) thick. Cut strips 1 cm wide by 30 to 35 cm long ($\frac{1}{2}$ inch by 12 to 14 inches). Moisten one edge of each dough strip with water. With the dry side next to the metal, wind each strip around a horn mould (*inset*) and trim off excess.

Stacking Baked Puff and Pastry Cream

1 **Baking the dough.** Roll puff dough thinly into a large rectangle, 3mm ($\frac{1}{8}$ inch) thick. Cut the dough into three equal pieces and place them on baking trays. Prick the dough with a fork (*above*). Cover the trays, and refrigerate the dough for 30 minutes. Bake the dough in a 220°C (425°F or Mark 7) oven until it is crisp and golden—about 20 minutes.

2 **Trimming the pastry.** Leave the pastry rectangles to cool, then stack them on a chopping board. With a large, sharp knife, trim the edges of the pastry (*above*). For a light filling, mix pastry cream (*page 13*) with lightly whipped cream, flavoured with vanilla sugar.

2 **Glazing the pastry.** Put the horns on a buttered baking tray with the loose end of their coils downwards to keep the horns neatly rolled. Refrigerate them for 1 hour. With a pastry brush, paint the top sides with egg beaten with milk. Bake in a 220°C (425°F or Mark 7) oven until crisp—about 25 minutes.

3 **Filling the horns.** Slip the horns from their moulds and return the pastries to the oven for a few minutes to dry out. Cool them on a wire rack. Gather the filling ingredients—here, apricot jam, whipped cream flavoured with vanilla sugar, and chopped pistachio nuts. Hold each horn upright (*above*), and drop in about 1 teaspoon of the apricot jam.

4 **Completing the filling.** Fit a piping bag with a nozzle—here, a star nozzle. Fill the bag with whipped cream. Holding each horn upright, pipe in the cream, filling the horn to just above its rim. Sprinkle pistachio nuts on top.□

3 **Assembling the pastry layers.** Put one pastry rectangle on a flat serving platter. With a spatula, spread on half the cream mixture; cover it with another layer of pastry and spread this with the rest of the cream. Put the third rectangle on top (*above, left*). For a light sugar topping, put icing sugar in a sieve. Move the sieve— tapping it gently with your finger—along the pastry (*above, right*).

4 **Decorating the pastry.** Hold the end of a thin steel skewer in a flame until it is red hot. To make a decorative pattern, lay the skewer across the top of the pastry in parallel lines (*above*). Rest the skewer on the pastry for only a second or so— just long enough to caramelize the sugar. Reheat the skewer if necessary.□

Fruit Cases Fashioned from Puff

Pre-baked puff dough can yield pastry cases of all shapes and sizes, ready for filling with fruits, cream or pastry cream. Fully risen puff, however, would be too fragile for this purpose. To restrict its expansion—as well as helping the dough to rise evenly—some or all of the shaped dough must be pricked before baking.

In the demonstration on the right, pricked and baked puff pastry is built up into a roomy basket. One piece of pastry forms the base of the basket, while the sides are constructed from stacked pastry rings. Layers of meringue hold the pastry pieces together; a final spell in the oven sets the meringue and browns it lightly. The more rings you bake the deeper the basket will be: here, three rings produce a capacious container for lightly sugared strawberries (*recipe, page 150*).

In the demonstration below, strips of puff pastry dough form a rim around a puff base to create a pastry tray; further strips of dough subdivide the tray into several compartments, each of which can be filled, after baking, with a different fruit or cream (*recipe, page 150*). The strips, brushed with egg to make them adhere, are placed on the base before cooking. Only the base of the pastry is pricked, to prevent it from rising too much and buckling; the strips of dough must rise to their full height in order to provide effective—and attractive—partitions.

You can make such a free-form pastry case as small or as large as you like, so long as it will fit inside your oven. The number of partitions is equally variable. In this demonstration, the basic tray is subdivided into eight, and once it has cooled, the compartments are filled with poached cherries and apricots, and with chilled pastry cream (*page 13*).

A Layered Basket for Sugared Berries

1 Cutting the puff dough. Make puff dough (*page 56*) and roll it to a thickness of 3 mm (⅛ inch). Use an inverted plate as a guide to cut four pieces of dough (*page 64*); transfer them to ungreased baking sheets. Using a similarly shaped but smaller plate, cut out the centres from three of the pieces (*above*). Choose a plate that will leave a pastry rim about 2 cm (¾ inch) wide. With a fork, prick the dough all the way through at even intervals and refrigerate it for 20 to 30 minutes. Bake the dough in an oven preheated to 220°C (425°F or Mark 7) for 20 to 25 minutes.

A Patchwork of Fruit and Pastry Cream

1 Making the case. Roll out puff dough to a thickness of 5 mm (¼ inch); cut out a large rectangular base, put it on an ungreased baking sheet and prick it with a fork. Cut the remaining dough into long strips 2.5 cm (1 inch) wide. Brush the outside edge of the base with beaten egg and position the strips to make a rim and geometric partitions (*above*).

2 Preparing the fruits. Glaze the rims of the pastry with egg and bake it for about 30 minutes, until risen and golden-brown. Cool it on a rack. Stem cherries and stone them with a cherry stoner. Halve, stone and poach apricots in sugar syrup (*page 8*) for 8 to 10 minutes. Peel them (*above*), then drain on paper towels.

2 **Constructing the case.** Prepare meringue mixture (*page 14*). When the pastry is cool, set the base on an ovenproof plate. With a metal spatula, spread the outer edge with a ring of meringue about as wide as the baked rims. Place a rim on top. Spread the rim with meringue, top it with another, and repeat to complete the container.

3 **Piping a decorative trim.** Fit a piping bag with a large star nozzle and fill the bag with the remaining meringue. Pipe the meringue along the top rim of the pastry case. Sprinkle the meringue with castor sugar. Bake the case in an oven preheated to 200°C (400°F or Mark 6) for about 10 minutes—until the peaks of the meringue turn lightly golden-brown.

4 **Filling the basket.** Pick the hulls from strawberries and put the fruit in a bowl. To heighten their flavour, sprinkle the berries with icing sugar, turn them gently with your hands and leave them for 10 to 15 minutes. Pile the strawberries in the case (*above*), leaving the excess juice which would make the pastry soggy. □

3 **Spooning in the cream.** Cook the cherries in a separate pan of sugar syrup for about 5 to 7 minutes, then lift them out with a slotted spoon and leave to drain and cool on paper towels. Prepare glazes from the two syrups (*box, page 9*) and allow them to cool before using. Spoon chilled pastry cream into alternate sections of the case (*above*) smoothing it with the back of a spoon.

4 **Arranging the fruit.** Pack the apricot halves and the cherries into the remaining sections of the pastry case, using separate sections for each fruit. With a pastry brush, coat each of the fruit sections with its respective glaze. To appreciate best the contrasts between crisp pastry, chilled cream and freshly cooked fruits, serve the tart as soon as possible, cut into rectangular portions of roughly equal size. □

The Potential of Paper-Thin Dough

Once you have made strudel dough and stretched it into a transparent sheet (*page 59*), it is easy to roll the whole dough around a filling to make strudel (*opposite page, above*), or cut the dough into rectangles and stack them with a filling to make baklava. Alternatively, as in the demonstration below, baklava can be based on phyllo—a dough similar in texture to strudel, but made with very strong flour and no eggs. Phyllo is often available ready-made in sheet form.

The multiple layer effect of a filled, cooked strudel (*Step 4, opposite page, above*) is achieved by using a floured cloth to help roll the dough repeatedly round a filling (*Step 3*). Soured cream and cottage cheese combined with butter, lemon rind, eggs, sugar and raisins are used to fill the strudel here (*recipe, page 153*); other interesting fillings are based on apples, nuts, poppy seeds and chocolate (*recipes, pages 153-155*). To absorb moisture from the filling and to keep the pastry crisp, scatter a layer of breadcrumbs all over the dough. For extra protection, as in this demonstration, a strip of semolina can be sprinkled on top of the breadcrumbs and the filling spooned over it (*Step 2*).

Do not be daunted by the thought of handling a very large piece of strudel dough—used to produce the pastry made here and shown in finished form on page 78. In fact, most cooks find a large sheet easier to handle than a small one; if the rolled strudel is too long to fit your baking tray, simply bend the roll into a horseshoe shape, or, as here, cut it into two or more lengths for cooking.

If you use the strudel dough to make baklava, cut the stretched dough into rectangles to fit a baking tray and layer the sheets with melted butter and chopped nuts, such as almonds or pistachios or, as here, walnuts (*recipe, page 154*). The baked pastry is then drenched with a honey or sugar syrup. For extra flavour, you can add rose water, whole cloves or lemon slices to the syrup (*recipe, page 153*).

A Traditional Cheese Strudel

1 **Making the filling.** Beat butter, sugar and egg yolks in a large bowl (*above*) until smooth. Stir in soured cream, raisins, grated lemon rind, flour and salt. Leave it for 15 minutes to thicken. Sieve cottage cheese, then stir it into the egg and soured cream mixture. Whisk egg whites until they are firm, then fold them into the other ingredients.

2 **Adding the filling.** Make strudel dough and stretch it on a cloth. Brush the dough all over with melted butter to prevent it drying out and to keep the layers separate. Scatter over some dry breadcrumbs. Sprinkle a 7.5 cm (3 inch) wide strip of semolina—about 7.5 cm (3 inches) from one edge; spoon the filling over the semolina (*above*).

A Confection of Nuts and Honey

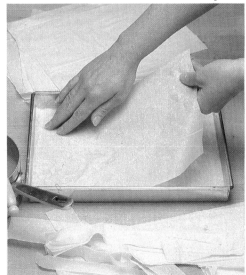

1 **Assembling the dough.** Cut strudel dough—or the ready-made phyllo dough used here—to fit a baking tray; you will need about 20 sheets. Stack 10 on a buttered baking tray (*above*). Brush each sheet generously with melted butter and intersperse the layers with some of the dough trimmings, also brushed with butter.

2 **Layering with nuts.** Use a sharp knife, or an electric grinder, to chop nuts finely—here, walnuts. Scatter about two-thirds of the nuts over the surface of the dough (*above*). Add the remaining sheets of dough, buttered as before, covering the second and fourth layers with the rest of the nuts and trimmings.

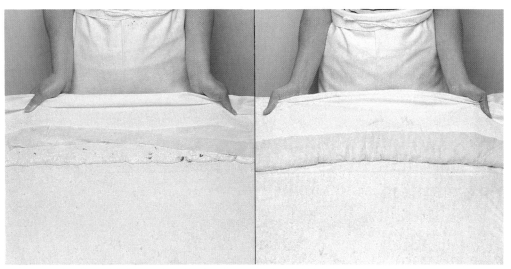

3 **Rolling the dough.** Use both hands to lift the cloth and push the edge of the dough over the filling (*above, left*). If the filling is very soft, tuck in the ends of the dough to prevent leakage during cooking. Pull the cloth—and the dough—towards you and gently lift the cloth a little at a time so that the dough gradually rolls itself around the filling (*above, right*). Use the cloth to tip the fully rolled strudel, seam side down, on to a buttered baking tray.

4 **Cooking and serving.** Cut the strudel, if necessary, to fit the baking tray. Brush the strudel with more melted butter (*above*) and bake it in an oven preheated to 200°C (400°F or Mark 6) for about 40 minutes or until it is crisp and golden. Remove the strudel from the oven, dust it with icing sugar and serve it warm.☐

3 **Scoring the baklava.** Score the top layers of the pastry (*above*), refrigerate it for 2 hours to firm the butter. Brush with melted butter and set in an oven preheated to 230°C (450°F or Mark 8); reduce the heat to 180°C (350°F or Mark 4) and bake for 7 minutes. Bake for about 30 minutes more at 170°C (325°F or Mark 3) until crisp and golden.

4 **Making the syrup.** Remove the pastry from the oven and allow it to cool. Heat water and honey in a heavy saucepan (*above*), allowing the mixture to boil for a few minutes and thicken. Then remove the pan from the heat.

5 **Finishing the pastry.** Pour the hot syrup over the cool pastry (*above*). Cut the pastry into diamond-shaped pieces along the scored lines and leave it for a few hours to absorb the syrup; serve with a spatula. Covered with plastic film or aluminium foil, baklava will keep for up to a week in a cool place.☐

Cream-Filled Éclairs Coated with Chocolate

Airy shells of choux are made by piping the dough (*page 60*) into mounds or, as here, strips, and baking them until the pastry is puffed and brown. In the oven, cavities form inside the shells as the moisture in the dough turns to steam and expands. These hollows can be filled with sweetened, lightly whipped cream or pastry cream (*page 13*) or with ice cream—flavoured, if you like, with vanilla, praline, chocolate or coffee (*recipe, page 155*).

Choux pastry that has browned on the outside but remains moist inside will collapse and toughen as it cools after cooking. To release any residual moisture, remove the choux from the oven during the last few minutes of baking and pierce the shells with the tip of a knife (*Step 2*). Return the choux to the oven to complete the baking and to dry out the inside of the pastries. When they are done, the shells will feel light and remain firm.

In the main demonstration here, thick fingers of choux, known as éclairs, are piped on to a baking tray. If you like, you can give the pastries a glossy finish by brushing the tops and sides lightly with a mixture of egg yolk and milk before baking them. Make sure that the glaze does not touch the baking tray or it will seal down the dough and prevent it from rising. After the éclairs are cooked, they are split in two and filled (*Step 3*)—pastry cream is used in this instance. The éclairs can then be covered with caramel (*page 8*), glacé icing (*page 15*) or, as here, chocolate fondant (*page 92*).

Cooking choux dough need not be confined to baking. If the dough is deep fried (*box, opposite page*), it will cook quickly before the expanding steam inflates the choux completely. The result is a crisp, closely textured pastry.

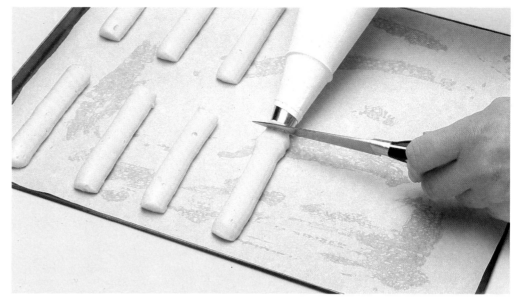

1 Piping the dough. To prevent the choux dough from sticking, cover a buttered baking sheet with greaseproof paper. Fit a 1 cm ($\frac{1}{2}$ inch) plain nozzle to a piping bag, fill the bag two-thirds full with dough and pipe the dough into strips about 7 to 10 cm (3 to 4 inches) long, cut off each length with a knife (*above*). Leave about 4 cm ($1\frac{1}{2}$ inches) between the strips to allow for expansion.

2 Baking the shells. Place the éclairs in an oven preheated to 200 °C (400°F or Mark 6). After about 15 minutes, reduce the heat to 190°C (375°F or Mark 5) to prevent burning; bake them for 10 more minutes or until they are firm and golden. Remove the éclairs from the oven and pierce the ends of each shell with a knife (*above*); bake for a few more minutes.

3 Filling the bases. While the pastry is baking, prepare the pastry cream filling and the icing—here, chocolate fondant. Keep the fondant soft in a bowl set over hot water. When the éclairs are cool, slice each one lengthwise and spoon the cream on to the bottom half (*above*). Replace the tops and put the éclairs on a wire rack for icing.

Deep Frying Strips of Choux

Deliciously crunchy pastries can be made by deep frying choux dough in a relatively flavourless oil such as the groundnut oil used here. You could flavour the choux dough with vanilla, rum or lemon juice (*recipe, page 157*). In this demonstration, the dough is piped directly into the hot oil; but instead of using a piping bag, you could simply drop spoonfuls of dough into the oil.

The dough swells as it comes in contact with the oil; the outside of the pastry fries to a crisp, golden-brown. To cook the dough quickly, but without burning, the temperature of the oil should be 180° to 190°C (350° to 375°F). Measure the temperature with a deep-frying thermometer, or test the heat by dropping a small piece of dough into the oil. If the dough sizzles on contact, the oil is hot enough. To keep the oil at a consistently high temperature, fry only a few pastries at a time.

1 Deep frying choux. Pour 7.5 cm (3 inches) of oil into a heavy-bottomed pan and heat it to 180° to 190°C (350° to 375°F). Fit a plain or star nozzle to a piping bag; fill it with dough. Pipe 20 to 30 cm (8 to 12 inch) lengths into the oil, cutting off the dough near the nozzle.

2 Serving the pastry. Fry the pastries for 5 to 7 minutes, or until they are golden. Remove them with a slotted spoon and drain on paper towels. Continue until the dough is used up. Sprinkle icing or, as here, castor sugar over the pastries and serve them warm or cold.

4 Icing the éclairs. Spoon the fondant over the top of each éclair. Use a spoon or knife to scrape up any drips of icing and add them to the fondant in the bowl, so that nothing is wasted. Arrange the éclairs on a dish (*right*) and serve.□

A Partnership of Choux and Shortcrust

Once you have learned to pipe strips of choux and bake them (*page 86*) you can use the same techniques to make and then assemble other choux pastry shapes.

For example, baked choux balls filled with pastry cream—also known as profiteroles—can be placed one on the other and topped with fondant (*box, opposite page; recipe, page 157*) or cut in half, filled with ice cream and covered with a hot cream and chocolate sauce (*page 10*). If you pipe the choux into a ring shape you can cut the baked pastry in half and fill it with sweetened whipped cream or pastry cream (*recipe, page 166*).

The *gâteau St. Honoré* on the right, (*recipe, page 156*) combines choux balls with a choux ring, arranged on a base of rich shortcrust (*page 52*). When baked, the choux ring case is filled with pastry cream—here, firmed with a little gelatine and aerated with whisked egg whites—and decorated with cream-filled choux balls coated with caramel.

Large rings of choux are most easily made by forcing the dough through a piping bag fitted with a plain nozzle. In the demonstration here, the small balls of choux are also piped, to give them a uniform appearance; a simpler but less precise method of shaping them is to scoop up spoonfuls of choux and drop the dough on to a baking sheet. The choux balls require less time to cook than the ring. Therefore, bake the choux balls and ring separately, in order to avoid opening the oven door to remove the balls while the ring is cooking; a change in temperature could cause the choux ring to sink.

To fill the cooked balls without cutting them in two, fit a small nozzle into a pastry bag, fill the bag with cream, and insert the tip of the nozzle into the pierced base of each ball (*Step 2*). By squeezing the bag with a firm, even pressure, you can force the cream from the bag into the hollow interior of the pastry. The undersides of the balls are then dipped in caramel (*page 8*) which serves as an adhesive to stick the balls to the ring of choux.

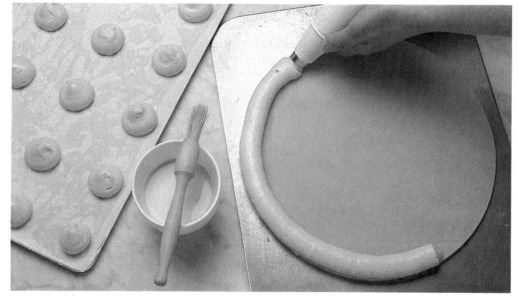

1 **Assembling the doughs.** With a 2 cm ($\frac{3}{4}$ inch) nozzle, pipe 15 walnut-sized choux balls on to a prepared baking sheet. Roll out rich shortcrust dough about 5 mm ($\frac{1}{4}$ inch) thick. Cut it into a 25 cm (10 inch) diameter circle, using a plate as a guide. Place this base on a baking tray, prick it with a fork and pipe choux round the rim (*above, right*). Glaze the choux with beaten egg and milk. Set in an oven preheated to 200°C (400°F or Mark 6); bake the balls for 15 to 20 minutes and the ring for 25 to 30 minutes.

4 **Constructing the case.** In a small, heavy saucepan, make caramel to a rich amber colour (*page 8*); remove it from the heat to arrest cooking. Dip the base of each ball into the caramel, then attach it to the choux ring pastry (*above*). If the caramel hardens before you have finished, place the pan briefly over low heat to melt it again. Continue to dip and position the balls until you have completed a full circle. Use a spoon to dribble the remaining caramel over the surface of the balls (*inset*) until richly coated.

2 **Filling the balls.** A few minutes before the choux balls are done, pierce them with a fork to release steam; complete the baking, then remove from the oven and cool. Do the same to the choux ring. Make pastry cream (*page 13*). Cool about one-third of the cream in a bowl, then pipe it into each ball (*above*).

3 **Preparing the cream.** In a saucepan, soften gelatine in a little cold water. Set the saucepan over low heat to dissolve the gelatine, then stir it into the remaining warm pastry cream. Beat egg whites and sugar until stiff. Fold the cream little by little into the egg whites (*above*).

5 **Finishing the case.** Spoon the pastry cream into the case up to the top of the choux ring. For a simple decoration, make shallow furrows in the cream by running the spoon edge across the surface. The pastry is best eaten immediately, but it can be kept in a cool place for several hours until you are ready to serve it. Using a sharp knife or cake server, cut in wedges and serve (*above*).□

A Miniaturized Assembly

Making small choux pastries. Pipe rounds of choux on to a lined and buttered baking tray (*Step 1, opposite*)—half of them about 2.5 cm (1 inch) across to form tops, and half of them about 5 cm (2 inches) across for bases. Bake the balls and fill them with pastry cream (*Step 2, above*). Dip the balls in fondant—both the filling and fondant used here are flavoured with coffee—and cool them on a rack. Set a small ball on top of a large one and decorate each pastry with a collar of butter cream (*above*).

A Fantasy of Choux and Caramel

Of all pastry constructions, *croquembouche*, demonstrated here, is one of the most dramatic. Its French name means "it cracks in the mouth"—a mundane but nevertheless correct description of this soaring cone of cream-filled choux balls, veiled with amber threads of caramel (*recipe, page 155*).

The towering assembly is not so precarious as it might at first appear. Bake the choux balls and fill them with pastry cream (*page 88*)—or sweetened whipped cream as here (*page 13*). To build the cone, dip the choux balls individually into sugar syrup, cooked to a light golden caramel (*page 8*) and set one ball on top of the other. As the syrup cools, it will harden to hold the balls firmly in place.

You can build the *croquembouche* directly on a serving stand or on a pre-baked base of meringue, plain shortcrust pastry or, as demonstrated in Step 1 (*right*), rich shortcrust pastry (*recipe, page 165*). To decorate the assembly, use a fork to spin a fine web of sugar syrup or caramel around the cone (*Step 3, inset*).

If you like, you can also pipe stars of whipped cream or butter cream around the *croquembouche* or stud the construction with glacé cherries that have been dipped in caramel to help them adhere.

1 **Making the base.** Place a pre-baked 20 cm (8 inch) pastry base (*page 72*) on a dish. Bake and fill about 150 choux balls (*page 88*). Make a caramel (*page 8*) and, to keep it liquid, place the pan in a larger pan of hot water. Dip a side of each ball into the syrup and set it on the pastry, flat base on the inside (*above*).

2 **Building the cone.** Complete the first layer by covering the base with more balls dipped in syrup. Continue building layers—each one slightly smaller than the last—to make a conical shape. If the syrup begins to harden, refill the larger pan with more hot water.

3 **Decorating and serving.** Use a fork to lift threads of caramel and drape them around the completed assembly until it is covered by a fine web (*inset*). Serve the pastry—starting at the top and gently snapping away one or two balls at a time with a spoon and fork (*far right*). □

Anthology
of Recipes

The cake and pastry recipes in the Anthology that follows have been selected by the Editors and consultants from among the best published during the past four centuries. The 128 authors whose work is represented range from such 17th-century forerunners of the French classical cuisine as Pierre de Lune and Nicolas de Bonnefons to such exponents of the English tradition as May Byron and Dorothy Hartley. The choice of recipes, drawing upon the cooking literature of 30 countries, extends from the syrupy, aromatic pastries of the Middle East to the fruit pies and layer cakes of rural America. Many have been selected from rare and out-of-print books in private collections; a large number of the recipes included in the Anthology have never before been published in English.

Throughout the Anthology, as in the first half of the book, the emphasis is on techniques fully accessible to the home cook and on doing justice to fresh, high-quality ingredients. Since many early cookery writers did not specify quantities, the missing information has been judiciously included and, where appropriate, introductory notes in italics have been added by the Editors.

Modern terms have been substituted for archaic language, but to preserve the character of the original and to create a true anthology, the author's texts have been changed as little as possible. Some instructions have necessarily been expanded, but in cases where the cooking directions seem somewhat abrupt, the reader need only refer to the appropriate demonstration in the front of the book to find the technique in question explained in words and pictures. Cooking terms and ingredients that may be unfamiliar are explained in the combined Index and Glossary at the end of the book.

For ease of use, the Anthology is organized in the same order as the techniques section of the book—beginning with fillings and icings and going on to cover cakes, pies and pastries. Within these categories, recipes are grouped according to ingredients. Standard preparations—basic pastry doughs, sponge cake batter, pastry cream—appear at the end. The serving suggestions included in some recipes are, of course, optional.

All recipe ingredients are listed in order of use, with both metric and imperial weights for each ingredient in separate columns. The two sets of figures are not exact equivalents, but are consistent for each recipe. Working from either metric or imperial weights and measures will produce equally good results, but the two systems should not be mixed for the same recipe. Where only one dimension is given for a cake or pie tin, it is assumed that the tin is round. All spoon measures are level.

Fillings and Icings

Almond Paste

Almond paste—often called almond icing or marzipan—is used to cover rich cakes before royal or glacé icing is applied. The paste is often coloured and flavoured and then moulded into various shapes to be used for cake decoration. A whole egg or egg whites may be used instead of egg yolks. Egg yolk gives a richer and yellower paste, whilst egg white gives a whiter, more brittle paste. (Economically, the yolks can be used for almond paste and the whites used for royal icing.) This quantity of paste is sufficient to cover the top and sides of a 20 cm (8 inch) cake.

To make 750 g (1½ lb) almond paste

350 g	ground blanched almonds	12 oz
175 g each	icing sugar and castor sugar, or 350 g (12 oz) icing sugar	6 oz each
½	lemon, juice strained	½
¾ tsp	orange flower water	¾ tsp
¾ tsp	vanilla extract	¾ tsp
1 or 2	egg yolks	1 or 2

Sieve the icing sugar into a bowl and mix with the ground almonds and castor sugar. Add the lemon juice, orange flower water, vanilla extract and enough egg yolk to bind the ingredients into a pliable but dry paste. Knead thoroughly with your hands until smooth.

MRS. ISABELLA BEETON
MRS. BEETON'S EVERYDAY COOKERY

Fondant Icing

For chocolate flavouring, add about 3 tablespoons grated chocolate or 2 tablespoons cocoa, or to taste. For coffee flavouring, add 2 tablespoons coffee essence, or to taste.

To make 45 cl (¾ pint) icing

500 g	sugar	1 lb
15 cl	water	¼ pint
1½ tsp	glucose, or a pinch of cream of tartar	1½ tsp

Dissolve the sugar in the water over a low heat, add the glucose or cream of tartar, bring to the boil quickly, and boil to a temperature of 115°C (238°F). Pour on to an oiled or wetted slab, let it cool slightly (if worked when too hot it will grain), and work well with a palette knife, keeping the mass together as much as possible. When the paste is sufficiently cool, knead well with your hands. Wrap in greaseproof paper or plastic film and store in an airtight tin.

When required, put into a basin over a saucepan containing sufficient hot water to come half way up the sides of the basin. Stir over a very low heat until the icing has the consistency of thick cream. Flavour and colour as required. Allow to cool slightly before using.

MRS. ISABELLA BEETON
MRS. BEETON'S EVERYDAY COOKERY

Butter Cream

La Crème au Beurre

This cream may be lightened by folding in a cooked meringue (*the boiled icing used on the devil's food cake, page 109*). It is preferable to use the butter cream immediately, but it may be kept in a covered bowl in the refrigerator overnight.

To make 500 g (1 lb) butter cream

250 g	butter	8 oz
125 g	lump sugar	4 oz
10 cl	water	3½ fl oz
5	egg yolks	5
1 tbsp	coffee extract, or vanilla extract, or praline (*page 94*), or liqueur (rum, kirsch, Grand Marnier, etc.), or 90 g (3 oz) plain chocolate melted over hot water	1 tbsp

Cook the sugar and water together until a syrup is formed that spins a thin thread when the spoon is lifted. Remove from the heat. Place the egg yolks in a bowl and gradually pour on the hot syrup, whisking vigorously. Continue to whisk until the mixture is cool; it will be light and fluffy. Work the butter until it is creamy. Add the yolk mixture, stirring with a spatula until the cream is firm and shiny. Stir in the flavouring of your choice, and the cream is ready to use.

JEAN KELLER
LES PÂTISSERIES ET LES BONBONS

Royal Icing

Glace Royale

This icing may be stored for a week in the refrigerator, one layer of plastic film pressed to the surface of the icing and another covering the bowl.

The exact amount of egg white needed for this icing depends on what size eggs are used and what the royal icing is needed for. If for a wedding cake or for smooth, thinly spread icing, the icing consistency need not be as thick as for heavy piping.

To make 30 cl (½ pint) icing

500 g	icing sugar	1 lb
2½	egg whites	2½
½	lemon, juice strained	½

Beat together in a basin three-quarters of the icing sugar with the whites of egg and lemon juice. Beat for about 15 minutes if working by hand with a wooden spatula or for about 8 minutes if using an electric mixer.

When the mixture is smooth, clear, white and comparatively light, add the rest of the icing sugar. Beat again for 2 minutes. Should the mixture still not be stiff enough, add some more sugar. If a machine is used, do not over-beat: excess aeration will create too many large air pockets.

When ready, the icing must be covered with a well-moistened cloth to prevent a skin from forming or the icing drying out. Before use, the icing must again be well beaten.

WILLIAM BARKER
THE MODERN PÂTISSIER

Almond Cream

Frangipane

To make 1 litre (1¾ pints) pastry cream

4 tbsp	finely chopped blanched almonds	4 tbsp
1	egg	1
8	egg yolks	8
200 g	flour	7 oz
150 g	sugar	5 oz
	salt	
60 cl	milk	1 pint
200 g	butter, cut into small pieces	7 oz
½	vanilla pod, split lengthwise, seeds removed and reserved	½

Put into a saucepan the egg, egg yolks, flour, sugar and a small pinch of salt. Mix over a low heat with a wooden spoon, gradually stir in the milk, and put the mixture through a fine

sieve. Return it to the saucepan and add 50 g (2 oz) of the butter, the almonds and the seeds from the vanilla pod.

Heat the mixture slowly, stirring constantly, until it thickens. Take it off the heat and stir vigorously until smooth and thick. Return it to the fire and, stirring continuously, allow the mixture just to come to the boil. Remove from the heat.

In a small pan, heat the remaining butter until it turns hazelnut-brown. Stir the browned butter into the cream.

URBAIN DUBOIS
CUISINE DE TOUS LES PAYS

Whipped Chocolate Filling

Ganache Soufflé

To make about ½ litre (16 fl oz) filling

125 g	bitter chocolate	4 oz
125 g	plain chocolate	4 oz
¼ litre	double cream	8 fl oz
1 tbsp	dark rum	1 tbsp

Combine the cream and both kinds of chocolate in a saucepan. Place over a low to medium heat and bring to the boil, stirring to melt the chocolate and prevent scorching. As soon as the mixture boils, remove it from the heat. Cool, stirring once in a while, until the mixture starts to thicken and set. When cool, place in the bowl of an electric mixer. Add the rum and mix at high speed for 4 to 5 minutes. The filling will lighten in colour and approximately double in volume. Use immediately; the filling quickly becomes hard and unspreadable.

JACQUES PÉPIN
LA TECHNIQUE

Praline

Le Pralin

To make 400 g (14 oz) praline

200 g	sugar	7 oz
½ tsp	lemon juice	½ tsp
10 cl	water	3½ fl oz
200 g	blanched almonds, coarsely chopped and lightly toasted	7 oz

Cook the sugar, lemon juice and water together over a medium heat, washing down the sides of the pan with a brush dipped in water. When the syrup is a light caramel colour, put in the almonds and mix with a wooden spoon. When the praline mixture returns to the boil, pour it out on to an oiled marble slab. Allow it to cool completely, then break the praline into pieces and crush them to powder in a mortar. The praline is now ready to use, but it may be kept for several months in a tightly sealed tin or jar.

JEAN KELLER
LES PÂTISSERIES ET LES BONBONS

Glacé Icing

For coffee icing replace half a teaspoon of the water with a half teaspoon coffee essence. For lemon icing, substitute strained lemon juice for all or part of the water. For orange icing, substitute orange juice for all or part of the water.

To make 15 cl (¼ pint) icing

125 g	icing sugar	4 oz
1 tbsp	warm water	1 tbsp

Sieve the icing sugar and put it into a small bowl over hot water. Add the warm water gradually. Stir until all the sugar is dissolved and the icing is smooth and warm. Do not allow it to get too hot, or the icing will lose its gloss. Add flavouring and colouring as desired, a drop at a time. The icing should be thick enough to coat the back of a spoon; if too thin add more sugar, if too thick add more water. When of the correct consistency, cool slightly, then use at once. This quantity will coat the top of a 15 to 20 cm (6 to 8 inch) cake.

MRS. ISABELLA BEETON
MRS. BEETON'S EVERYDAY COOKERY

Mincemeat

For baking this mincemeat, take some out of a jar, if not moist enough add a little hot water, and strew a few whole raisins over each pie. Instead of boiled beef, either beef's-heart or roasted beef may be used for this recipe.

To make 7 litres (12 pint) mincemeat

2.5 kg	boneless stewing beef	5 lb
	salt	
1.5 kg	beef suet	3 lb
2 kg	raisins, seeded and cut	4 lb
2 kg	currants, washed and dried	4 lb
500 g	candied citron, thinly sliced	1 lb
4 kg	tart apples, cored and peeled, finely chopped	9 lb
60 g	ground cinnamon	2 oz
30 g	ground cloves	1 oz
30 g	ground ginger	1 oz
4	nutmegs, grated	4
2	lemons, rind grated, juice strained	2
1 tsp	pepper	1 tsp
1 kg	sugar	2 to 2½ lb
1 litre	apple juice, boiled until reduced by half, or currant or grape juice	1¾ pints
1 litre	molasses or syrup	1¾ pints
	syrup from sweet pickles (optional)	
125 g	butter	4 oz

Put the beef to boil in enough water to cover it; take off the scum that rises when it reaches the boiling point, then simmer, adding hot water from time to time until it is tender. Remove the lid from the pot, salt the meat, let it boil till almost dry, turning the meat over occasionally in the liquor, take from the heat, and let stand overnight to get thoroughly cold. Pick any bones, gristle or stringy bits from the meat, chop very fine, mincing the suet at the same time. Put in a pan with the raisins, currants, citron, apples, spices, lemons, 1 tablespoon of salt, the pepper and the sugar.

Put in an enamelled saucepan the apple, currant or grape juice, molasses or syrup, sweet pickle syrup and butter. Let this mixture come to boiling point, and pour it over the ingredients in the pan, mixing thoroughly.

Pack the mincemeat in jars and put in a cool place, and, when cold, pour molasses over the top, 3 mm (⅛ inch) thick, and cover tightly. This will keep 2 months.

THE BUCKEYE COOKBOOK: TRADITIONAL AMERICAN RECIPES

Cakes

Yule Log with Chestnuts

Bûche de Noël aux Châtaignes

The techniques of rolling and decorating a yule log cake are demonstrated on page 32.

To prepare the chestnuts for the chestnut filling, they should be shelled, blanched and simmered in 45 cl (¾ pint) of milk with 60 g (2 oz) of sugar and ½ tsp of vanilla extract for 20 minutes. To make the *beurre manié* for the filling, work together equal parts of butter and flour with a fork.

To make one rolled cake
approximately 20 cm (8 inches) long

4	egg yolks	4
90 g	sugar	3 oz
90 g	flour	3 oz
3	egg whites, stiffly beaten	3
30 g	butter, melted	1 oz
	Chestnut filling	
1 kg	cooked chestnuts	2 to 2½ lb
100 g	*beurre manié*	3½ oz
2	egg yolks	2
150 g	plain chocolate, melted in 4 tbsp of water	3½ oz
	sweetened whipped cream or icing sugar	

Beat the egg yolks and sugar in a bowl with a wooden spatula until the mixture turns pale. Gradually sift in the flour. Add the egg whites to the mixture along with the melted butter. Cover a baking tray with buttered greaseproof paper.

Pour on the mixture, spreading it evenly to a thickness of about 1.5 cm (½ inch). Cook in a hot oven preheated to 220°C (425°F or Mark 7) for 8 to 10 minutes or until the cake is firm but not coloured. Remove the baking tray from the oven and turn the cake out on to a stainless steel or marble surface, with the paper side up. Peel off the paper and cover the cake with a cloth so that it stays light and does not harden, and is easy to roll. Let it cool completely.

For the filling, purée the chestnuts by sieving them or putting them through a food mill. Beat in the *beurre manié*, the egg yolks and 100 g of the melted chocolate. Spread three-quarters of this mixture on the cake and roll it up to form a log. Cover and decorate the log with the remaining chestnut mixture and the rest of the melted chocolate icing.

Make stripes in this chestnut-chocolate mixture with a fork, to imitate the bark of the log. Snowy effects can be achieved with sweetened whipped cream or icing sugar. Use your imagination to make sprigs of holly or mistletoe.

ZETTE GUINAUDEAU-FRANC
LES SECRETS DES FERMES EN PERIGORD NOIR

Yule Log

La Bûche de Noël

For this recipe, the sponge cake mixture (recipe, page 167) is baked in a shallow Swiss roll tin 20 by 30 cm (8 by 12 inches), in an oven preheated to 230°C (450°F or Mark 8), for about 10 minutes. For instructions on rolling and decorating the yule log, see the demonstration on page 32.

To make one 30 cm (12 inch) cake roll

1	baked rectangular sheet of sponge cake	1
10 cl	sugar syrup, made by boiling 60 g (2 oz) of sugar in 10 cl (3½ fl oz) of water for 5 minutes, then flavouring the syrup with 1 tsp vanilla extract or 1 tbsp kirsch	3½ fl oz
½ tsp	vanilla extract	½ tsp
500 g	butter cream (*page 92*)	1 lb
70 g	plain chocolate, melted	2½ oz
	icing sugar	
	almond paste (*page 92*), coloured with spinach green (*page 120*) or green food colouring (optional)	

Sprinkle the cake sheet with the sugar syrup. Add the vanilla to 100 g (3½ oz) of the butter cream. Mix the remaining butter cream with the melted chocolate.

Spread the cake with one-third of the chocolate cream, and roll it up, starting at the long side. Cut the ends of the roll diagonally to resemble a sawn log. Place two flattened balls of vanilla-flavoured butter cream on the logs to resemble knots in the wood. Place the remaining chocolate cream in a piping bag with a fluted tip, and pipe it in strips the length of the log to resemble bark. Spread the centres of the cut ends with vanilla cream to represent the heart of the log. Refrigerate the log until the cream is firm.

Dip a knife tip in hot water and make holes in the chocolate cream over the discs of vanilla cream, so that the knots show through. Sprinkle the log with icing sugar, and decorate it as desired with ivy or holly formed from green almond paste. The log may be refrigerated overnight before serving.

JEAN KELLER
LES PÂTISSERIES ET LES BONBONS

Hazelnut Roll with Whipped-Cream Filling

Ground nuts replace flour in this unusual cake roll. The hazelnuts may be bought ground. If you grind your own in a blender or food processor, spread them out on a baking sheet and let them dry overnight.

To make one 42 cm (17 inch) long cake roll		
175 g	ground hazelnuts	6 oz
7	eggs, yolks separated from whites, whites stiffly beaten	7
200 g	sugar	7 oz
2 tsp	baking powder	2 tsp
	icing sugar	
35 cl	double cream	12 fl oz
1 tbsp	rum	1 tbsp

Oil a 27 by 42 cm (11 by 17 inch) Swiss roll tin or baking sheet, line it with greaseproof paper, letting the paper extend over the ends, and oil again. Set aside.

In the bowl of an electric mixer beat the egg yolks at medium speed. Gradually add the sugar and beat for 5 to 7 minutes until the mixture is thick and will "form the ribbon"—that is, until part of it will fall from the beaters and look like a ribbon on the surface of the rest. Mix the baking powder with the hazelnuts and add them to the egg yolk mixture. Beat at low speed, just enough to mix.

Stir a quarter of the egg whites into the nut mixture to lighten it, then gently fold in the remaining whites. Spread the mixture in the prepared tin and bake in an oven preheated to 180°C (350°F or Mark 4) for 15 minutes.

Let the cake cool for a few minutes with paper towels spread over it to prevent a crust from forming. Remove the towels, loosen the cake from the edges of the tin, and dust the cake generously with icing sugar.

Lay two strips of greaseproof paper, overlapping lengthwise, on a table or board. Dust the paper with icing sugar, invert the baking tin over the paper, then lift the tin off the cake and peel away the paper lining.

In a bowl set over ice, whip the cream with a whisk. Add 2 tablespoons of icing sugar and stir in the rum. Spread the whipped cream on the cake, then roll up the cake, starting on one long side. Use the paper to help you in rolling the cake. Transfer the roll to a long serving board. Remove all the paper. Sift icing sugar over the cake before serving.

JULIE DANNENBAUM
JULIE DANNENBAUM'S CREATIVE COOKING SCHOOL

Raspberry Roll

Hallonrulltårta

To make one 27cm (11 inch) rolled cake		
3	eggs	3
About 160 g	sugar	About 5½ oz
50 g	flour, sifted	2 oz
1 tsp	baking powder	1 tsp
	Raspberry filling	
750 g	raspberries	1½ lb
35 cl	double cream, stiffly whipped	12 fl oz
	sugar	

Preheat the oven to 220°C (425°F or Mark 7). Line a Swiss roll tin with buttered aluminium foil. Beat the eggs with 100 g (3½ oz) of the sugar until the mixture is thick and pale. Mix the flour and baking powder and stir into the egg batter. Blend well. Spread the batter thinly and evenly in the tin, and bake for 5 to 6 minutes, or until golden. Sprinkle the cake with the remaining sugar and invert it on to a wire rack lined with greaseproof paper. Let the cake cool covered with the tin. Mix half of the cream with the raspberries, saving a handful of these for the garnish. Add sugar to taste and spread the raspberry filling over the cold cake. Roll it up, starting from one short side. Cover the roll with the remaining cream and garnish with the reserved berries.

GOREL KRISTINA NASLUND
SWEDISH BAKING

Strawberry Roll

To make one 42 cm (17 inch) long Swiss roll		
350 g	strawberries, sliced	12 oz
5	eggs, yolks separated from whites, whites stiffly beaten	5
150 g	sugar	5 oz
1 tsp	vanilla extract	1 tsp
3 tbsp	flour	3 tbsp
35 cl	double cream, whipped	12 fl oz
2 tbsp	icing sugar	2 tbsp
	whole strawberries for garnish	

Oil a 27 by 42 cm (11 by 17 inch) Swiss roll tin, line it with greaseproof paper, and oil the paper. Set aside.

Beat the egg yolks, add 60 g (2 oz) of the sugar, and beat until very thick and pale yellow. Add the vanilla, then carefully fold in the flour and egg whites. Spread the batter in the prepared pan and bake in an oven preheated to 180°C (350°F or Mark 4) for 15 minutes or until the cake is springy. Loosen the edges of the cake, sprinkle it with half of the remaining sugar, and turn it out, sugar side down, on two overlapping sheets of greaseproof paper. Carefully remove the paper from the bottom of the cake, and sprinkle the bottom with the remaining sugar.

Sweeten two-thirds of the whipped cream with the icing sugar. Fold in the sliced strawberries. Spread this mixture on the cake and roll it up. Decorate the roll with the remaining whipped cream, piped in rosettes down the length of the cake. Put a whole strawberry on each rosette. The cake may be made early in the same day and kept refrigerated until serving time.

JULIE DANNENBAUM
MENUS FOR ALL OCCASIONS

Meringue Cake
Le Succès

If you wish to make this cake with layers of sponge cake alternating with the meringue layers, as in the demonstration on page 34, treble the quantity of praline-flavoured butter cream to sandwich the extra layers.

To make one two-layer 20 cm (8 inch) cake

100 g	ground almonds	3½ oz
60 g	sugar	2 oz
75 g	icing sugar	2½ oz
4	egg whites	4
350 g	butter cream (*page 92*)	12 oz
50 g	praline (*page 94*)	2 oz
	chopped blanched almonds	

Preheat the oven to 170°C (325°F or Mark 3). Butter and flour a baking sheet.

In a bowl, mix the ground almonds and sugar with 60 g (2 oz) of the icing sugar. In another bowl, beat the egg whites until they form stiff peaks. With a spatula, fold the almond mixture into the whites, being careful not to make the whites collapse. Put the mixture into a piping bag, and pipe it into two spiral rounds on the baking sheet. Bake for 1 hour, reducing the oven temperature if the meringue

rounds colour too rapidly. Allow them to cool completely before removing them from the baking sheet.

Meanwhile, make the butter cream and fold in the praline. Spread one of the meringue rounds with a 1 cm (½ inch) layer of cream, top with the other layer, and spread the top and sides of the cake with a coating of butter cream. Sprinkle the top with the remaining icing sugar, and press chopped almonds into the sides. The cake may be made in advance and refrigerated overnight.

JEAN KELLER
LES PÂTISSERIES ET LES BONBONS

Meringue Cake with Peaches

To make one two-layer 20 cm (8 inch) cake

2	peaches, peeled and diced	2
125 g	butter	4 oz
300 g	sugar	10 oz
4	eggs, yolks separated from whites	4
4 tbsp	milk	4 tbsp
½ tsp	vanilla extract	½ tsp
125 g	flour, sifted with 1 tsp baking powder	4 oz
⅛ tsp	salt	⅛ tsp
30 g	shelled walnuts or pecans, chopped	1 oz
¼ litre	double cream, whipped	8 fl oz
2 tbsp	icing sugar	2 tbsp

Grease two sandwich tins and line the bottoms with grease-proof paper. Preheat the oven to 180°C (350°F or Mark 4).

In an electric mixer bowl, cream the butter, slowly add 100 g (3½ oz) of the sugar, and beat until light and fluffy. Beat in the egg yolks, one at a time, then add the milk and vanilla. Add the flour, beating slowly until mixed. The mixture will be thick. Scrape the sides of the bowl, and continue beating for at least 2 minutes. Divide the batter between the two tins, smoothing the tops with a spatula.

Beat the egg whites with the salt until stiff. Add the remaining sugar, a tablespoonful at a time, beating constantly. Continue to beat until the mixture is like marshmallow and feels smooth when you pinch it. Spread the meringue over the cake batter in the tins, then sprinkle one layer only with the chopped nuts. Bake for 30 minutes.

To assemble the cake, whip the cream and sweeten it with the icing sugar. Fold in the peaches. Place the unnutted layer, meringue side down, on a serving plate. Spread with all of the peaches and cream. Place the second layer, nut side up, on top. Refrigerate before serving.

JULIE DANNENBAUM
MENUS FOR ALL OCCASIONS

Macadamia Nut Cake with Rum-Flavoured Butter Cream

La Hawaiienne

To make one 20 cm (8 inch) cake

115 g	unsalted macadamia nuts or blanched almonds, very finely chopped	4 oz
70 g	flour	2½ oz
½ tsp	baking powder	½ tsp
60 g	unsalted butter, at room temperature	2 oz
4	egg whites	4
	salt	
100 g	sugar	3½ oz
	Macadamia butter cream	
85 g	unsalted macadamia nuts or blanched almonds, pulverized in a mortar or food processor	3 oz
85 g	unsalted butter	3 oz
115 g	icing sugar	4 oz
4 tbsp	dark rum	4 tbsp
7 or 8	pistachio nuts, blanched and roughly chopped	7 or 8

Butter a deep cake tin generously. If it does not have a removable base, put a piece of buttered greaseproof paper on the bottom. Sift the flour with the baking powder. Beat the butter into the chopped nuts until the mixture is very creamy. Add the flour.

Beat the egg whites with a pinch of salt until they form soft peaks. Sprinkle on the sugar and continue beating until the meringue holds fairly stiff peaks. Stir one quarter of the whites into the nut mixture to lighten it, then delicately fold in the rest. Turn the batter into the prepared tin.

Bake in an oven preheated to 190°C (375°F or Mark 5) for 20 to 25 minutes, until the cake has risen nicely, has pulled away from the sides of the pan, and is slightly golden. Remove the pan to a cooling rack. After 10 minutes, run a knife around the inside edges and unmould the cake; remove the paper if you have used it.

To make the butter cream, beat the butter, sugar and 2 tablespoons of the rum into the pulverized nuts.

When the cake has cooled completely, slice it in half to make two even layers. Sprinkle the remaining rum over the cut surfaces of the cake, then spread one layer with about one-third of the butter cream. Place the second layer firmly on top, and spread the remaining butter cream smoothly over the top and sides of the cake. Sprinkle the chopped pistachios around the edges. The *Hawaiienne* will store well for a day or two in the refrigerator. Remove it to room temperature 30 minutes before serving so that the butter cream will be creamy.

SIMONE BECK AND MICHAEL JAMES
NEW MENUS FROM SIMCA'S CUISINE

Almond Meringue Cake

Gâteau à la Bennich

To make one 18 cm (7 inch) cake

100 g	ground almonds	3½ oz
140 g	castor sugar	4½ oz
4	egg whites, stiffly beaten	4
	Butter cream	
100 g	castor sugar	3½ oz
4 tbsp	double cream	4 tbsp
4	egg yolks	4
150 g	butter	5 oz
	toasted almond strips	

Add the ground almonds and sugar to the stiffly beaten egg whites. Pour into two buttered sandwich tins and bake in a cool oven, preheated to 150°C (300°F or Mark 2), for 30 minutes or until a skewer inserted in the centre comes out clean. Turn the cakes out on to wire racks to cool.

To make the butter cream, beat the sugar, double cream and egg yolks in a saucepan over a low heat until the mixture thickens, but do not let it boil. Remove the pan from the heat and, when the mixture cools, stir in the butter.

Sandwich the cakes with butter cream and spread some of the cream on top. Sprinkle with toasted almond strips.

INGA NORBERG
GOOD FOOD FROM SWEDEN

Praline Meringue Cake

Gâteau Progrès

This cake was invented by Bruno Comin, pastry chef at New York's Four Seasons restaurant. Though rich, it has a deceptively simple appearance and flavour. If you cannot buy almond flour, simply pulverize blanched almonds in your blender (not too many at a time) to achieve an equally good result. Praline paste may be bought in jars from delicatessens and some good confectioners.

To make one 22 by 15 cm (9 by 6 inch) cake

10	egg whites	10
400 g	sugar	14 oz
30 g	cornflour	1 oz
750 g	almond flour	1½ lb
60 g	praline paste	2 oz
40 g	bitter chocolate, melted	1½ oz
30 g	almonds, toasted and sliced	1 oz

Praline butter cream

60 g	praline paste	2 oz
250 g	butter, softened	8 oz
200 g	sugar	7 oz
½ tsp	cream of tartar	½ tsp
8 cl	water	3 fl oz
5	egg yolks, beaten until thick and fluffy	5
	kirsch	

Beat the egg whites with the sugar. When thick, add the cornflour. Mix in the almond flour gently with your hands. With a pastry bag or spatula, make three thin rectangular layers of the mixture on buttered greaseproof paper on a baking sheet. Bake in a preheated 100°C (200°F or Mark ¼) oven for 30 minutes. When you take this meringue from the oven it will be soft. Turn the rectangles over on to wire racks. Cool. Remove the paper.

While the meringue is baking, prepare the butter cream by combining the sugar, cream of tartar and water in a saucepan. Stir over a low heat until the sugar is completely dissolved. Bring to the boil and cook without stirring until the syrup reaches the soft ball stage (115°C or 238°F). Add the syrup to the egg yolks in a thin stream, beating constantly. Beat until cool. The mixture will become thick and light. Cool completely. Beat in the butter, then the praline paste and a drop of kirsch.

Spread a quarter of the butter cream on one of the meringue layers. Cover with another layer. Spread this with another quarter of the butter cream. Repeat with the remaining meringue layer. Spread the remaining butter cream over the top and sides of the cake.

Mix the praline paste with the melted chocolate. Refrig-erate for 1 hour. Work the mixture with a wooden spoon, then roll it into a sausage shape. Flatten it and use it to make a diagonal band across the cake. Sprinkle the almonds all over the top except on the chocolate band.

CHARLOTTE ADAMS
THE FOUR SEASONS COOKBOOK

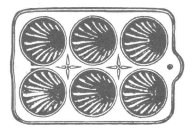

St. George's Cake

Pastel Sant Jordi

St. George's cake is a particular speciality of Barcelona.

To make one 20 by 8 or 10 cm (8 by 3 or 4 inch) cake

6	eggs, yolks separated from whites	6
160 g	sugar	5½ oz
200 g	flour	7 oz

Cocoa butter cream filling

1 tbsp	cocoa powder	1 tbsp
200 g	butter	7 oz
300 g	icing sugar	10 oz

Beat the egg whites with the sugar until stiff. Lightly beat the yolks and add them to the whites. Finally, add the flour, mixing everything gently so that the beaten egg whites do not liquefy. Pour the mixture into a rectangular baking tin greased with lard. Bake in an oven preheated to 200°C (400°F or Mark 6) for 40 minutes, or until the top is nicely browned. Take it out, remove the cake from the tin and leave to cool on a wire rack.

Meanwhile, prepare the filling: work the butter with a beater until it is fluffy; add the icing sugar and the cocoa and beat until a fine cream is obtained. Cut the cake crosswise into three slices and stack them one on top of the other, spreading a coating of butter cream between each layer. The top layer of cake should not be spread with the cream. Place the cake in a refrigerator. Just before serving, sprinkle it with a little icing sugar.

MARIA DEL CARMEN CASCANTE
150 RECETAS DE DULCES DE FÁCIL PREPARACIÓN

Pound Cake

True pound cakes are made without baking powder. The raising agent is the air introduced in the creamed mixture and in the egg white foam.

To make one loaf

125 g	butter	4 oz
125 g	sugar	4 oz
125 g	flour, sifted	4 oz
2	eggs, yolks separated from whites, whites stiffly beaten	2

Cream the butter, add the sugar, and cream well together. Add the egg yolks, one at a time, beating after each addition. Beat in the flour. Fold in the beaten egg whites. Pour the mixture into a prepared 500 g (1 lb) loaf tin. Bake in an oven preheated to 180°C (350°F or Mark 4) for about 45 minutes or until the cake shrinks slightly from the sides of the pan. The top of the cake will crack due to internal steam pressure. Allow the cake to cool completely in the tin, and keep it for 24 hours before slicing it.

MADELEINE KAMMAN
THE MAKING OF A COOK

Old Cape Pound Cake

The dried and grated rind of half an orange may be substituted for the tangerine peel.

To make one 30 cm (12 inch) cake

500 g	butter, softened	1 lb
500 g	castor sugar	1 lb
12	eggs, yolks separated from the whites, each well beaten	12
500 g	flour	1 lb
1 tsp	mixed dried and powdered tangerine peel, cinnamon and nutmeg	1 tsp
60 g	sponge finger biscuits, ground to fine crumbs	2 oz

Stir the butter to a cream; beat in the sugar, then the beaten egg yolks, followed by the flour and spices, previously well mixed. Lastly, fold in the beaten egg whites. Thickly butter a cake tin, and dust it with biscuit crumbs. Pour in the cake mixture, place a buttered paper on top of the tin and bake in an oven preheated to 180°C (350°F or Mark 4) for 2 hours or until the cake shrinks slightly from the sides of the tin.

HILDAGONDA J. DUCKITT
HILDA'S "WHERE IS IT?" OF RECIPES

Almond Cake

Gâteau d'Amandes

For this recipe, the almonds may be ground in an electric blender or food processor, then combined by hand or machine with the other ingredients.

To make one 20 cm (8 inch) cake

175 g	almonds, blanched	6 oz
1	lemon, rind grated	1
3	eggs, lightly beaten	3
175 g	flour	6 oz
175 g	butter, softened	6 oz
175 g	sugar	6 oz

Pound the almonds in a mortar with the lemon rind. Add the remaining ingredients gradually, pounding them together to obtain a thick paste. Spread the paste evenly in a buttered tart tin. Bake in an oven preheated to 170°C (325°F or Mark 3) for about 1 hour or until the cake is golden on top.

NOUVEAU MANUEL DE LA CUISINIÈRE BOURGEOISE ET ÉCONOMIQUE

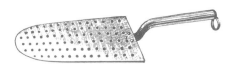

Catalan Sponge Cake

Pa de-Pessic

To make one 22 cm (9 inch) square cake

250 g	sugar	8 oz
8	eggs, yolks separated from whites, whites stiffly beaten	8
1 tsp	vanilla extract	1 tsp
1	lemon, rind grated	1
120 g	flour	4 oz
120 g	cornflour	4 oz
50 g	butter, melted and cooled	2 oz

Beat the sugar, egg yolks, vanilla and lemon rind together until the mixture is pale and fluffy. Stir in, alternately, a tablespoon or so of flour and one of cornflour, until both are used up. Beat in the butter. Fold in the egg whites.

Put the mixture into a 4 to 5 cm (2 inch) deep square buttered cake tin, and bake in an oven preheated to 180°C (350°F or Mark 4) for 30 to 35 minutes or until the cake springs back when touched in the centre.

ELIANE THIBAUT COMELADE
LA CUISINE CATALANE

Marbled Cake

Gâteau Marbré

To make one 20 cm (8 inch) cake

White batter

4	egg whites, stiffly beaten	4
250 g	sugar	8 oz
125 g	butter	4 oz
250 g	flour	8 oz
2 tsp	baking powder	2 tsp
½ tsp	salt	½ tsp
10 cl	milk	3½ fl oz
1 tsp	vanilla extract	1 tsp

Brown batter

125 g	butter	4 oz
125 g	brown sugar	4 oz
4	egg yolks	4
½ tsp	bicarbonate of soda	½ tsp
15 cl	molasses	¼ pint
250 g	flour	8 oz
2 tsp	baking powder	2 tsp
½ tsp	salt	½ tsp
½ tsp	grated nutmeg	½ tsp
1 tsp each	ground cinnamon and ground ginger	1 tsp each
4 tbsp	milk	4 tbsp

To prepare the white part of the cake, add half the sugar to the stiffly beaten egg whites. Cream the butter with the rest of the sugar. Sieve the flour, baking powder and salt and add this mixture to the creamed butter and sugar a little at a time, alternating with the milk. Add the vanilla extract. Fold the egg whites into the batter.

To prepare the brown part of the cake, cream the butter with the sugar. Beat in the egg yolks. In a saucepan over a low heat dissolve the bicarbonate of soda in the molasses. Sieve the flour with the baking powder, the salt and the spices. Combine all of these ingredients and add them to the butter little by little, alternating with the milk, and mix well.

Butter a deep cake tin and place heaped tablespoons of the white and brown mixtures alternately in the tin to create a marbled effect.

Bake in an oven preheated to 180°C (350°F or Mark 4) for 1 hour or more, until an inserted skewer comes out clean.

LA SOCIÉTÉ ST. THOMAS D'AQUIN
LA CUISINE ACADIENNE (ACADIAN CUISINE)

Victoria Sandwich

This cake is traditionally sandwiched together with jam and the top sprinkled with icing sugar.

To make one two-layer 20 cm (8 inch) cake

125 g	butter	4 oz
125 g	castor sugar	4 oz
2	eggs, beaten	2
1 tbsp	warm water	1 tbsp
125 g	flour	4 oz
1 tsp	baking powder	1 tsp

Cream the butter and sugar until fluffy. Add the eggs gradually, then add the warm water and beat well. Sift the flour with the baking powder, add to the beaten mixture and stir in thoroughly until the mixture will spread easily.

Put into two well-greased and floured sandwich tins. (Don't forget to put a small piece of greaseproof paper at the bottom to ease turning out.) Bake in an oven preheated to 180°C (350°F or Mark 4) for about 20 minutes or until the cakes are springy to the touch. Allow the layers to cool before sandwiching them together.

MISS READ
MISS READ'S COUNTRY COOKING

Seed Cake

To make one 18 cm (7 inch) cake

2 tsp	caraway seeds	2 tsp
125 g	butter	4 oz
150 g	castor sugar	5 oz
2	eggs	2
150 g	flour, sifted	5 oz
30 g	cornflour	1 oz
½ tsp	baking powder	½ tsp
40 g	glacé cherries, finely chopped	1½ oz
½ tsp	vanilla extract	½ tsp

Beat the butter and sugar together until white, then add each egg separately. Gradually stir in the flour, cornflour, baking powder, caraway seeds, cherries and vanilla extract. Pour into a cake tin lined with paper and bake in an oven preheated to 170°C (325°F or Mark 3) for 1¼ hours, or until an inserted skewer comes out clean. Turn on to a wire rack to cool.

FREDA MURRAY
LACOCK TEA TIME RECIPES

Mother's Cake

Pastel de la Madre

To make one 20 cm (8 inch) cake

200 g	sugar	7 oz
100 g	butter	3½ oz
2	eggs	2
250 g	flour, sieved with 2 tsp baking powder	8 oz
¼ litre	muscatel wine	8 fl oz
250 g	strawberry jam	8 oz

Place a pan over a low heat until it is barely warm, then remove it from the heat and put in the sugar and butter. Beat steadily until the mixture is creamy, then add the eggs and continue to beat until fluffy, about 5 minutes. Add the flour and baking powder; a minute later, stir in the muscatel. Pour the mixture into a greased, floured cake tin and bake in an oven preheated to 180°C (350°F or Mark 4) for 35 minutes or until the top of the cake is springy to the touch. Cool the cake before removing it from the tin. Spread the top with the strawberry jam.

CANDIDO LOPEZ
EL LIBRO DE ORO DE LA GASTRONOMIA

Traditional Christmas Cake

To make one 22 cm (9 inch) cake

175 g	candied peel, chopped	6 oz
175 g	glacé cherries, quartered	6 oz
500 g each	sultanas and currants	1 lb each
350 g	raisins	12 oz
125 g	almonds, blanched and chopped	4 oz
300 g	flour	10 oz
300 g	butter	10 oz
300 g	soft brown sugar	10 oz
1	orange, rind grated	1
1	lemon, rind grated	1
1 tbsp	black treacle	1 tbsp
6	eggs, beaten	6
½ tsp each	salt, mixed spice and grated nutmeg	½ tsp each
4 to 6 tbsp	rum, brandy, whisky or sherry	4 to 6 tbsp

In a large bowl, coat all of the fruit and the nuts with a tablespoon of the flour. In a separate bowl, cream the butter and sugar until light and fluffy, beat in the grated orange and lemon rind and the black treacle. Beating with a wooden spoon, gradually add the beaten eggs, with a sprinkling of flour to stop the mixture from curdling. Then stir in the remaining flour, sifted with the salt and spices, and enough of the rum to make a batter that will drop easily when shaken from the spoon. Lastly, stir in the fruit and nuts.

Turn the batter into a 12 cm (5 inch) deep cake tin, well greased and lined with 2 thicknesses of greaseproof paper. Tie a band of brown paper round the outside of the tin for extra protection. Hollow out the centre of the batter quite deeply to ensure a flat top for icing; the cake will rise in the centre. Cover the top of the tin with 2 thicknesses of greaseproof paper to prevent it from browning too fast.

Put the cake into a preheated 170°C (325°F or Mark 3) oven and after 20 minutes, reduce the heat to 150°C (300°F or Mark 2). Bake for a further 40 minutes, then reduce the heat to 140°C (275°F or Mark 1). The cake will need about 5 hours' baking altogether. It is done when it stops "singing" and a warm skewer inserted in the centre comes out clean. Let the cake cool for 1 hour before turning it out.

MARGARET COSTA
MARGARET COSTA'S FOUR SEASONS COOKERY BOOK

Danish Christmas Cake

Grossmutters Wunderkuchen

To make two 22 cm (9 inch) cakes

400 g	flour	14 oz
400 g	rye flour	14 oz
½ tsp each	pepper, ground cloves, ground ginger and ground cardamom	½ tsp each
2 tsp	ground cinnamon	2 tsp
	salt	
400 g	sugar	14 oz
400 g	honey	14 oz
60 g	butter	2 oz
1 tbsp	baking powder, dissolved in 3 to 4 tbsp warm milk	1 tbsp
10	eggs, lightly beaten	10
200 g	raisins, washed and dried	7 oz
200 g	prunes, washed, dried and cut into quarters	7 oz
150 g	dried figs, washed, dried, pips removed and cut into quarters	5 oz
100 g	mixed candied peel, chopped	3½ oz
100 g	almonds, blanched and slivered	3½ oz

Sieve the flour, rye flour, spices and salt together. Put half of the sugar into a saucepan and stir it on a low heat until it browns and begins to melt. Add the honey and let it melt with the sugar. When both are liquid, stir in the rest of the sugar and two-thirds of the butter. Allow the mixture to cool, then stir in the baking powder dissolved in milk, the eggs and the sieved flour mixture. Beat the mixture well. Lastly fold in the fruit and almonds, mix well and pour into two greased cake tins. Only fill the tins half way to the top, allowing the cakes room to rise. Bake in an oven preheated to 170°C (325°F or Mark 3) for 1½ hours, or until a skewer inserted into the centre comes out clean. Let the cakes cool completely in the tins before turning them out. They will keep for months in an airtight tin.

GRETE WILLINSKY
KULINARISCHE WELTREISE

Twelfth Night Cake

On Twelfth Night at London's Theatre Royal, Drury Lane, a rich cake is eaten, accompanied by Port Negus, with the toast "To the memory of actor and one-time pastrycook, Robert Baddeley." Except during the war years, this ceremony has taken place every year since Baddeley died in 1794, for in his will he left £100 to be invested at 3 per cent for providing the little feast. It is for all those acting at Drury Lane Theatre (where Baddeley once acted) on Twelfth Night.

To make one 20 cm (8 inch) cake

250 g	flour	8 oz
15 g	baking powder	½ oz
	salt	
	grated nutmeg	
250 g	butter	8 oz
250 g	castor sugar	8 oz
4	eggs	4
500 g	currants, rubbed with flour on a sieve	1 lb
125 g	candied mixed peel, sliced	4 oz
60 g	almonds, blanched and chopped	2 oz
5 tbsp	brandy	5 tbsp
500 g	icing sugar, sifted	1 lb
2	egg whites, slightly beaten	2
1	small lemon, juice strained	1
	assorted crystallized fruits	

Sift the flour with the baking powder and a pinch each of salt and nutmeg. Cream the butter with the castor sugar until the mixture is light and fluffy, and beat in the whole eggs with a little of the flour mixture. Stir in the rest of the flour and add the currants, candied peel, almonds and then the brandy.

Grease and line the cake tin, pour in the mixture and make a depression in the centre. Bake the cake in an oven preheated to 170°C (325°F or Mark 3) for about 3 hours or until an inserted skewer comes out clean. When the cake is cooked, keep it in the oven with the heat off for a short while, then lift the cake out and turn it on to a rack to cool.

Put the icing sugar into a basin and add the egg whites and the lemon juice, both in small quantities at a time, beating constantly with a wooden spoon. When this icing is thick, smooth and white, put it on to the cake and smooth the surface with a knife dipped in hot water. Before the icing has time to set, decorate it with the crystallized fruits, pressing them in slightly. Let it harden before serving.

GERTRUDE MANN
A BOOK OF CAKES

Dundee Cake

To make one 20 cm (8 inch) cake

175 g	butter	6 oz
175 g	castor sugar	6 oz
4	eggs	4
60 g	ground almonds	2 oz
300 g	flour	10 oz
½ tsp	salt	½ tsp
1 tsp	baking powder	1 tsp
125 g each	currants, sultanas and raisins	4 oz each
60 g	candied mixed peel, chopped	2 oz
30 g	whole almonds, blanched and split	1 oz

Beat the butter and sugar to a light, fluffy cream and then beat in the eggs, one at a time, along with the ground almonds. Sift the flour with the salt and baking powder and gradually add it to the creamed mixture along with the fruit and peel. Put the mixture in a lined cake tin, smooth it over and arrange the split almonds on top.

Preheat the oven to 240°C (475°F or Mark 9). Put the cake in the oven on the middle shelf. Reduce the heat immediately to 170°C (325°F or Mark 3), and bake the cake for 1½ hours. Then gently take the cake out and listen to it: if it is "purring" it is still cooking so put it back and listen occasionally until the "purring" stops. An inserted skewer should come out clean when the cake is done.

JANET MURRAY
WITH A FINE FEELING FOR FOOD

inches) of the top of the tin and place two layers of greaseproof paper over the top. Bake in an oven preheated to 140°C (275°F or Mark 1) for about 3 hours. The last hour of baking, remove the paper from the cake and decorate the top with fruit and nuts. Insert a straw or cake tester into the centre of the cake to see when it is done. If it is not, cover the top with fresh greaseproof paper and continue cooking until the tester comes out clean. Remove it from the oven and let it cool in the tin, then remove. If desired pierce the top of the cake in several places with a long, thin skewer and spoon in the wine.

MARION BROWN
THE SOUTHERN COOK BOOK

Tennessee White Fruit Cake

This recipe is from "Nancy Nash" (Mrs. B. Frank Womack), Foods Editor, The Nashville Tennessean Magazine. Reserve a few whole cherries and nuts to decorate the cake.

To make one 30 cm (12 inch) cake

1	large coconut, grated	1
500 g	candied pineapple, chopped	1 lb
500 g	sultanas, chopped	1 lb
500 g	white or red glacé cherries, chopped	1 lb
250 g	green glacé cherries, chopped	8 oz
250 g	candied citron peel, chopped	8 oz
500 g	ground almonds	1 lb
500 g	ground pecans	1 lb
350 g	flour	12 oz
500 g	sugar	1 lb
350 g	butter	12 oz
7	eggs	7
10 cl	buttermilk	3½ fl oz
½ tsp	bicarbonate of soda	½ tsp
	salt	
1	nutmeg, grated	1
20 cl	bourbon whiskey	7 fl oz
1	large orange, juice strained	1
6 tbsp	sweet white wine (optional)	6 tbsp

Dredge the coconut, fruit and ground nuts with 250 g (8 oz) of the flour. Cream the sugar and butter together until the mixture is pale and fluffy and beat in the eggs, one at a time. Mix well after each addition. Beat in the buttermilk, soda, a pinch of salt, and the remaining flour and mix well. Stir the nutmeg into the whiskey and add to the mixture along with the orange juice. Fold in the fruit and nuts last.

Butter a cake tin and line it with two layers of buttered greaseproof paper. Pour in the cake mixture to within 5 cm (2

Simnel Cake

To make one 20 cm (8 inch) cake

250 g	flour	8 oz
60 g	ground rice	2 oz
1 tsp	baking powder	1 tsp
	salt	
250 g	butter	8 oz
250 g	castor sugar	8 oz
5	eggs	5
500 g	currants, rubbed in a sieve with a little flour	1 lb
125 g	mixed candied peel, finely chopped	4 oz
1	egg yolk, lightly beaten	1
	Almond paste	
500 g	ground almonds	1 lb
3	eggs, well beaten	3
500 g	castor sugar	1 lb
2 to 3 drops	almond extract	2 to 3 drops
1 tbsp	brandy	1 tbsp

For the almond paste, beat together the eggs, ground almonds, sugar, almond extract and brandy. Knead the mixture well, until it forms a smooth ball, then put it aside.

Sift the flour with the ground rice, baking powder and a pinch of salt. Cream the butter and sugar together until the mixture is very pale, and then beat in the eggs one at a time, adding 1 tablespoon of the flour mixture to prevent curdling. Add the rest of the flour and stir in the currants and peel.

Grease and line a spring-form cake tin and put in half of the cake mixture. Cover it evenly and lightly with half of the almond paste. Now add the rest of the cake mixture. Bake it in an oven preheated to 180°C (350°F or Mark 4) for 1½ hours or until the cake shrinks slightly from the sides of the tin.

Form the rest of the almond paste into a roll about 65 cm

(26 inches) long and join the ends to form a ring the size of the cake. Lay this on top of the cake, mark a pattern on the paste with a fork and brush it with the egg yolk.

Return the cake to the oven at 150°C (300°F or Mark 2) until the paste has coloured lightly—about 15 minutes. Let the cake cool for a while before turning it from the tin.

An alternative way to make Simnel is to bake the cake without the almond paste filling and leave it for a day to cool thoroughly. Then, saving one-third of the almond paste, form the rest into a round and press it on to the top of the cake after first brushing the surface with beaten egg white. Make small balls with the remaining paste and press them lightly around the edge of the top. Brush the top and the balls with beaten egg yolk and colour the paste in the oven preheated to 150°C (300°F or Mark 2).

GERTRUDE MANN
A BOOK OF CAKES

———————— ◆ ————————

Lawn Tennis Cake

A similar recipe by Mrs. Isabella Beeton is available from the Wimbledon Lawn Tennis Museum.

To make one 18 cm (7 inch) cake

125 g	butter	4 oz
90 g	castor sugar	3 oz
30 g	candied mixed peel, very finely chopped	1 oz
4 or 5 drops	vanilla extract	4 or 5 drops
$\frac{1}{8}$ tsp	ground cinnamon	$\frac{1}{8}$ tsp
125 g	flour	4 oz
30 g	rice flour	1 oz
125 g	sultanas, minced	4 oz
125 g	glacé cherries, minced	4 oz
2	eggs, yolks separated from whites, whites stiffly beaten	2
10 cl	maraschino or noyau liqueur	$3\frac{1}{2}$ fl oz
1 tsp	baking powder	1 tsp
	salt	
125 g	almond paste *(page 92)*	4 oz
	glacé icing *(page 94)*	
	glacé cherries and angelica (optional)	

Cream the butter with the sugar, then add the candied peel, vanilla and cinnamon. Gradually and lightly stir in all of the remaining ingredients, except the egg whites. Last of all, fold in the whites. Bake in a greased, paper-lined cake tin in an oven preheated to 180°C (350°F or Mark 4) for about 1½ hours or until a skewer inserted in the centre comes out clean.

When the cake is completely cooled, roll out the almond paste and cover the top of the cake with it. When this has set, ice the cake with glacé icing. It can be decorated with crystallized cherries and angelica.

MAY BYRON
MAY BYRON'S CAKE BOOK

———————— ◆ ————————

Black Bun

Black Bun is the traditional Scottish Twelfth Night cake, which was transferred to Hogmanay (New Year) after the banning of Christmas and its subsidiary festival, Twelfth Night, by the Reformers.

To make two 25 cm (10 inch) cakes, or one deep 35 cm (14 inch) cake

1 kg	currants, washed and dried	2 lb
1 kg	muscatel raisins, stoned	2 lb
250 g	almonds, blanched and chopped	8 oz
250 g	mixed candied peel, chopped	8 oz
500 g	flour, sifted	1 lb
125 g	sugar	4 oz
15 g	ground cloves or cinnamon	$\frac{1}{2}$ oz
15 g	ground ginger	$\frac{1}{2}$ oz
1 tsp	ground allspice	1 tsp
$\frac{1}{2}$ tsp	ground black pepper	$\frac{1}{2}$ tsp
1 tsp	bicarbonate of soda	1 tsp
About 30 cl	buttermilk or beaten eggs	About $\frac{1}{2}$ pint
1 tbsp	brandy	1 tbsp
750 g	shortcrust dough *(page 165)*	$1\frac{1}{2}$ lb
1 or 2	eggs, beaten	1 or 2

Put the currants, raisins, almonds and mixed peel in a bowl. Mix the flour with the sugar, spices and soda, and add to the currant mixture. Add just enough buttermilk or beaten egg, with the brandy, to moisten the mixture.

Roll out two-thirds of the dough and use to line one or two greased cake tins. Trim the edges. Fill the tins with the fruit mixture, smoothing the top. Roll out the remaining dough and use it to cover the tins. Moisten the edges of the dough with cold water and press firmly to seal, making all secure and neat. With a skewer, make four holes in each cake right down to the bottom of the tin. Prick the tops all over with a fork, brush with beaten egg, and bake in an oven preheated to 180°C (350°F or Mark 4) for 3 hours or longer for the large cake, or about 2 hours for the smaller cakes. The cakes are done when a skewer inserted in the centre comes out clean.

F. MARIAN McNEILL
THE SCOTS KITCHEN

Cherry Cake

To make one 20 cm (8 inch) cake

250 g	glacé cherries, quartered	8 oz
250 g	butter	8 oz
250 g	castor sugar	8 oz
4	eggs, lightly beaten	4
250 g	flour	8 oz
½ tsp	baking powder	½ tsp
60 g	candied citron peel, chopped	2 oz
125 g	ground almonds	4 oz
1	lemon, rind grated, juice strained	1

Cream the butter and sugar thoroughly, then beat in the eggs and, with the last of the egg, add the flour and baking powder. Mix the cherries and citron peel with the ground almonds and add them to the cake batter, together with the lemon rind and juice. Turn into a prepared cake tin and bake in a preheated, 180°C (350°F or Mark 4) oven for approximately 2 hours or until the cake has shrunk slightly from the sides of the tin.

MARGARET BATES
TALKING ABOUT CAKES

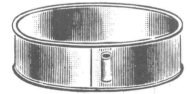

Cherry and Almond Cake

To make one 20 cm (8 inch) cake

125 g	ground blanched almonds	4 oz
125 g	glacé cherries, rolled in a little flour	4 oz
250 g	butter	8 oz
250 g	castor sugar	8 oz
3	eggs	3
250 g	flour	8 oz
	salt	
½ tsp	baking powder	½ tsp
	almond extract	

Cream the butter and sugar until they are light and fluffy. Beat in each egg separately. Add the flour, a pinch of salt and the baking powder, then add the ground almonds, the cherries and a few drops of almond extract. Put into a lined cake tin and bake in an oven preheated to 170°C (325°F or Mark 3) for 1¼ hours or until a skewer inserted into the centre comes out clean. Turn on to a wire rack to cool.

FREDA MURRAY
LACOCK TEA TIME RECIPES

Blueberry Cake

To make one 25 cm (10 inch) cake

350 g	blueberries	12 oz
60 g	butter, softened	2 oz
400 g	sugar	14 oz
2	eggs	2
300 g	flour, sifted	10 oz
¼ litre	soured milk	8 fl oz
1 tsp	bicarbonate of soda	1 tsp

Cream together the butter and sugar until the mixture is light and fluffy. Gradually beat in the eggs, one at a time, then add the flour, milk and bicarbonate of soda. Mix until well blended, then stir the blueberries into the batter. Grease and flour the cake tin, and pour the batter into it. Bake in an oven preheated to 180°C (350°F or Mark 4) for 1½ hours or until the centre of the cake is firm to the touch.

THE LADIES AUXILIARY OF THE LUNENBURG HOSPITAL SOCIETY
DUTCH OVEN

Carrot Cake

Rüeblitorte

To make one 20 cm (8 inch) cake

275 g	carrots, peeled and grated	9 oz
5	eggs, yolks separated from whites, whites stiffly beaten	5
300 g	sugar	10 oz
½	lemon, rind grated	½
300 g	ground blanched almonds	10 oz
60 g	flour	2 oz
1 tsp	baking powder	1 tsp
	salt	
2 tbsp	jam, preferably apricot, thinned down with 1 tbsp water	2 tbsp
8	small marzipan carrots, for decoration	8
	Lemon icing	
160 g	icing sugar	5½ oz
2 tbsp	lemon juice	2 tbsp
1 tbsp	water	1 tbsp

Beat together the egg yolks and sugar until foamy, add the lemon rind, almonds and carrots. Sift together the flour, the baking powder and a pinch of salt and add to the mixture. Fold in the stiffly beaten egg whites and turn the cake mixture into a well-greased and floured cake tin. Bake in an oven preheated to 190°C (375°F or Mark 5) for 50 minutes, or until a skewer inserted into the centre comes out clean. Leave to cool.

To make the icing, thoroughly mix the sugar with the lemon juice and water. Brush the cold cake with the thinned-down jam and then coat it with the icing. Decorate with the marzipan carrots and keep in an airtight tin until the following day, at the earliest, before serving.

EVA MARIA BORER
TANTE HEIDI'S SWISS KITCHEN

Rhubarb Cake

Rhabarberkuchen

To make one 25 cm (10 inch) cake

600 g	rhubarb, cut into 2 cm (¾ inch) pieces	1¼ lb
150 g	butter, softened	5 oz
350 g	sugar	12 oz
220 g	flour	7½ oz
2 tsp	baking powder	2 tsp
	salt	
3	eggs, lightly beaten	3
1	lemon, rind grated, juice strained	1
4 tbsp	milk	4 tbsp
1 tsp	ground cinnamon	1 tsp
	icing sugar	

Cream the butter with 150 g (5 oz) of the sugar until the mixture is light and fluffy. Mix together the flour, baking powder and a pinch of salt. Add the flour mixture to the butter alternately with the eggs. Beat in the lemon rind and juice, and lastly the milk. Put the dough into a greased spring-form cake tin and level the top.

Mix the rhubarb with the cinnamon and the remaining sugar, and spread on top of the dough. Bake in an oven preheated to 190°C (375°F or Mark 5) for 40 to 45 minutes, or until the rhubarb is soft and the cake has shrunk slightly from the sides of the tin. Leave the cake to cool completely in the tin. When cold, remove it from the tin and sprinkle the top with icing sugar.

HANS KARL ADAM
DAS KOCHBUCH AUS SCHWABEN

Cinnamon Apple Cake

Kaneläppelkaka

To make one 25 cm (10 inch) cake

3	apples, peeled, cored and cut into wedges	3
2 tsp	ground cinnamon	2 tsp
4 tbsp	fine dry breadcrumbs	4 tbsp
4	eggs	4
250 g	sugar	8 oz
250 g	butter, melted	8 oz
175 g	flour, sifted	6 oz
1 tsp	baking powder	1 tsp

Preheat the oven to 180°C (350°F or Mark 4). Butter a 25 cm (10 inch) cast-iron skillet or cake tin, then sprinkle it with the breadcrumbs.

Beat the eggs with 200 g (7 oz) of the sugar until the mixture is thick and pale. Add the butter and the flour sifted with the baking powder and blend well. Pour this batter into the skillet or cake tin. Dip the apples in the remaining sugar mixed with the cinnamon. Put the apples into the cake batter.

Bake for 30 to 35 minutes or until the top is golden and a skewer inserted into the cake comes out clean. Serve the cake hot or at room temperature.

GOREL KRISTINA NASLUND
SWEDISH BAKING

Fig Cake

Pastel de Higos

To make one 25 by 30 cm (10 by 12 inch) cake

100 g	dried figs, stems removed, cut into small pieces	3½ oz
½ litre	milk	16 fl oz
75 g	butter, cut into small pieces	2½ oz
450 g	flour, sifted with 2 tsp baking powder	15 oz
125 g	sugar	4 oz
12.5 cl	dark rum	4 fl oz
2	egg whites, stiffly beaten	2

Heat the milk almost to boiling point. Remove it from the heat and add the butter. When the butter melts, gradually stir in the flour. Then add the sugar, rum and figs. Fold in the egg whites. Pour the mixture into a greased, floured, shallow baking tin, smooth the top, and bake in an oven preheated to 180°C (350°F or Mark 4) for about 50 minutes or until an inserted skewer comes out clean.

CANDIDO LOPEZ
EL LIBRO DE ORO DE LA GASTRONOMIA

Lemon Cake

Zitronenkuchen

To make one 20 cm (8 inch) cake

2	lemons, rind grated and juice of one strained	2
175 g	butter	6 oz
200 g	sugar	7 oz
3	eggs	3
200 g	flour, sieved with 2 tsp baking powder	7 oz
100 g	cornflour	3½ oz
12.5 cl	milk	4 fl oz
	Lemon icing	
1	lemon, juice strained	1
200 g	icing sugar	7 oz

Cream the butter in a bowl and beat in first the sugar and then the eggs and lemon juice. Beat for 10 minutes or until the mixture is creamy. Beat in the flour mixture and the cornflour by the tablespoon. Then add the lemon rind and finally the milk, a little at a time. Put the mixture into a buttered cake tin and bake in an oven preheated to 180°C (350°F or Mark 4) for 45 minutes or until the top is light brown.

Mix the icing sugar with the lemon juice and spread the resulting icing over the cake while it is still warm.

HERMINE KIEHNLE AND MARIA HÄDECKE
DAS NEUE KIEHNLE-KOCHBUCH

Eggless Orange Sponge

Coconut cream is a white solid which is available in tubs from health food shops.

You might think that a cake like this, made without eggs and with wholewheat flour, would be decidedly rock-like. I was afraid so too, but had to try it—and was amazed and delighted at the light, springy cake that resulted.

For a chocolate sponge, omit the orange and add a tablespoonful of cocoa to the mixture, sifting it with the flour and baking powder. Cover the sponge with chocolate icing.

To make one flat cake 30 by 20 cm (12 by 8 inches)

150 g	wholewheat flour	5 oz
1 tsp	baking powder	1 tsp
100 g	butter, softened	3½ oz
100 g	soft brown sugar	3½ oz
½	orange, rind grated, juice strained	½
12.5 cl	milk	4 fl oz

No-sugar icing

100 g	coconut cream, grated	3½ oz
2 tbsp	boiling water	2 tbsp
	honey	

Sift together the flour and baking powder. Cream the butter and sugar, then gently add the sifted ingredients and the orange rind alternately with the milk and orange juice; if the mixture looks a bit lumpy, beat it well and it will smooth out again. Spread into a greased Swiss roll tin and bake in a moderate oven preheated to 180°C (350°F or Mark 4), for 25 minutes or until golden. Cool the sponge in the tin.

For the icing, mix the coconut cream, water, and a dash of honey. Stir until creamy. Pour the icing over the sponge. Cut into fingers when the icing has set.

ROSE ELLIOT
BEANFEAST, NATURAL FOODS COOK BOOK

Orange Mazurka

Mazurek Pomarańczowy

Mazurkas are traditional Polish Easter cakes. They should be baked in shallow rectangular tins.

To make one 20 by 25 cm (8 by 10 inch) cake

4	oranges, pricked in a few places	4
300 g	icing sugar	10 oz
500 g	flour	1 lb
1 tsp	baking powder	1 tsp
150 g	sugar	5 oz
150 g	butter	5 oz
2	egg yolks	2
4 to 6 tbsp	soured cream	4 to 6 tbsp
100 g	almonds, blanched and chopped	3½ oz

Cover the oranges with water, bring to the boil, and cook them gently for about 5 minutes or until they begin to soften. Remove and cool the oranges, then slice them, removing the pips. Dissolve the icing sugar in the orange-cooking water and boil this mixture for about 10 minutes to make a syrup.

Poach the orange slices in the syrup for about 10 minutes or until the rind is tender. Cool the slices in the syrup.

Combine the flour, baking powder and sugar, and rub in the butter to make a crumbly mixture. Add the egg yolks and enough soured cream to make a soft and workable dough. Roll out the dough, put it in a greased tin, and bake in an oven preheated to 180°C (350°F or Mark 4) for about 1 hour or until the cake is lightly coloured.

Turn the cake out of the tin and place it right side up on a floured baking sheet. Arrange a layer of poached orange slices over the top, draining them of excess syrup. Sprinkle on the almonds. Put the cake back into the oven for a few minutes to allow the orange slices to dry. Serve cold.

J. DMOCHOWSKA-GORSKA
DOMOWE CIASTA I DESERY

Pumpkin Cake

Le Milla Sarladais

If wished, you may leave out the baking powder in this recipe. Instead, separate the egg yolks and mix them into the paste. Then beat the egg whites until stiff, folding them into the mixture which will swell like a soufflé and can be eaten hot, with a spoon.

To make one 22 cm (9 inch) cake

500 g	pumpkin, peeled and sliced	1 lb
200 g	cornflour	7 oz
1 tsp	baking powder	1 tsp
150 g	castor sugar	5 oz
	salt	
75 g	butter, melted or 2 tbsp oil	2½ oz
5	eggs	5
½ litre	milk	16 fl oz
2 tbsp	rum or 2 tbsp vanilla sugar or 1 lemon, rind grated	2 tbsp
	vanilla sugar	

Cook the pumpkin for 10 to 15 minutes in 15 cl (¼ pint) lightly salted water. Drain it and pass the pumpkin through a fine meshed sieve to make a rather dry purée. Beat in the cornflour, baking powder, sugar, salt and the butter. Add the eggs one at a time and the milk, which should be poured gradually. The paste should be thick but runny. Finally, add your chosen flavouring. Bake the cake in an oven preheated to 180°C (350°F or Mark 4) in a well-greased deep tart tin for 45 minutes. It will turn a lovely copper colour. Serve cold sprinkled with vanilla sugar.

ZETTE GUINAUDEAU-FRANC
LES SECRETS DES FERMES EN PERIGORD NOIR

Devil's Food Cake

Coffee-flavoured butter cream (recipe, page 92) may be used for this cake instead of the boiled icing. The addition of baking powder produces a fluffier cake; omit it for a denser, moister cake. Use as dark a chocolate as possible for this recipe, preferably the French Chocolat Menier.

To make one three-layer 20 cm (8 inch) cake

300 g	soft brown sugar	10 oz
175 g	butter, creamed	6 oz
3	eggs	3
17.5 cl	boiling water	6 fl oz
90 g	plain chocolate, broken into pieces	3 oz
300 g	plain flour	10 oz
¼ tsp	baking powder (optional)	¼ tsp
1½ tsp	bicarbonate of soda	1½ tsp
17.5 cl	soured cream	6 fl oz
1 tsp	vanilla extract	1 tsp

American frosting (boiled icing)

500 g	sugar	1 lb
1 tbsp	instant coffee powder (optional)	1 tbsp
30 cl	water	½ pint
	cream of tartar	
2	egg whites, stiffly beaten	2

Add the sugar, a little at a time, to the creamed butter. Beat until light and fluffy. Add the eggs one at a time, beating well. Pour the boiling water over the broken-up chocolate in a heavy pan. Stir over a low heat until smooth and thick. Cool a little, add to the creamed mixture and blend well. Sift the flour with the baking powder, if using, and the bicarbonate of soda. Add to the creamed chocolate mixture alternately with the soured cream and vanilla extract.

Pour the mixture into three buttered sandwich tins, and bake in an oven preheated to 190°C (375°F or Mark 5) for about 25 minutes or until the cakes shrink slightly from the sides of the tins. Turn the cakes out of the tins on to wire racks to cool completely.

For the icing, put the sugar, and the coffee powder if you like, into a saucepan with the water. Stir over a low heat until the sugar has quite dissolved. Bring to the boil without stirring and heat to 115°C (238°F) or until a small amount of the syrup dropped in cold water forms a soft ball. Remove from the heat, add a pinch of cream of tartar, and beat hard until the syrup is cloudy. Pour on to the egg whites, whisking hard all the time. Whisk until the icing thickens and loses its shiny look. Use at once to sandwich the three cake layers together and to frost the top and sides.

MARGARET COSTA
MARGARET COSTA'S FOUR SEASONS COOKERY BOOK

Chocolate Cake

Gâteau au Chocolat

To make one 20 cm (8 inch) cake

125 g	plain chocolate, grated	4 oz
5	eggs, yolks separated from whites, whites stiffly beaten	5
250 g	castor sugar	8 oz
125 g	butter, softened	4 oz
125 g	flour, sifted	4 oz

Beat the egg yolks with the sugar until the mixture is thick and pale and forms a ribbon. Add the butter and chocolate, and beat while gradually adding the flour. Fold in the beaten egg whites, and pour the mixture into a buttered cake tin. Bake in an oven preheated to 180°C (350°F or Mark 4) for 30 minutes or until a toothpick inserted into the centre of the cake comes out clean. Turn it out on to a rack to cool.

FERNAND POINT
MA GASTRONOMIE

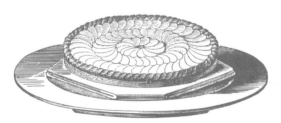

German Chocolate Cake

Schokoladentorte

To make one 18 cm (7 inch) cake

100 g	plain chocolate	3½ oz
100 g	butter, softened	3½ oz
160 g	icing sugar	5½ oz
7	eggs, yolks separated from whites, whites stiffly beaten	7
150 g	flour	5 oz
60 g	apricot jam	2 oz
12.5 cl	double cream, lightly whipped	4 fl oz
60 g	chocolate pralines	2 oz

Put the chocolate into a heatproof dish and put it in an oven preheated to 170°C (325°F or Mark 3) to melt. Put the butter in a bowl and beat in the sugar, egg yolks and the chocolate. Beat for 20 minutes or until the mixture is smooth and creamy. Fold in the beaten egg whites and the flour.

Butter a cake tin, and dust it with flour. Put in the mixture and bake in an oven preheated to 180°C (350°F or Mark 4) for about 40 minutes or until the cake shrinks slightly from the sides of the tin and a skewer inserted into the centre comes out clean. Cool the cake in the tin for 10 minutes and then turn it on to a rack to cool completely.

Cut the cake in half horizontally. Spread the bottom layer with apricot jam and put half of the cream on top of the jam. Replace the other half of the cake and top it with the remaining cream. Garnish with the chocolate pralines.

MARIA HAJKOVA
MÚČNIKY

Sacher Cake

Sachertorte

To make one 22 cm (9 inch) cake

200 g	butter	7 oz
200 g	sugar	7 oz
10	eggs, yolks separated from whites, whites stiffly beaten	10
300 g	plain chocolate	10 oz
150 g	flour, sieved	5 oz
50 g	rusk crumbs	2 oz
	breadcrumbs	
	apricot jam	

Beat the butter until it is creamy. Add the sugar and egg yolks alternately, beating for 30 minutes or until the mixture is very light and fluffy.

Put 200 g (7 oz) of the chocolate in a double saucepan or a bowl over hot water, and heat gently until the chocolate is melted. Beat it into the butter mixture. Fold in the flour and rusk crumbs, and finally fold in the beaten egg whites. Pour the mixture into a buttered and crumbed spring-form cake tin, and bake in an oven preheated to 180°C (350°F or Mark 4) for 1 hour or until the cake shrinks slightly from the sides of the tin. Cool the cake for 10 minutes in the tin, then turn it out on to a rack to cool completely.

The following day, spread the top and sides of the cake with apricot jam. Leave it to set. Melt the remaining chocolate over hot water, and spread it evenly over the jam coating. The cake becomes smooth and shiny if it is put very briefly into a warm oven (170°C, 325°F or Mark 3) for a minute or two after the chocolate is spread on it.

ELIZABETH SCHULER
MEIN KOCHBUCH

A Very Rich Chocolate Cake with Cherries

Le Montmorency

For the cherries in this recipe, you may substitute a purée of fresh figs; or chopped dried prunes or dried apricots, plumped in water and a little kirsch and flavoured with orange marmalade. To do the cake full justice, it *must* be made a day ahead, or even two or three. Then all the flavours of chocolate and fruit will rest and ripen, and be even more rich.

To make one 22 cm (9 inch) cake

400 g	plain chocolate, broken into bits	14 oz
2 tbsp	instant coffee granules	2 tbsp
10 cl	kirsch	3½ fl oz
4	eggs, yolks separated from whites	4
175 g	unsalted butter, at room temperature	6 oz
50 g	flour	2 oz
	salt	
125 g	sugar	4 oz
500 g	cherries, stoned	1 lb

Line the bottom of a deep cake tin with a piece of greaseproof paper, then spread the pan evenly with butter.

In a heavy-bottomed saucepan set over a low heat, melt 250 g (8 oz) of the chocolate with 1 tablespoon of the coffee granules and half of the kirsch, stirring occasionally until smooth. Off the heat, stir in the egg yolks, one at a time, then return the pan to the heat and stir the mixture briefly until the yolks are warmed and have thickened the chocolate slightly. Off the heat, beat in the butter by tablespoons, stirring until smooth. Stir in the flour.

Beat the egg whites with a pinch of salt until they form soft peaks. Sprinkle on 60 g (2 oz) of the sugar and continue beating until the whites form fairly stiff and shiny peaks. Fold the warm chocolate mixture delicately into the meringue and turn the batter into the prepared pan. Bake in an oven preheated to 190°C (375°F or Mark 5) for 25 to 30 minutes, until the cake has puffed and a knife inserted in the centre comes out with only a slightly creamy layer. Do not overcook. Set the pan on a rack to cool for at least 45 minutes before unmoulding. As it cools, the cake will sink and the surface crack slightly.

While the cake is baking and cooling, place the cherries in a saucepan with the remaining sugar and 2 tablespoons of the remaining kirsch. Reserve a few cherries for decoration if desired. Cook the mixture over a medium-low heat, partially covered, for 30 to 40 minutes, stirring occasionally. Uncover the pan for the last 10 minutes or so; the cherries should reduce to a thick compote. Allow them to cool, then chop roughly. Invert the cake on to a serving platter and remove the paper.

Using a large spoon, trace a 12.5 cm (5 inch) circle in the centre of the cake, then scoop out the top part of the circle, leaving at least 1 cm (½ inch) of cake at the bottom. Add the scooped-out cake to the cherries and stir together well. Return the mixture to the cake, smoothing it nicely.

In a heavy-bottomed saucepan, melt the remaining chocolate, coffee granules and kirsch, and 3 tablespoons of water, stirring occasionally until smooth. Allow to cool slightly, then spread evenly over the top and sides of the cake. Refrigerate until 30 minutes before serving. Serve the cake garnished with the reserved cherries.

SIMONE BECK AND MICHAEL JAMES
NEW MENUS FROM SIMCA'S CUISINE

Black Forest Cherry Cake

Schwarzwälder Kirschtorte

To make one 20 cm (8 inch) cake

750 g	sour cherries, stoned	1½ lb
300 g	sugar	10 oz
4	eggs, yolks separated from whites, whites stiffly beaten	4
6 tbsp	water	6 tbsp
125 g	butter	4 oz
200 g	flour	7 oz
50 g	cornflour	2 oz
1 tsp	baking powder	1 tsp
50 g	cocoa powder	2 oz
1 to 2 tbsp	arrack or rum	1 to 2 tbsp
½ litre	double cream, whipped and slightly sweetened with sugar	16 fl oz
50 g	plain chocolate chips	2 oz

In a bowl, beat together 250 g (8 oz) of the sugar, the egg yolks and the water for 20 minutes or until the mixture is foamy. Melt the butter and add it to the mixture. Sieve the flour with the cornflour, baking powder and cocoa and slowly add to the yolk mixture, stirring well. Stir the beaten whites into the mixture. Put this batter into a spring-form cake tin and bake in an oven preheated to 180°C (350°F or Mark 4) for 45 minutes or until the cake shrinks slightly from the sides of the tin and a skewer inserted in the centre comes out clean.

Leave the cake to cool or, better still, leave until the next day. Then slice the cake horizontally in three. The bottom layer should be soaked with the arrack or rum, and the cherries placed upon it, along with the remaining sugar. Cover with whipped cream and add the second layer of cake. Add another layer of cream, and put on the top layer of cake. Finally, the cake should be covered with cream and sprinkled with the chocolate chips (the sides as well).

HERMINE KIEHNLE AND MARIA HÄDECKE
DAS NEUE KIEHNLE-KOCHBUCH

Chocolate Cake with Almonds

Gâteau au Chocolat et aux Amandes

To make one 18 cm (7 inch) cake

250 g	plain chocolate	8 oz
125 g	ground almonds	4 oz
5 tbsp	water	5 tbsp
4	eggs, yolks separated from whites, whites stiffly beaten	4
250 g	sugar	8 oz
125 g	butter, softened and cut into pieces	4 oz
75 g	flour	2½ oz

Heat the water and in it melt the chocolate. Remove the mixture from the heat and stir in the egg yolks, one at a time, then the sugar and the butter. When the butter has melted, stir in the almonds and the flour. Last of all, fold in the stiffly beaten egg whites. Pour the mixture into a well-greased cake tin and bake in an oven preheated to 180°C (350°F or Mark 4) for 45 to 50 minutes or until a warm skewer inserted into the cake comes out clean.

GINETTE MATHIOT
JE SAIS FAIRE LA PÂTISSERIE

Mashed-Potato Chocolate Cake

The quantity of mashed potato used for this cake may be made from two medium-sized potatoes, boiled until tender and mashed with 4 tablespoons of hot milk and 15 g (½ oz) of butter.

To make one two-layer 22 cm (9 inch) cake

250 g	mashed potato, kept hot over hot water	8 oz
90 g	plain chocolate, melted over hot, not boiling water	3 oz
125 g	butter, at room temperature	4 oz
400 g	sugar	14 oz
1½ tsp	bicarbonate of soda, dissolved in 4 tbsp water	1½ tsp
4	large eggs, yolks separated from whites, yolks beaten until very light, whites stiffly beaten	4
250 g	flour	8 oz
2 tsp	baking powder	2 tsp
½ tsp	salt	½ tsp
12.5 cl	milk	4 fl oz
1 tsp	vanilla extract	1 tsp

Mocha-cocoa icing

5 tbsp	very strong black coffee	5 tbsp
4 tbsp	cocoa powder	4 tbsp
75 g	unsalted butter	2½ oz
500 g	icing sugar	1 lb
½ tsp	salt	½ tsp
1 tsp	vanilla extract	1 tsp

Preheat the oven to 190°C (375°F or Mark 5). Butter and flour two round layer-cake tins.

Cream the butter and sugar together until light and fluffy. Add the hot mashed potato and the melted chocolate, and mix well. Add the dissolved soda, stir well, and add the egg yolks to this batter. Sift together the flour, baking powder and salt, and then sift the mixture again into the batter, adding it alternately with the milk, beating well with a spoon. Stir in the vanilla extract and, last of all, fold in the egg whites carefully.

Spread the mixture in the two cake tins, dividing it equally, and place in the preheated oven to bake for about 40 minutes, or until a skewer inserted into the centre comes out clean. Turn the layers out on to cake racks to cool thoroughly before icing the cake.

To make the icing, cream the butter until very smooth and soft. Sift together the icing sugar, salt and cocoa. Add the sugar mixture gradually to the butter. Stir in the coffee until the icing is the right consistency to spread. Flavour with the vanilla extract. Spread the icing between the two layers and over the top and sides of the cake.

JUNE PLATT
JUNE PLATT'S NEW ENGLAND COOK BOOK

Chocolate Pancake

Galette au Chocolat

To make one 18 cm (7 inch) cake

125 g	plain chocolate, melted	4 oz
60 g	butter, softened	2 oz
125 g	sugar	4 oz
3	eggs, yolks separated from whites, whites stiffly beaten	3
2 tbsp	flour	2 tbsp

In a bowl, cream the butter and sugar together until light and fluffy. Gradually beat in the egg yolks, then the chocolate and flour. Fold in the egg whites.

Butter a tart tin and put in the mixture, which should be

about 2.5 cm (1 inch) thick. Bake for 10 minutes in an oven preheated to 220°C (425°F or Mark 7). When the top is nicely golden, invert another buttered tart tin, of the same size, over the pancake. Turn the tins over, holding them together, so that the pancake is inverted into the second tin. Bake for another 10 minutes. The inside of the cake should remain soft. Serve cold.

X. MARCEL BOULESTIN
SIMPLE FRENCH COOKING FOR ENGLISH HOMES

Triple Chocolate Cake

Gâteau au Chocolat de la Maréchale de Lannes

For the technique of melting and using chocolate, see the demonstration on page 10.

To make one three-layer 18 cm (7 inch) cake

90 g	plain chocolate, melted in a tablespoonful of water	3 oz
4	eggs, yolks separated from whites, whites stiffly beaten	4
200 g	castor sugar	7 oz
100 g	flour	3½ oz
	Chocolate cream	
125 g	plain chocolate, melted in a tablespoonful of water	4 oz
100 g	castor sugar	3½ oz
17.5 cl	water	6 fl oz
3	egg yolks	3
400 g	butter	14 oz
	Chocolate icing	
60 g	plain chocolate	2 oz
90 g	icing sugar	3 oz
15 g	butter	½ oz
1	egg yolk, lightly beaten	1

To prepare the cake, first put the egg yolks and sugar into a bowl and whisk the mixture to a pale foam that forms a slowly dissolving ribbon when the whisk is lifted from the bowl.

Gradually fold in the chocolate, flour and egg whites. Blend thoroughly and pour the mixture into a deep, buttered cake tin. Bake in an oven preheated to 180°C (350°F or Mark 4) for approximately 30 minutes. The cake is baked when the skewer used to prick it comes out dry. Remove the cake from the tin and set it on a rack to cool.

To make the chocolate cream, dissolve the sugar in the water in a saucepan and simmer over a low heat until the syrup is very smooth. Remove the syrup from the heat and beat in the egg yolks, one at a time, beating until a light cream

forms. Leave this to get quite cold. Cream the butter and beat in the melted chocolate. Mix in the syrup and yolk mixture.

Cut the cake in three horizontally and reassemble it after spreading a thick layer of chocolate cream between the slices. The cake is now formed.

To make the icing, melt the chocolate with the icing sugar and butter over a low heat. Remove the pan from the heat and bind the icing with the beaten egg yolk. Carefully pour the icing over the cake so that it is evenly glazed.

LES PETITS PLATS ET LES GRANDS

Chocolate Cake with Cinnamon

Torta de Chocolate

This Chilean recipe is adapted from El Cocinero Chileno, *originally published in Spanish in 1875.*

To make one 22 cm (9 inch) cake

175 g	plain chocolate, melted	6 oz
500 g	sugar	1 lb
4 tsp	ground cinnamon	4 tsp
1 tsp	ground cloves	1 tsp
14	eggs, yolks separated from whites	14
175 g	black bread, grated	6 oz

Mix together the sugar, cinnamon, cloves and chocolate. Beat in the 14 egg yolks one at a time and beat thoroughly until the mixture becomes very thick and forms a ribbon. Fold in the 14 egg whites along with the grated black bread. Pour the mixture into a cake tin, greased with unsalted butter. Place the cake immediately in an oven preheated to 150°C (300°F or Mark 2), and bake for about 1 hour or until a skewer inserted into the centre comes out clean. Cool the cake in the tin before turning it out on to a flat plate.

MARTHA VON ZOBELTITZ
DAS KASSEROL: ABSONDERLICHE GAUMENLETZEN AUS ALLER ZEIT

Dutch Chocolate Cake

Holländische Schokoladentorte

To make one 20 cm (8 inch) cake

180 g	butter, softened	6 oz
180 g	sugar	6 oz
8	eggs, yolks separated from whites, whites stiffly beaten	8
120 g	plain or bitter chocolate, grated	4 oz
1 tsp	ground cinnamon	1 tsp
1	small lemon, rind grated, juice strained	1
250 g	ground blanched almonds, or half this quantity mixed with 125 g (4 oz) of sieved rusks or sponge cake crumbs	8 oz
	Filling	
35 cl	milk	12 fl oz
80 g	sugar	2½ oz
3	egg yolks	3
50 g	cocoa powder	2 oz
45 g	butter, cut into small pieces	1½ oz
	Chocolate glaze	
90 g	plain chocolate	3 oz
175 g	sugar	6 oz
12.5 cl	water	4 fl oz

Put the butter into a bowl and beat in the sugar and egg yolks. Beat for about 30 minutes, or until the mixture is foamy. Melt the chocolate with 2 tablespoons of hot water and spoon it into the foamy butter and egg mixture. Mix well. Then add the cinnamon, lemon rind and juice, and almonds, and fold in the stiffly beaten egg whites.

Bake the cake in a buttered baking tin, in an oven preheated to 180°C (350°F or Mark 4) for about 1 hour or until the edges shrink slightly from the sides of the tin and a skewer inserted in the centre comes out clean. Leave the cake to cool, and cut it into three horizontal rounds.

To make the filling, put the milk, sugar, egg yolks, cocoa powder and butter in a double saucepan or in a bowl standing in a saucepan of water, and stir until you have a thick cream. Spread it between the three layers of cake and put one layer on top of the other.

To make the glaze, melt the chocolate in a bowl set over a pan of hot water. In a small saucepan, boil the sugar and water together until the syrup reaches the soft ball stage. Cool slightly, then stir the syrup into the chocolate. When the glaze is still warm, but beginning to thicken, spread it on the top and sides of the cake.

HERMINE KIEHNLE AND MARIA HÄDECKE
DAS NEUE KIEHNLE-KOCHBUCH

Granny's Vinegar Cake

This recipe comes from Kirkcudbrightshire, Scotland.

To make one 22 cm (9 inch) cake

250 g	butter	8 oz
500 g	flour	1 lb
250 g	sugar (brown, if you like)	8 oz
250 g	currants	8 oz
125 g	seedless or seeded raisins	4 oz
1	egg, beaten (optional)	1
17.5 cl	milk	6 fl oz
3 tbsp	distilled white vinegar	3 tbsp
1 tsp	bicarbonate of soda	1 tsp

Rub the butter into the flour with your fingers until the mixture is crumbly. Add the sugar and fruit, and then the egg, if using. Put 15 cl (¼ pint) of the milk into a large jug and add the vinegar. Warm the remaining milk, stir in the soda until dissolved and add to the jug. Stir this mixture quickly into the cake dough. Pour into a greased and floured cake tin, and put into an oven preheated to 190°C (375°F or Mark 5) for 30 minutes, then lower the temperature to 150°C (300°F or Mark 2). Continue to bake for a further 30 minutes or until firm to the touch.

PETITS PROPOS CULINAIRES I

Betsy Cake

A Betsy cake is an English harvest cake.

To make one 20 cm (8 inch) cake

125 g	butter	4 oz
125 g	sugar	4 oz
1 tbsp	golden syrup	1 tbsp
250 g	barley flour	8 oz
250 g	flour	8 oz
¼ litre	milk	8 fl oz
250 g	sultanas	8 oz
1½ tsp	baking powder	1½ tsp
½ tsp	salt	½ tsp

Beat the butter and sugar to a cream. Add the syrup, then the flour and milk alternately, the fruit, baking powder and salt last. Mix into a dough, put into a buttered tin and bake in an oven preheated to 170°C (325°F or Mark 3) for 1½ to 2 hours.

MRS. C. F. LEYEL
CAKES OF ENGLAND

Cree Cake

Teisen Griwsion

The small, crisp pieces left over when pork fat was rendered to yield lard were commonly known in Welsh as *criwsion* or *creision*. Cree, scruggins and scrutchins were the English equivalents used in different parts of Wales. Tossed in oatmeal and seasoned with salt and pepper, they were eaten with bread and butter. Alternatively they were put in a cake mixture instead of ordinary fat. This recipe is from Swansea.

To make one 20 by 16 cm (8 by 6 inch) cake

500 g	self-raising flour	1 lb
350 g	cree, finely chopped	12 oz
275 g	sugar	9 oz
About 15 cl	milk and water mixed	About ¼ pint

Put the flour, cree and 250 g (8 oz) of sugar into a mixing bowl and gradually add the milk and water mixture to make a soft dough, mixing it together first with a rounded knife and finally with your fingers. Turn the dough out on to a well-floured board and roll it out to a thickness of about 2.5 cm (1 inch). Place in a greased shallow tin, sprinkle with a little sugar and then bake in an oven preheated to 190°C (375°F or Mark 5) for about 30 minutes or until the cake sounds hollow when it is gently tapped and the top is brown.

S. MINWEL TIBBOTT
WELSH FARE

Potato Cake

Poten Dato

The quantities of ingredients used in this recipe may be varied according to taste. Up to 60 g (2 oz) extra butter will give this cake a richer flavour.

Poten dato was baked regularly in the Welsh counties of Cardiganshire and Pembrokeshire, where potatoes were plentiful in the autumn. Prepared in large quantities, it would be baked in the brick wall-oven. This oven would be heated at least once a week for baking bread, and as the bricks retained some heat for several hours it was the custom to bake cakes and puddings in this "after heat" overnight.

To make one 22 cm (9 inch) cake

600 g	mashed boiled potatoes	1¼ lb
125 g	butter, cut into small pieces	4 oz
60 g	sugar	2 oz
60 g	currants	2 oz
125 g	flour	4 oz
2 tsp	ground mixed spice	2 tsp
	salt	
1	egg, beaten	1
About 15 cl	milk	About ¼ pt

Put the potatoes into a large bowl. Add a few lumps of butter and mash thoroughly. Mix in the other dry ingredients and beat in the egg and a little milk to give the mixture a fairly soft consistency. Put the mixture into a greased shallow tin and bake in an oven preheated to 180°C (350°F or Mark 4) for 45 minutes or until golden-brown on top. Eat hot.

S. MINWEL TIBBOTT
WELSH FARE

Shearing or Threshing Cake

Cacen Gneifio neu Ddyrnu

To make one 20 cm (8 inch) cake

250 g	bacon dripping	8 oz
375 g	flour	12 oz
250 g	sugar	8 oz
250 g each	currants and raisins	8 oz
2	large eggs, well beaten	2
1 tsp	bicarbonate of soda, dissolved in 4 tbsp mixed tepid water and buttermilk	1 tsp
About ¼ litre	buttermilk	About 8 fl oz

Rub the fat into the flour and work in the sugar, currants and raisins. Gradually mix in the beaten eggs, the bicarbonate of soda and sufficient buttermilk to give a fairly soft consistency. Grease a cake tin, put the mixture into it and bake in an oven preheated to 180°C (350°F or Mark 4) for approximately 1½ hours or until a skewer inserted into the centre comes out clean. Cool the cake in the tin for 10 minutes and turn it on to a wire rack to cool completely.

S. MINWEL TIBBOTT
WELSH FARE

Cider Cake

This recipe is from Somerset. The cake has a subtle flavour of cider and is particularly good served with a purée of apples and with plenty of cream; or at a picnic with apples and with cider to drink.

To make one 18 cm (7 inch) square cake

15 cl	cider	$\frac{1}{4}$ pint
125 g	butter	4 oz
125 g	sugar	4 oz
2	eggs, beaten	2
250 g	flour	8 oz
1 tsp	bicarbonate of soda	1 tsp
1 tsp	grated nutmeg	1 tsp

Cream the butter and the sugar, add the beaten eggs, then half of the flour, sifted with the soda and the nutmeg. Pour the cider over and beat the batter thoroughly until the acid of the cider acts on the alkali of the soda and makes the mixture froth. Then stir in the remaining flour and quickly pour the mixture into a well-greased square cake tin. Bake in an oven preheated to 180°C (350°F or Mark 4) for 40 minutes or until the cake shrinks slightly from the sides of the tin.

ELISABETH AYRTON
THE COOKERY OF ENGLAND

Porter Cakes

To make two 18 cm (7 inch) cakes

250 g	butter	8 oz
350 g	sugar	12 oz
30 cl	stout	$\frac{1}{2}$ pint
2	eggs, well beaten	2
750 g	currants	$1\frac{1}{2}$ lb
500 g	flour	1 lb
1 tsp	bicarbonate of soda	1 tsp
$\frac{1}{2}$ tsp	ground mixed spice	$\frac{1}{2}$ tsp

Melt the butter over a very gentle heat without letting it foam. Remove the pan from the heat and stir in the sugar, stout and eggs. Transfer the mixture to a large bowl. Mix the currants with the flour and stir them into the stout mixture. Lastly, add the bicarbonate of soda and the mixed spice. Stir thoroughly for several minutes so all of the ingredients are well incorporated. Divide the mixture equally between two tins and bake in an oven preheated to 180°C (350°F or Mark 4)

for at least 2 hours or until a skewer inserted into the centre comes out clean. Cool the cakes for 10 minutes in the tins and turn them on to wire racks to cool completely.

ANN PASCOE
CORNISH RECIPES OLD AND NEW

Ginger Cake

Teisen Sinsir

To make one 25 cm (10 inch) cake

500 g	treacle	1 lb
125 g	butter	4 oz
60 g	brown sugar	2 oz
30 g	candied mixed peel, minced	1 oz
2	eggs, beaten	2
500 g	flour	1 lb
30 g	ground ginger	1 oz
1 tsp	bicarbonate of soda	1 tsp
About 20 cl	milk	About 7 fl oz

In a saucepan over a low heat, stir together the treacle, butter and sugar until they are thoroughly melted.

Mix the minced peel into the beaten eggs. Put the dry ingredients in a bowl, and gradually stir in first the egg mixture, then the treacle mixture, and finally enough milk to make a fairly liquid batter. Pour the batter into a well-greased, shallow tin, and bake in a moderate oven, preheated to 180°C (350°F or Mark 4), for 45 minutes or until a knife inserted into the cake comes out clean.

WALES GAS HOME SERVICE
A WELSH WELCOME

Ukrainian Honey Cake

To make one 18 cm (7 inch) cake

$\frac{1}{4}$ litre	liquid honey, warmed by setting the pot or bowl in a pan of hot water	8 fl oz
3	large eggs or 4 medium-sized eggs, beaten until foamy	3
175 g	flour	6 oz
1 tsp	baking powder	1 tsp

Beat the warmed honey until frothy, and add the eggs, flour and baking powder. Pour the mixture into a shallow, buttered tin and bake for 15 to 20 minutes in an oven preheated to 190°C (375°F or Mark 5). Check the cake after 15 minutes; if it is done, it will shrink slightly from the sides of the tin. Turn it out immediately on to greaseproof paper. Allow to cool. Store in an airtight tin for a day or so before using.

BRITISH COLUMBIA WOMEN'S INSTITUTES
ADVENTURES IN COOKING

Raisin Gingerbread

To make one 22 cm (9 inch) square cake

75 g	raisins, washed and dried	2½ oz
150 g	sugar	5 oz
15 cl	molasses	¼ pint
15 cl	boiling water	¼ pint
30 g	butter	1 oz
1 tsp	bicarbonate of soda	1 tsp
60 g	walnuts or pecans, chopped	2 oz
1	egg, well beaten	1
175 g	flour, sifted	6 oz
1 tsp each	ground cinnamon and ginger	1 tsp each
¼ tsp	ground cloves	¼ tsp
¼ litre	double cream, lightly beaten	8 fl oz

Preheat the oven to 180°C (350°F or Mark 4). Mix together the sugar, molasses and boiling water. While the mixture is still hot, stir in the butter and the bicarbonate of soda. Cool. Add the raisins, nuts and beaten egg. Sift together the flour and spices, and stir them into the molasses mixture. Pour the mixture into a well-buttered cake tin and bake in the preheated oven for 35 to 40 minutes, or until an inserted skewer comes out clean. Serve hot or cold with cream.

JUNE PLATT
JUNE PLATT'S NEW ENGLAND COOK BOOK

Lady Constance Howard's Ginger Cake

To fill one 1 kg (2 lb) loaf tin

600 g	flour	1¼ lb
1 tsp	baking powder	1 tsp
125 g	butter	4 oz
125 g	sugar	4 oz
2 tbsp	ground ginger	2 tbsp
250 g	raisins	8 oz
2	eggs, well beaten	2
15 cl	dark treacle	¼ pint
15 cl	milk	¼ pint

Mix the flour and the baking powder; rub in the butter; add the sugar, the ginger and the raisins. Add to the eggs the treacle and milk; then mix the whole well together, and put it in the oven at once in a loaf tin lined with buttered paper. Bake for about 2 hours in a moderate oven, preheated to 180°C (350°F or Mark 4), or until the cake shrinks slightly from the sides of the tin.

W. T. FERNIE
KITCHEN PHYSIC

Molasses Cake

To make one 25 cm (10 inch) square cake

½ litre	molasses	16 fl oz
1 kg	flour	2 to 2½ lb
250 g	butter	8 oz
250 g	sugar	8 oz
2 tbsp	ground ginger	2 tbsp
1 tbsp	bicarbonate of soda	1 tbsp
3 tbsp	warm water	3 tbsp
¼ litre	soured milk	8 fl oz

Put the flour in a large basin and rub in the butter until the mixture is quite smooth; then mix in the sugar and the ginger. Dissolve the bicarbonate of soda in the warm water and stir in the soured milk and molasses to make a fairly sticky dough. Work the dough thoroughly. If it is a little too stiff, more water can be added, or, if not stiff enough, a little more flour. Put the dough in a buttered cake tin and bake in an oven preheated to 190°C (375°F or Mark 5) for 50 minutes or until an inserted skewer comes out clean. When cut, the interior should be quite dark.

OSCAR TSCHIRKY
THE COOKBOOK BY "OSCAR" OF THE WALDORF

Old Polish Honey Cake

Staropolski Piernik Świąteczny

This cake may be iced with chocolate icing and decorated, but even served plain it would be the first among traditionally festive Polish cakes at the Christmas table.

To make one three-layer 20 by 25 cm (8 by 10 inch) cake

500 g	honey	1 lb
500 g	sugar	1 lb
250 g	lard or butter	8 oz
1 kg	flour	2 lb
3	eggs	3
3 tsp	bicarbonate of soda, dissolved in 12.5 cl (4 fl oz) milk	3 tsp
½ tsp	salt	½ tsp
1 tsp each	ground cinnamon, cloves, ginger and cardamom	1 tsp each
30 g	nuts, chopped (optional)	1 oz
3 tbsp	finely slivered orange rind, fried in 15 g (½ oz) butter with 2 tbsp sugar (optional)	3 tbsp
	powidel (Polish prune jam) or marzipan	

Gradually heat the honey, sugar and lard together almost to boiling point. Cool. Working the dough with your hands, gradually add the flour, eggs, soda and milk, salt and spices. Add the nuts and orange rind, if desired. Shape the dough into a ball and put it in a bowl covered with a towel. Leave in a cool place for several hours or overnight to mature.

Divide the dough into three parts, roll them out, and place each piece in a rectangular baking tin. Bake in an oven preheated to 180°C (350°F or Mark 4) for 40 minutes or until the cakes are slightly browned and firm to the touch. The cakes are hard at first, but after 2 or 3 days become tender and melt in the mouth. When cool, the layers may be sandwiched together with *powidel* jam or marzipan. Two different fillings may be used.

After filling, the cake should be covered with a sheet of paper and weighted down with a board or books. The cake keeps for a long time, particularly if stored in a cool place.

M. LEMNIS AND H. VITRY
W STAROPOLSKIEJ KUCHNI I PRZY POLSKIM STOLE

Catalan Cake

"Cake" a la Catalana

To make one 20 by 25 cm (8 by 10 inch) cake

165 g	butter	5½ oz
165 g	sugar	5½ oz
3	eggs	3
200 g	flour, sifted with 1 tsp baking powder	7 oz
150 g	peeled pine-nuts, toasted	5 oz
165 g	candied orange slices, cut into small pieces	5½ oz
12.5 cl	dark rum	4 fl oz

Cream the butter and sugar together until very creamy; add the eggs, one by one, beating well until completely blended. Add the flour mixture, toasted pine-nuts and candied orange pieces, then stir in the rum.

Pour the mixture into a greased and floured rectangular tin, smoothing the top with a spatula. Bake in an oven preheated to 180°C (350°F or Mark 4) for 45 minutes or until an inserted skewer comes out clean. Cool the cake in the tin before turning it out.

CANDIDO LOPEZ
EL LIBRO DE ORO DE LA GASTRONOMIA

Date and Nut Loaf

To make two 21 by 11.5 cm (8½ by 4½ inch) loaves

500 g	stoned dates, roughly chopped	1 lb
250 g	walnuts, roughly chopped	8 oz
275 g	brown sugar	9 oz
250 g	butter	8 oz
3	eggs	3
1 tsp	bicarbonate of soda, dissolved in 1 tbsp hot water	1 tsp
	salt	
325 g	flour, sifted	11 oz

Cream together the sugar and butter until the mixture is light in colour. Beat in the eggs, one at a time. Add the dissolved bicarbonate of soda with a pinch of salt and the walnuts and dates. Stir in the flour and divide the batter beween two loaf tins. Bake the loaves in an oven preheated to 170°C (325°F or Mark 3) for 1½ to 2 hours or until the loaves pull away from the sides of the tins.

BRITISH COLUMBIA WOMEN'S INSTITUTES
ADVENTURES IN COOKING

Clunie Rock Buns

To make 18 buns

60 g	butter	2 oz
250 g	flour	8 oz
100 g	castor sugar	3½ oz
2 tbsp	grated plain chocolate	2 tbsp
60 g	nuts (walnuts, hazelnuts or almonds), chopped	2 oz
60 g	raisins, stoned	2 oz
¼ tsp	mixed spice	¼ tsp
1 tsp	baking powder	1 tsp
1	egg, lightly beaten	1
	milk	

Rub the butter into the flour. Stir in 90 g (3 oz) of the sugar, the chocolate, nuts, raisins, mixed spice and baking powder. Add the egg and enough milk to make a stiff dough. Shape the dough into balls, with floured hands. Place the balls about 5 cm (2 inches) apart on a lightly floured baking sheet. Bake in an oven preheated to 180°C (350°F or Mark 4) for about 20 minutes or until golden-brown. Dredge with the remaining castor sugar while still hot.

ELIZABETH CRAIG
THE SCOTTISH COOKERY BOOK

Portugal Cakes

To make 12 small cakes

125 g	sugar	4 oz
4	egg yolks	4
1 tbsp	rum	1 tbsp
60 g	almonds, blanched	2 oz
5	egg whites, 4 stiffly beaten	5
15 cl	orange juice	5 fl oz
1 tbsp	grated orange rind	1 tbsp
	icing sugar	

Place in a basin the sugar, egg yolks and rum, and beat up with a whisk for 10 minutes. Pound the almonds in a mortar with the unbeaten egg white to a smooth pulp, rub through a sieve into a bowl, add the orange juice and rind and mix thoroughly. Fold the beaten whites into the yolk mixture; mix well, then add the almond and orange mixture and blend well.

Line the bottom of a small, square, buttered baking tin with a sheet of buttered paper; then spread the preparation in the tin, sprinkle a little icing sugar over, and set in an oven preheated to 180°C (350°F or Mark 4) for 25 minutes or until

lightly browned. Allow to cool in the tin for 10 minutes, then turn out the cake, remove the paper, cut the cake into 12 equal parts, dredge a little icing sugar over them while still warm, and serve.

MAY BYRON
MAY BYRON'S CAKE BOOK

George Mardikian's All-Purpose Cake

This cake, with its hard caramel base, is delicious for afternoon tea, or for dessert with fruit.

To make one 22 cm (9 inch) square cake

300 g	brown sugar	10 oz
250 g	flour, sifted	8 oz
125 g	butter	4 oz
¼ litre	soured cream	8 fl oz
1 tsp	bicarbonate of soda	1 tsp
1	egg, beaten	1
1 tsp	grated nutmeg	1 tsp
	chopped nuts (any variety)	
	ground cinnamon	

Butter a square baking tin. Blend together the sugar, flour and butter as for a pastry dough, by pinching the mixture with the fingers. Set aside half of this crumbly mixture. Mix the soured cream, bicarbonate of soda, egg and nutmeg, and add this to the other half of the sugar mixture.

Spread the reserved half of the crumbly mixture over the base of the baking tin. Top with the soured cream mixture. Sprinkle with chopped nuts and cinnamon. Bake in an oven preheated to 180°C (350°F or Mark 4) for about 40 minutes or until a skewer inserted in the centre comes out clean. Do not open the oven door for the first 30 minutes of baking.

Cool the cake and turn it out, then turn it right side up so that the caramel layer is on the bottom.

GEORGE MARDIKIAN
DINNER AT OMAR KHAYYAM'S

Butter-Cream Layer Cake

Marjolaine

Rapid baking at high temperatures demands an accurate oven thermostat that can be adjusted with precision. At a high temperature a cake may require 1 minute more, or less, baking time and must be watched closely while it is in the oven.

To make one four-layer 12 by 50 cm (5 by 20 inch) cake

200 g	almonds, blanched	7 oz
150 g	shelled hazelnuts	5 oz
300 g	castor sugar	10 oz
30 g	flour	1 oz
8	egg whites, stiffly beaten	8
	chocolate shavings (*page 11*)	
	icing sugar	
	Chocolate cream	
350 g	plain chocolate, melted	12 oz
$\frac{1}{4}$ litre	double cream	8 fl oz
	White cream	
$\frac{1}{4}$ litre	double cream, whipped and flavoured with vanilla sugar	8 fl oz
60 g	butter, softened	2 oz
	Praline cream	
100 g	praline (*page 94*)	$3\frac{1}{2}$ oz
$\frac{1}{4}$ litre	double cream, whipped and flavoured with vanilla sugar	8 fl oz
60 g	butter, softened	2 oz

Roast the almonds and the hazelnuts on separate tins in a 200°C (400°F or Mark 6) oven for 10 minutes or until lightly browned. Rub the skins off the hazelnuts in a towel. Grind the nuts together in a mortar or blender, then add the sugar and the flour and grind everything together very finely.

Gently fold the nut mixture into the egg whites, sprinkling it on lightly as you fold. Spread the mixture into four buttered and lightly floured long shallow baking tins. Bake in an oven preheated to 200°C (400°F or Mark 6) for 3 to 4 minutes or until evenly browned and swelled in the centre. Cool.

To make the chocolate cream, stir the cream into the chocolate. Bring the mixture to the boil, stirring constantly, then remove from the heat and cool.

To make the white cream, put the whipped cream into a sieve and drain off as much water as possible. Add the cream to the butter, little by little, until no more can be absorbed.

Make the praline cream in the same way as the white cream, folding in the praline powder at the end.

Spread half of the chocolate cream on to the first cake layer, top with the second layer, and spread this with all of the white cream. Top with the third layer, spread with all of the praline cream, then top with the fourth layer. Spread the entire cake with the remaining chocolate cream. Press chocolate shavings into the sides of the cake, and sprinkle the top with icing sugar. Refrigerate for 24 hours before serving.

FERNAND POINT
MA GASTRONOMIE

Pistachio Cake

Vert-Vert

For the green colouring used in the cream, blanch a few leaves of spinach in boiling water, then rub them through a fine sieve. Heat the resulting purée, pour off the water that separates from it, and use the thick purée that remains.

To make one 22 cm (9 inch) three-layer cake

50 g	shelled pistachio nuts, ground	2 oz
4	eggs	4
125 g	sugar	4 oz
4 tbsp	kirsch	4 tbsp
60 g	flour, sieved	2 oz
60 g	ground rice, sieved	2 oz
$\frac{1}{2}$	lemon, rind grated	$\frac{1}{2}$
60 g	butter, melted	2 oz
	Pistachio cream	
80 g	shelled pistachio nuts, blanched	$2\frac{1}{2}$ oz
10 cl	kirsch	$3\frac{1}{2}$ fl oz
1 tbsp	spinach green	1 tbsp
1	egg	1
2	egg yolks	2
80 g	sugar	$2\frac{1}{2}$ oz
1 tsp	flour	1 tsp
	salt	
$\frac{1}{4}$ litre	milk	8 fl oz
60 g	butter	2 oz

For the cake, place the eggs and sugar in a bowl set over a pan of hot water. Never letting the mixture become more than warm, whisk over a very low heat for 10 to 15 minutes, until it is very thick and light and forms a ribbon. Mix the pistachio nuts with the kirsch and add this paste to the egg mixture with the flour, ground rice and grated lemon rind, working with a wooden spoon until everything is thoroughly blended. Finally, stir in the melted butter. Pour the mixture into a buttered and floured cake tin, and bake in an oven preheated to 180°C (350°F or Mark 4) for 25 to 30 minutes or until the cake shrinks slightly from the sides of the tin. Turn the cake out on a rack to cool.

For the cream, pound the pistachio nuts, gradually adding the kirsch. When you obtain a fine paste, transfer it to a bowl and add the spinach green. Beat the egg and yolks with the sugar until the mixture whitens; add the flour and a pinch of salt, whisk for 1 minute more, then add the milk. Heat this custard until it comes to the boil, then pour it on to the pistachio paste and stir until the mixture cools slightly. Work in 30 g (1 oz) of the butter.

Slice the cake horizontally into three layers. Spread each layer with a quarter of the pistachio cream, and stack the layers. Spread a thin layer of cream around the sides. Heat the remaining cream slightly, and incorporate the remaining butter. Decorate the cake with this mixture, using a piping bag. The cake is just as good the next day.

MME. JEANNE SAVARIN (EDITOR)
LA CUISINE DES FAMILLES (MAGAZINE)

Nut-Glazed Cake

The soured milk called for in this recipe can be made by adding two teaspoons of lemon juice or vinegar to fresh milk.

To make one 22 cm (9 inch) square cake

125 g	walnuts, chopped	4 oz
45 g	butter	1½ oz
60 g	brown sugar	2 oz
1 tbsp	water	1 tbsp
30 g	bitter chocolate	1 oz
125 g	shortening	4 oz
275 g	sugar	9 oz
2	eggs	2
200 g	flour, sifted with ¾ tsp bicarbonate of soda and 1 tsp salt	7 oz
¼ litre	soured milk or buttermilk	8 fl oz

Melt the butter in the bottom of the cake tin, and mix in the brown sugar and the water. Sprinkle with the walnut pieces.

Melt the chocolate in a dish set over a pan of simmering water, then take the dish from the heat and let the chocolate cool for a few minutes, taking care it does not harden again.

Cream the shortening with the sugar until it is fluffy textured, and add the eggs, one at a time, beating thoroughly after each addition. Beat in the chocolate. Blend the flour into the creamed mixture alternately with the soured milk. Spoon the batter over the walnuts in the tin.

Bake the cake in an oven preheated to 180°C (350°F or

Mark 4) for about 50 minutes or until a skewer inserted into the centre comes out clean. Let the cake stand for 5 minutes. Invert the tin carefully over a serving plate to remove the cake. Serve warm, plain or with whipped cream.

BRITISH COLUMBIA WOMEN'S INSTITUTES
ADVENTURES IN COOKING

Dead Man's Cake

Pan di Mort

To make about twenty 10 by 4 cm (4 by 1½ inch) cakes

400 g	demerara sugar	14 oz
50 g	cocoa	2 oz
60 g	plain chocolate, melted	2 oz
17.5 cl	white wine	6 fl oz
1 tbsp	honey	1 tbsp
300 g	flour	10 oz
300 g	almonds, blanched and roughly chopped	10 oz
100 g	candied mixed peel	3½ oz
100 g	pine-nuts	3½ oz
1 tbsp	mixed spice	1 tbsp
	icing sugar	

In a large bowl, knead together thoroughly all of the ingredients except the icing sugar. Form the mixture into 20 small, elongated oval loaves. Arrange them on a buttered baking sheet, lined with buttered greaseproof paper if desired, and bake in oven preheated to 180°C (350°F or Mark 4) for 1 hour or until the cakes feel firm to the touch. Sprinkle with icing sugar while still hot.

OTTORINA PERNA BOZZI
VECCHIA MILANO IN CUCINA

Coffee and Walnut Cake

Torta Rustica di Noci al Caffè

To make one 20 cm (8 inch) cake

10 to 15 cl	strong coffee	3½ to 5 fl oz
200 g	shelled walnuts, very finely chopped	7 oz
100 g	butter, softened	3½ oz
300 g	castor sugar	10 oz
2	eggs, lightly beaten	2
200 g	flour, sieved with 1 tbsp baking powder	7 oz

Cream the butter and sugar together until light and fluffy, then beat in the eggs. Add the flour alternately with the coffee until the mixture is soft and smooth. Add the nuts. Pour the mixture into a buttered cake tin and bake in an oven preheated to 180°C (350°F or Mark 4) for about 1 hour or until a skewer inserted in the centre comes out clean.

MARIÙ SALVATORI DE ZULIANI
LA CUCINA DI VERSILIA E GARFAGNANA

Nut and Anisette Cake

Brustengolo

*To make one 20 by 30 cm
(8 by 12 inch) cake*

100 g	pine-nuts	3½ oz
200 g	shelled walnuts, roughly chopped	7 oz
4 tbsp	anisette	4 tbsp
350 g	cornmeal	12 oz
1 litre	water, lightly salted and heated to boiling	1¾ pints
1	apple, peeled, cored and thinly sliced	1
1	lemon, juice strained, rind grated	1
100 g	sugar	3½ oz
8 cl	olive oil	3 fl oz

Put the cornmeal into a bowl. Gradually pour in the water, stirring all the time with a wooden spoon.

Sprinkle the apple with the lemon juice. Mix together the apple, lemon rind, pine-nuts and walnuts; flavour with the sugar, oil and anisette. Mix them into the cornmeal.

Thoroughly butter a baking tin and pour in the mixture, spreading it out evenly. Bake in an oven preheated to 180°C (350°F or Mark 4) for about 40 minutes or until the top is golden-brown. Serve cold.

LUIGI VOLPICELLI AND SECONDINO FREDA
L'ANTIARTUSI: 1000 RICETTE

Claricinha Coffee Cake

Bôlo de Café Claricinha

To make one 25 cm (10 inch) cake

¼ litre	strong coffee	8 fl oz
2	eggs, lightly beaten	2
200 g	sugar	7 oz
350 g	honey	12 oz
15 g	butter, softened	½ oz
125 g	candied fruits, chopped	4 oz
150 g	raisins	5 oz
125 g	plain chocolate, grated	4 oz
1 tsp	ground cinnamon	1 tsp
1	clove, crushed	1
1 tbsp	baking powder	1 tbsp
350 g	flour	12 oz

Mix all the ingredients together and beat them well. Put the mixture into a greased cake tin and bake in an oven preheated to 180°C (350°F or Mark 4) for 1½ hours or until the cake shrinks slightly from the sides of the tin.

DONA TITA
RECEITAS EXPERIMENTADAS

Wild Rice-Bourbon Cake

To make one 1 kg (2 lb) loaf

90 g	wild rice, cooked in water only until the grains pop, about 30 minutes	3 oz
15 cl	bourbon whiskey	¼ pint
500 g	flour, sifted	1 lb
½ tsp	salt	½ tsp
2 tsp	baking powder	2 tsp
15 cl	milk	¼ pint
1 tsp	vanilla extract	1 tsp
500 g	butter, softened	1 lb
400 g	sugar	14 oz
8	eggs, at room temperature	8

Sift the flour with the salt and baking powder. Set aside. Combine the bourbon, milk and vanilla and set aside.

Cream the butter and sugar together until light and fluffy. Add the eggs, one at a time, beating well after each addition. Add one-third of the flour mixture at a time alternately with one-third of the bourbon and milk mixture. Blend in the wild rice, mixing thoroughly.

Generously butter and flour a loaf tin. Pour the batter into this and bake in an oven preheated to 150°C (300°F or Mark 2) for $1\frac{1}{4}$ to $1\frac{1}{2}$ hours or until a straw or wooden toothpick inserted near the centre comes out clean. Set the cake on a wire rack and cool it in the tin for about 10 minutes. Then turn the cake out of the tin on to the rack.

To maintain maximum moistness in the cake, place it, not yet quite cooled, on a cake plate and cover it with a tea towel. The cake is especially good served when not thoroughly cooled, but cool enough so that it will slice well.

BETH ANDERSON
WILD RICE FOR ALL SEASONS COOKBOOK

Moss Rose Cake

To make one two-layer 20 cm (8 inch) cake

4	eggs	4
400 g	sugar	14 oz
$\frac{1}{2}$ tsp	almond extract	$\frac{1}{2}$ tsp
$\frac{1}{4}$ litre	milk, heated to boiling point	8 fl oz
250 g	flour, sifted	8 oz
2 tsp	baking powder	2 tsp

Orange-coconut icing

330 g	sugar	11 oz
10 cl	water	$3\frac{1}{2}$ fl oz
2	egg whites, stiffly beaten	2
1 tsp	vanilla extract	1 tsp
250 g	grated coconut	8 oz
1	large orange, rind grated, juice strained	1

Break the eggs over the sugar and beat for 12 minutes—this must be done. Add the almond extract to the hot milk and leave to cool slightly. Re-sift the flour with the baking powder. Add the flour to the egg and sugar mixture. Add the warm milk, slowly, and beat for 3 minutes. Bake in two cake tins in an oven preheated to 180 °C (350 °F or Mark 4) for 25 minutes

or until the cakes shrink slightly from the sides of the tins. Put them out on to wire racks to cool completely.

For the icing, combine 300 g (10 oz) of the sugar with the water in a small pan and boil for about 15 minutes or until the sugar syrup spins a small thread. Pour the sugar syrup slowly over the stiffly beaten egg whites and beat the mixture until it is thick enough to spread. Add the vanilla extract and spread the icing on the two cake layers, but do not put the two layers together.

Mix the coconut with the orange rind and juice, and sweeten to taste with the remaining sugar. When the icing has begun to set, but is not hard, pat the orange-coconut mixture into it and put the layers together.

MARION BROWN
THE SOUTHERN COOK BOOK

Maple Upside-Down Cake

To make one 25 by 15 cm (10 by 6 inch) cake

$\frac{1}{4}$ litre	pure maple syrup	8 fl oz
30 g	butter	1 oz
3 tbsp	sugar	3 tbsp
1	large egg, well beaten	1
125 g	flour	4 oz
2 tsp	baking powder	2 tsp
$\frac{1}{4}$ tsp	salt	$\frac{1}{4}$ tsp
10 cl	milk	$3\frac{1}{2}$ fl oz
6	pecans, halved	6
30 cl	double cream	$\frac{1}{2}$ pint

Preheat the oven to 190 °C (375 °F or Mark 5). Heat the syrup to the boiling point and pour it into a 5 cm (2 inch) deep rectangular ovenproof glass dish. Cream the butter and sugar together until they are light and fluffy and beat in the egg. Sift together the flour, baking powder and salt, then sift again into the butter mixture, adding the flour alternately with the milk to make a smooth batter. Pour the batter on to the hot syrup, spreading it evenly.

Bake in the preheated oven until the cake is brown on top, and until a skewer inserted into the centre comes out clean—about 25 to 30 minutes. Allow the cake to cool for 10 minutes before turning it out, bottom side up, on to a hot platter, running a knife around the edge first to help loosen the cake. Dot with the pecan halves, cut the cake into six equal portions, and serve while still warm, accompanied by the cream, slightly whipped or plain.

JUNE PLATT
JUNE PLATT'S NEW ENGLAND COOK BOOK

Glenna McGinnis Lane Cake

To toast the pecans, put them on a baking sheet and put into a moderate 180°C (350°F or Mark 4) oven for 15 minutes.

This is traditionally a handsome four-layer cake, but can be made as two two-layer cakes.

To make one 22 cm (9 inch) four-layer cake

250 g	butter	8 oz
500 g	sugar	1 lb
1 tsp	vanilla extract	1 tsp
400 g	flour, sifted	14 oz
3½ tsp	baking powder	3½ tsp
1 tsp	salt	1 tsp
¼ litre	milk	8 fl oz
8	egg whites, stiffly beaten	8
	Filling-frosting	
12	egg yolks	12
400 g	sugar	14 oz
½ tsp	salt	½ tsp
175 g	butter	6 oz
10 cl	rye or bourbon whiskey	3½ fl oz
200 g	pecans, coarsely chopped, toasted	7 oz
200 g	fresh coconut, shredded	7 oz
200 g	seeded raisins, chopped	7 oz
	toasted halved pecans (optional)	

Grease four 22 cm (9 inch) round layer cake tins with a little butter. Fit the bottoms of the tins with greaseproof paper and butter the papers. If you have only two tins this size, bake only two layers at a time.

Cream the butter until very fluffy; this is easiest done within the large bowl of an electric mixer. Cream in the sugar gradually. The mixture should be very light. Add the vanilla and beat for a few seconds to mix. Sift the dry ingredients together several times. Add alternately with the milk to the creamed mixture. If you are using an electric mixer, turn if off, sprinkle in the flour mixture, then resume mixing at the lowest speed, and slowly pour the milk in the centre. Do not overmix, but mix just enough to incorporate the flour evenly.

Fold the stiffly beaten egg whites into the cake batter carefully, using a rubber spatula or whisk. Spread the batter evenly in the four cake tins. Bake in an oven preheated to 180°C (350°F or Mark 4) for about 25 minutes or until the cake has shrunk from the sides of the tins and the centres spring back when pressed lightly with the finger. Transfer the tins to wire racks and let them stand 10 minutes to cool. Loosen the cakes from the tins and turn out the layers on the racks to cool thoroughly. While they cool, make the filling-frosting.

Put the egg yolks in the top of a double saucepan and beat lightly with a rotary or electric beater. Add the sugar, salt and butter. Cook over simmering water—the water should not touch the pan containing the yolks—stirring constantly until the sugar is dissolved, the butter melted, and the mixture slightly thickened. Do not overcook or the eggs will separate and harden like scrambled eggs. Remove from the heat, add the bourbon or rye whiskey, beat for 1 minute with a rotary or electric beater, and stir in the pecan nuts, coconut and raisins.

Cool the filling-frosting and spread it between the layers and on the top and sides of the cake. After an hour, if any of the frosting has dripped from the cake, spread it back on. If you like, decorate the top, or top and sides, with toasted halved pecans. This cake is much better if it is left in an airtight tin to age for at least 3 to 5 days, in a cool, dry place. It will keep well for as long as 3 to 4 weeks stored in this manner. The cake also freezes well.

JAMES BEARD
JAMES BEARD'S AMERICAN COOKERY

Black Bread Torte

To make one 22 cm (9 inch) cake

100 g	fresh black bread or pumpernickel crumbs	3½ oz
4 tbsp	rum	4 tbsp
6	eggs, yolks separated from whites	6
	salt	
200 g	sugar	7 oz
1 tsp	vanilla extract	1 tsp
30 g	shelled walnuts, finely grated	1 oz
100 g	plain chocolate, grated	3½ oz
35 cl	double cream, whipped, sweetened and flavoured with rum	12 fl oz

Pour the rum over the breadcrumbs and set aside. Beat the egg whites with a pinch of salt until they hold soft peaks. Add the sugar, a tablespoonful at a time, beating well after each addition. Continue beating for at least 5 minutes, or until the egg whites are very firm.

Stir the yolks with a fork to break them up. Add the vanilla. Fold a quarter of the whites into the yolks. Pour this mixture over the remaining whites. Add the breadcrumb mixture, nuts and grated chocolate. Carefully fold all together. Pour into a deep spring-form tin, which has been greased on the bottom but not on the sides.

Bake in an oven preheated to 180°C (350°F or Mark 4) for 50 to 60 minutes or until the top of the cake is brown and springy to the touch. Let it cool in the pan before removing. It will shrink quite a bit. Serve with the cream.

PAULA PECK
THE ART OF FINE BAKING

Orange Pecan Crown Cake

You can garnish this cake with fresh strawberries, and serve a small mound of icing sugar on the side for dipping them.

To make one 20 cm (8 inch) tube cake

1	large orange, rind grated	1
75 g	pecans, finely chopped	2½ oz
90 g	butter, softened	3 oz
100 g	sugar	3½ oz
1	egg	1
½ tsp	vanilla extract	½ tsp
125 g	flour, sifted	4 oz
½ tsp	baking powder	½ tsp
½ tsp	bicarbonate of soda	½ tsp
⅛ tsp	salt	⅛ tsp
10 cl	buttermilk	3½ fl oz
6 tbsp	finely cut stoned dates, rolled in 2 tbsp flour	6 tbsp
	icing sugar, sifted	
	Rum syrup	
6 tbsp	fresh strained orange juice	6 tbsp
60 g	sugar	2 oz
2 tbsp	rum	2 tbsp

In a mixing bowl, cream together the butter and sugar thoroughly. Add the egg and vanilla, and beat until the mixture is light and fluffy. Sift together the flour, baking powder, soda and salt; beat the flour into the creamed mixture alternately with the buttermilk. Stir in the orange rind. Mix together the dates and pecans; add them to the batter and mix well.

Turn the mixture into a buttered and floured *kugelhopf* mould, or other tubed cake mould without a removable bottom, with a capacity of about 1.25 litres (2 pints). Bake in an oven preheated to 180°C (350°F or Mark 4) for 50 minutes or until the cake springs back when lightly touched. With a fine skewer, poke holes at 1 cm (½ inch) intervals down through the cake to the bottom of the tin.

Stir together the syrup ingredients, then slowly spoon the syrup over the warm cake, letting the syrup soak in. Cool the cake in its tin on a rack. When cool, cover or wrap tightly and allow to stand for 2 to 3 days. With a thin knife, loosen the cake at the edges and turn it out. Dust it with sifted icing sugar. Gently cut into fairly thick slices.

VICTOR J. BERGERON
TRADER VIC'S RUM COOKERY AND DRINKERY

Martinique Rice Cake

The cake is very good with any sweet jam or plain as an accompaniment for stewed fruit or fruit fool.

To make one 25 cm (10 inch) cake

250 g	rice	8 oz
90 cl	hot milk	1½ pints
½ tsp	vanilla extract	½ tsp
125 g	butter	4 oz
4	eggs, yolks separated from whites, whites stiffly beaten	4
40 g	castor sugar	1½ oz
1 tbsp	ground almonds	1 tbsp
	Topping	
	guava jelly or other fruit jam	
	double cream, whipped (optional)	

Blend the milk and vanilla in a saucepan, add the rice and cook gently for about 20 minutes or until the rice is tender.

In a bowl, cream the butter. Add the egg yolks, beating all the time, and continue beating for 5 minutes. Beat in the sugar and the almonds, then add the cooled rice, draining off any unabsorbed milk. Fold the egg whites into the mixture. Pour into a buttered cake tin, put this in a pan of hot water coming half way up the cake tin and bake in a moderately hot oven, preheated to 190°C (375°F or Mark 5), for 1 hour or until an inserted skewer comes out clean.

Turn out the cake, cool and top with guava jelly and, if liked, unsweetened whipped cream.

MARY SLATER
CARIBBEAN COOKING FOR PLEASURE

Rum Barada

To make one 20 cm (8 inch) ring cake

125 g	butter	4 oz
125 g	castor sugar	4 oz
2	eggs, beaten	2
125 g	flour, sieved 3 times with 1 tsp baking powder	4 oz
$\frac{1}{4}$ tsp	vanilla extract	$\frac{1}{4}$ tsp
1 tbsp	castor sugar, mixed with 2 tbsp of water	1 tbsp
3 tbsp	rum	3 tbsp
2 tbsp	apricot jam, sieved	2 tbsp
	glacé cherries	
	angelica leaves	

Vanilla filling

60 g	butter	2 oz
60 g	castor sugar	2 oz
2 tbsp	rum (optional)	2 tbsp
1	egg yolk	1
60 g	ground almonds or cashew nuts, flavoured with a few drops of almond extract	2 oz
2 tbsp	double cream	2 tbsp
1	large piece preserved ginger, finely chopped (optional)	1

Beat the butter and sugar together to a pale cream. Beat in first the beaten eggs, and then the sieved flour and baking powder and the vanilla extract. Put the mixture into a buttered and floured ring mould and bake in an oven preheated to 180°C (350°F or Mark 4) for about 30 minutes, or until the cake is pale golden-brown on top and begins to ease away from the sides of the mould slightly. Cool the cake for 10 minutes in the mould, then turn it on to a wire rack to cool completely.

With a small-pronged fork, prick the cake all over on the underside, and here and there on the top and sides, taking care not to damage the "crust". Mix the dissolved castor sugar with 2 tablespoons of the rum and pour the mixture liberally on to the underside of the cake with a teaspoon. Moisten the rest at the fork pricks to ensure that the inside will not be dry in any part. Place the cake on a serving dish.

In a small saucepan, mix thoroughly the apricot jam and the remaining rum. Set the mixture over a very low heat and stir very gently until it is hot and clear in appearance. Use a clean dry pastry brush to coat the whole of the outside crust of the cake and down into the centre cavity with the apricot and rum glaze. Take care not to disturb the crumbs of the crust. The cake should now have a clear jellied appearance. Chill thoroughly in the refrigerator.

Prepare the filling by beating the butter until soft. Add the sugar, and cream the mixture together for a few minutes until light and fluffy, then beat in the rum, if using, by degrees. Beat all together until the mixture is pale in colour and thick. Add the yolk, mix well, then add the nuts and cream and beat again for a few minutes. If the ginger is used, it should be added now. Chill the mixture in the refrigerator, then pile it up in the hollow centre of the cake, rounding it nicely.

Put any remaining filling mixture into a cone made of double greaseproof paper with a plain meringue tube in the end. Pipe a neat decoration all round the edge of the centre filling of cream resting on top of the cake and decorate all round the base of the cake in the same manner. Put an alternate garnish of cherries and angelica leaves on this decoration (top and bottom), and arrange a cluster of cherries and angelica leaves on top of the centre filling. Refrigerate until required, and serve ice-cold.

HILDA DEUTROM (EDITOR)
CEYLON DAILY NEWS COOKERY BOOK

Coconut Cake

To make coconut milk, place the grated flesh of half a coconut, or 60 g (2 oz) desiccated coconut, in a bowl and pour on 15 cl ($\frac{1}{4}$ pint) boiling water. Allow to stand for 10 minutes, then strain through a cloth, squeezing to extract all the milk.

To make four 18 cm (7 inch) cakes

$1\frac{1}{2}$	coconuts, flesh removed and grated	$1\frac{1}{2}$
12.5 cl	coconut milk	4 fl oz
500 g	castor sugar	1 lb
500 g	butter	1 lb
8	eggs, yolks separated from whites, whites stiffly beaten	8
350 g	semolina	12 oz
125 g	flour, sifted	4 oz
1 tsp	baking powder	1 tsp
2	small nutmegs, grated	2
$\frac{1}{2}$ tsp	each caraway seeds, ground cinnamon and ground ginger	$\frac{1}{2}$ tsp

Beat together to a cream the sugar and butter. Add the egg yolks, one by one, beating the mixture constantly. Stir in the beaten egg whites and the semolina; mix well, then add a little at a time, the flour mixed with the baking powder, the nutmeg, caraway seeds, cinnamon and ginger. When these are thoroughly mixed, stir in the grated coconut. Lastly pour in the coconut milk. Bake the cake in shallow buttered tins in an oven preheated to 180°C (350°F or Mark) for 20 minutes or until the cake shrinks slightly from the sides of the tins.

MRS. J. BARTLEY
INDIAN COOKERY GENERAL FOR YOUNG HOUSEKEEPERS

Echenon Cornmeal Cake

Gâteau aux Gaudes d'Echenon

This recipe was contributed by Dr. Guichard of Saint-Jean-de-Losne. Echenon is a small village on the River Ouche, a tributary of the Saône. The grains from the locally grown maize, dried in a special way, produce the celebrated *gaudes* used in this delicious cake. Cornmeal may be substituted.

To make one 18 cm (7 inch) cake

60 g	*gaudes* or cornmeal	2 oz
125 g	unsalted butter	4 oz
125 g	flour	4 oz
125 g	castor sugar	4 oz

Melt the butter slowly in a small pan. In a bowl, mix the *gaudes* or cornmeal with the flour and sugar. Pour in the melted butter, mix well, and pour the mixture into a flan ring placed on a baking sheet. Spread the somewhat grainy mixture into an even layer, smoothing it with the back of a spoon.

Bake in an oven preheated to 190°C (375°F or Mark 5) for 20 minutes. Watch over the cake carefully, since it burns easily. When the cake is lightly browned, turn it out at once and cut it into slices: it hardens quickly. It is good served either hot or cold with tea.

70 MÉDECINS DE FRANCE
LE TRÉSOR DE LA CUISINE DU BASSIN MÉDITERRANÉEN

Cornmeal Fruit Cake

Torta Detta "La Putana"

To make one 22 cm (9 inch) cake

300 g	cornmeal	10 oz
1 litre	milk	1¾ pints
200 g	flour	7 oz
2	pears, peeled, cored and diced	2
2	apples, peeled, cored and diced	2
200 g	sultanas	7 oz
200 g	dried figs, cut up	7 oz
100 g	butter, cut into pieces	3½ oz
200 g	sugar	7 oz
½ tsp	salt	½ tsp
2 tsp	baking powder	2 tsp
3 tbsp	dry breadcrumbs	3 tbsp

Bring the milk to the boil and gradually stir in the flour and cornmeal to make a thick cream. When the mixture returns to the boil, add all of the fruit, the butter, sugar, salt and baking powder. Cook for about 30 minutes, stirring often.

Butter a cake tin and sprinkle it with the breadcrumbs. Pour in the cooked mixture and bake in an oven preheated to 180°C (350°F or Mark 4) for 1½ hours or until an inserted skewer comes out clean, watching carefully to see that the top of the cake does not burn.

LUIGI VOLPICELLI AND SECONDINO FREDA
L'ANTIARTUSI: 1000 RICETTE

Cornmeal Cheesecake

Torta Dolce di Polenta e Ricotta

To make one 30 cm (12 inch) cake

300 g	cornmeal	10 oz
350 g	very fresh *ricotta* or curd cheese	12 oz
175 g	castor sugar	6 oz
	salt	
60 g	sultanas, washed	2 oz
60 g	pine-nuts	2 oz
1 tsp	ground cinnamon	1 tsp
	lard	

Bring 60 cl (1 pint) of water to the boil and gradually pour in the cornmeal. Cook over a medium heat, stirring continuously, for 30 minutes or until the *polenta* acquires an elastic texture and comes away from the sides of the saucepan.

In a large bowl, mash the *ricotta* or curd cheese in a little warm water, and add the sugar and a pinch of salt. Gradually blend in the cooked *polenta*, moistening with additional warm water if necessary to make a firm but workable dough. Stir in the sultanas.

Pour the mixture into a greased cake tin, smooth the surface, and scatter the pine-nuts over the top. Dot the surface with lard. Bake in an oven preheated to 180°C (350°F or Mark 4) for about 45 minutes or until golden-brown on top. Turn the cake out of the tin while still warm, and allow to cool completely before serving.

LUIGI CARNACINA AND VINCENZO BUONASSISI
IL LIBRO DELLA POLENTA

Grecian Sugar Cake

Ravaní

This delicious concoction is based on semolina and has a sugar syrup flavoured with lemon juice poured over it. The result is a light, fluffy, truly sweet cake and one you can make ahead for company. It can serve 20 to 30.

To make one 36 by 25 cm (14 by 10 inch) cake

620 g	sugar	1 lb 6 oz
¾ litre	water	1¼ pints
1 tbsp	lemon juice	1 tbsp
250 g	unsalted butter	8 oz
5	medium eggs, beaten	5
175 g	semolina or farina	6 oz
250 g	flour	8 oz
2 tbsp	baking powder	2 tbsp
2 tsp	vanilla extract	2 tsp
	double cream, whipped (optional)	
	chopped nuts (optional)	

First make the syrup by combining the water with 500 g (1 lb) of the sugar and the lemon juice. Boil in a small saucepan over a medium heat for 15 minutes. Set aside to cool. The syrup should be watery, but not sticky.

Melt the butter over a low heat (do not brown). Transfer the butter to a large bowl and add the remaining sugar. Cream until light, then beat in the eggs.

Stir the semolina or farina with the flour and baking powder. Combine them thoroughly with the egg and sugar mixture. Add the vanilla extract. Mix well with a beater or wooden spoon. The batter will be golden-yellow with the consistency of oatmeal at this point.

Set the oven at 180°C (350°F or Mark 4). Butter a tin 36 by 25 by 5 cm (14 by 10 by 2 inches) or use two small tins. The batter needs at least 2.5 cm (1 inch) space to rise in the tin. Smooth the batter out in the tin and place it on the middle shelf of the oven.

Bake for 30 to 35 minutes. The cake should be medium brown on top, and a cocktail stick or toothpick should come out clean when inserted into the cake. Cut the hot cake into squares or diamond shapes right in the tin. Pour some cooled syrup over the hot cake slowly and evenly. When the syrup has been absorbed, pour a little more over the cake. Repeat until the syrup is used up.

Allow the cake to cool before serving. Room temperature is best. Whipped cream and chopped nuts can be used for topping, but are not necessary.

ANNE THEOHAROUS
COOKING THE GREEK WAY

Semolina Cake

Polenta-Kuchen

To make one 20 cm (8 inch) cake

350 g	semolina	12 oz
1 litre	milk	1¾ pints
4	eggs	4
100 g	sugar	3½ oz
30 g	flour	1 oz
	salt	
115 g	butter, cut into small pieces	3¾ oz
70 g	raisins	2¼ oz
3	apples, peeled, cored and cut into pieces	3
5 tbsp	single cream	5 tbsp
2 tsp	ground cinnamon	2 tsp

Mix together 5 tablespoons of the milk, 2 eggs, 60 g (2 oz) of the sugar, the flour and a pinch of salt, as for a pancake batter, and leave to one side.

Stir the semolina into the rest of the milk, bring to the boil and add half the butter. Boil again, stirring frequently, until the mixture is a thick porridge consistency. Set it aside to cool.

Mix the raisins and apples into the batter mixture, then combine with the semolina mixture. Turn into a well-greased cake tin. Level the surface and make holes in it with the handle of a wooden spoon. Mix the two remaining eggs with the remaining sugar, the cream and the cinnamon and pour over the mixture in the tin. Fill the holes with the remaining butter, and bake in an oven preheated to 220°C (425°F or Mark 7) for 1 hour or until a skewer inserted into the centre comes out clean.

EVA MARIA BORER
TANTE HEIDI'S SWISS KITCHEN

Pies and Tarts

Free-Form Apple Tart

A *pâte sablée*, a very rich shortcrust, is the usual base also for jam tarts, a thin layer of jam replacing the apples in this recipe with a latticework of pastry strips pressed on top for decorative purposes. Any fairly thick puréed jam or fruit "butter" may replace the apricot jam as a glaze in this recipe—I usually make one of wild plums.

To make one 30 cm (12 inch) tart

	Tart filling	
500 g	apples	1 lb
	sugar (to sprinkle surface of tart)	
	puréed apricot jam	
	Sablée dough	
125 g	flour	4 oz
3 tbsp	sugar	3 tbsp
60 g	butter, softened	2 oz
	salt	
1	egg	1

Combine the dough ingredients in a mixing bowl, stirring and mashing with a fork until the dough is fairly smooth; then work it with your fingertips until everything is absorbed in a coherent mass. Transfer the dough to a floured pastry marble or board and knead it for a couple of minutes, pushing small sections of the mass against the floured surface and away from yourself with the heel of your hand; gather the dough together in a ball and begin again—it will, at this point, be soft and sticky; wrap it in plastic film or greaseproof paper and refrigerate it for at least a couple of hours.

If using a baking sheet, butter it lightly. If your oven is fitted with a solid metal plaque, remove it from the oven before heating and line it with lightly buttered greaseproof paper or aluminium foil.

Roll out the dough as rapidly as possible, being certain that it is always lightly coated with flour—it sticks easily. Turn the dough over two or three times while rolling it into a circular sheet approximately 32 cm (14 inches) in diameter. Fold the sheet and transfer it to the baking sheet or lined plaque; then unfold the sheet. The dough is extremely fragile; if it should tear, don't worry—patch it up. Roll the edges up to form a rim, pressing all round with the prongs of a fork.

Halve the apples, core and peel them (don't do it ahead of time—they will turn brown). Slice each of the halves cross-wise into 3 to 5 mm ($\frac{1}{8}$ to $\frac{1}{4}$ inch) thicknesses and arrange the slices, starting just inside the rim of the dough, in concentric rings, slices overlapping and rings overlapping. Sprinkle the surface with sugar and bake in an oven preheated to 180°C (350°F or Mark 4) for 50 minutes to 1 hour, checking the progress of the tart regularly after 45 minutes.

Paint the surface of the apple slices with the puréed jam, using a pastry brush—or simply dribble the jam around with a teaspoon, smearing it regularly over the surface of each apple slice with the back of the spoon. Slip the tart on to a large flat, round platter; serve hot, tepid or cold.

RICHARD OLNEY
SIMPLE FRENCH FOOD

Apple Pie

To make one 22 cm (9 inch) pie

1 kg	tart apples, peeled, cored and sliced	2 to 2$\frac{1}{2}$ lb
300 g	sugar	10 oz
$\frac{1}{8}$ tsp	salt	$\frac{1}{8}$ tsp
$\frac{3}{4}$ tsp	ground cinnamon	$\frac{3}{4}$ tsp
$\frac{1}{2}$ tsp	grated nutmeg	$\frac{1}{2}$ tsp
2 tbsp	flour	2 tbsp
$\frac{1}{2}$ tsp	grated lemon rind	$\frac{1}{2}$ tsp
1 tbsp	lemon juice (optional)	1 tbsp
1 to 2 tbsp	butter	1 to 2 tbsp
500 g	shortcrust dough (*page 165*)	1 lb

Line a pie plate with half the dough. Cover the remaining dough to keep it moist. Mix the sugar, the salt, the cinnamon, the nutmeg and the flour together in a large bowl. Add the sliced apples and mix well so that the apples are coated with the other ingredients. Place the apple slices in the pie plate, laying slices first along the outside and then working towards the centre until the bottom of the dough is covered.

Continue placing the slices in the same way until the pie plate is filled. Sprinkle with lemon rind and juice, if desired, and dot with butter. Moisten the edge of the bottom crust. Cover the pie with the remaining dough and trim the edge to 1 cm ($\frac{1}{2}$ inch) larger than the pie plate. Press the edges firmly together, flute and slash vents in the centre of the crust. Bake in an oven preheated to 220°C (425°F or Mark 7) for 50 to 60 minutes until the apples are done and the crust is golden-brown, lowering the heat if the crust browns too much.

LETHA BOOTH (EDITOR)
THE WILLIAMSBURG COOKBOOK

Normandy Apple Tart

Tarte Le Deun

To make one 25 cm (10 inch) tart

5	apples, peeled, cored and thinly sliced	5
100 g	flour	3½ oz
100 g	butter, cut into small pieces	3½ oz
100 g	almonds, blanched and chopped	3½ oz
200 g	castor sugar	7 oz
2 tbsp	vanilla sugar	2 tbsp
½ tsp	ground cinnamon	½ tsp
350 g	puff dough (*page 167*)	12 oz
	double cream (optional)	

In a bowl, combine the flour, butter, almonds, castor sugar, vanilla sugar and the cinnamon. Mix these briskly with your fingertips, until the mixture resembles fine crumbs.

Roll out the puff dough and line a greased tart tin with it. Fill the pastry case with the apples and cover them with the almond mixture. Bake in an oven preheated to 200°C (400°F or Mark 6) for 40 minutes or until the topping is golden-brown. Serve hot, with double cream if desired.

MARIE BISSON
LA CUISINE NORMANDE

Upside-Down Apple Tart

Tarte des Demoiselles Tatin

To make one 20 cm (8 inch) tart

500 g	apples, preferably pippins or reinettes, peeled, cored and quartered	1 lb
60 g	sugar	2 oz
60 g	butter, melted	2 oz
250 g	shortcrust dough (*page 165*)	8 oz

Thickly butter a 5 cm (2 inch) deep pie plate, preferably of tinned copper, and sprinkle the bottom with half the sugar. Fill the pie plate with the apples. Sprinkle with the remaining sugar and the melted butter. Cover the apples with the dough, rolled out 3 mm (⅛ inch) thick.

Bake in an oven preheated to 220°C (425°F or Mark 7) for about 30 minutes or until the apples are golden and slightly caramelized. To serve, carefully turn the tart out on to a serving plate so that the apples are on top. The tart can be eaten either hot or cold.

CURNONSKY
RECETTES DES PROVINCES DE FRANCE

Grandmother's Apple Tart

Tarte aux Pommes Grand-Mère

To make one 22 cm (9 inch) tart

750 g	apples, peeled, cored and sliced	1½ lb
3 to 4 tbsp	sugar	3 to 4 tbsp
1	egg	1
3 tbsp	double cream	3 tbsp
	kirsch	
250 g	shortcrust dough (*page 165*)	8 oz

Line a tart tin with the dough and arrange the apple slices on top. Sprinkle with 2 to 3 tablespoons of the sugar. Bake in an oven preheated to 180°C (350°F or Mark 4) for 15 minutes or until the pastry is firm but not brown.

Whisk together the egg, 1 tablespoon of sugar, double cream and a few drops of kirsch. Pour this mixture over the apples and continue to bake for 15 minutes or until the cream has set. Serve hot.

FELIX BENOIT AND HENRY CLOS JOUVE
LA CUISINE LYONNAISE

Apple, Apricot and Walnut Tart

La Tarte à la Bréalaise

To make the fruit purées for this recipe, the fruits—stones and cores removed—are cooked with sugar to taste, then puréed through a sieve or in a blender. If liked, 150 g (5 oz) apricot jam may be substituted for the apricot purée. For the "turning" technique required for the pastry, see page 56.

To make one 35 cm (14 inch) tart

300 g	apple purée	10 oz
300 g	apricot purée	10 oz
6 to 8	walnuts, shelled and quartered	6 to 8
	Dough	
500 g	flour	1 lb
2	eggs	2
375 g	butter	13 oz
	salt	
1 tbsp	sugar	1 tbsp
17.5 cl	milk	6 fl oz

Heap the flour on a board and make a well in the centre. Put in the eggs, 125 g (4 oz) of the butter, a pinch of salt and the sugar. Work together with the fingertips, gradually adding the milk to the dough as the flour is absorbed. Knead briefly, wrap the dough, and allow it to rest for 1 hour. Roll out the dough and enclose the remaining butter in it as for puff dough, then give the dough three "turns". Leave it to rest again for 1 hour, then roll it out and use about two-thirds of it to line a tart tin.

In a saucepan, blend the apple purée and 250 g (8 oz) of the apricot purée. Cook over a medium heat, stirring, until the mixture is of thick spreading consistency. Fill the tart case with this mixture. Criss-cross the top with strips of the remaining dough. Bake in an oven preheated to 220°C (425°F or Mark 7) for about 30 minutes, turning the heat down to 190°C (375°F or Mark 5) after the first 10 minutes. The tart is done when the pastry is crisp and golden.

When the tart is cold, place a walnut quarter in each of the spaces between the lattice strips. Cook the remaining apricot purée until it is reduced to a syrupy consistency, and use it to glaze the surface of the tart.

ÉDOUARD NIGNON
LES PLAISIRS DE LA TABLE

◄ ● ►

Apple Tart

Tarte aux Pommes

To prepare apple jelly for glazing the tart, cook the cores, seeds and peelings of the apples, in enough water to cover them, until soft. Drain the mixture through muslin, without pressing on the apple trimmings, and add an approximately equal bulk of sugar to the resulting apple juice. Boil the mixture over a medium heat until it is syrupy.

To make one 25 cm (10 inch) tart

1 kg	apples, peeled, cored and quartered or sliced	2 to 2½ lb
60 g	sugar	2 oz
	apple jelly (optional)	
	Dough	
250 g	flour	8 oz
100 g	butter, softened and cut into small pieces	3½ oz
75 g	sugar	2½ oz
	salt	
3 tbsp	water	3 tbsp
3	egg yolks	3

To make the dough, heap the flour on a board. Make a well in the centre of the heap, and into this put the butter, the sugar, a pinch of salt, the water and the egg yolks. Pound these ingredients together with your fingertips to make a smooth dough. Make the dough into a ball and leave it to rest for 20 minutes in the refrigerator.

Roll out the dough with a rolling pin and use it to line a flan ring placed on a baking sheet. Cut off the edges of the dough level with the top of the tin, and crimp the edges. Fill this pastry case with the apples. Sprinkle the top with 30 g (1 oz) of the sugar and bake in an oven preheated to 220°C (425°F or Mark 7) for 10 to 15 minutes, then reduce the temperature to 190°C (375°F or Mark 5) and bake for a further 15 minutes or until the edges of the pastry are golden and the apples are tender. Serve hot, sprinkled with the remaining sugar, or glazed with an apple jelly made from the boiled peelings.

J. B. REBOUL
LA CUISINIÈRE PROVENÇALE

Gooseberry Meringue Tart

To make one 20 cm (8 inch) pie

750 g	gooseberries, topped and tailed	1½ lb
2	egg yolks, beaten	2
60 g	butter, cut into small pieces	2 oz
2 tbsp	breadcrumbs	2 tbsp
	sugar	
1	egg white, lightly beaten with 1 tsp sugar	1
250 g	shortcrust dough (*page 165*)	8 oz
	Meringue	
2	egg whites, stiffly beaten	2
60 g	sugar	2 oz

Place the gooseberries in an earthenware jar, cover, and set in an oven preheated to 150°C (300°F or Mark 2) for 30 minutes or until quite soft, then rub the berries through a sieve into a bowl. Add the egg yolks, butter, breadcrumbs and sugar to taste. Line a pie dish round the sides and rims (not on the bottom) with the dough; glaze the edges with the egg white and sugar mixture. Put in the gooseberries. Bake in an oven preheated to 180°C (350°F or Mark 4) until the pastry is lightly browned, about 45 minutes.

Prepare the meringue by beating the sugar into the egg whites. Cover the gooseberries with the meringue, return to the oven for 10 minutes or until just set, and serve.

MAY BYRON
PUDDINGS, PASTRIES AND SWEET DISHES

Fruit Tartlets

Tartelettes aux Fruits

The following recipe calls for apples for half of the tartlets and strawberries for the other half. You can, if you wish, substitute other fresh fruits such as white grapes or raspberries, for example, using 200 g (7 oz) of each. For both these fruits, the pastry cases should be baked blind, sprinkled with the breadcrumb mixture, filled with the fruit, then glazed and finished with a little icing sugar. Use redcurrant jelly glaze for red fruits and apricot glaze for white fruits. Whichever tartlets you choose to make, keep them in their moulds until serving time to protect their delicate pastry shells. The technique for baking blind is demonstrated on page 72.

To make 12 tartlets

350 g	strawberries, hulled	12 oz
2	large eating apples, peeled, cored and cut into halves	2
1	lemon, rind grated and 2 tsp of strained juice reserved	1
175 g	peach jam	6 oz
4 tbsp	breadcrumbs	4 tbsp
150 g	sugar	5 oz
½ tsp	ground cardamom seed	½ tsp
¼	nutmeg, freshly grated	¼
60 g	unsalted butter, melted	2 oz
30 g	icing sugar	1 oz
500 g	shortcrust dough (*page 165*)	1 lb

Glazes

175 g	redcurrant jelly	6 oz
1 tbsp	framboise	1 tbsp
175 g	apricot jam	6 oz
1 tbsp	cognac, brandy or sherry	1 tbsp

Roll out the dough 5 mm (¼ inch) thick. Set the buttered tartlet moulds in a cluster, touching each other. Carefully lift the sheet of dough on the rolling pin and lay it over the moulds. Run the rolling pin over the dough to cut the correct size round for each mould. With your fingers, firm the dough against the bottoms and sides of the moulds. Brush a little melted butter on to each of these pastry cases.

Mix together the breadcrumbs, 60 g (2 oz) of the sugar, the cardamom and a pinch of grated nutmeg. Divide half of the mixture evenly among six of the pastry cases and put the other half aside, with the remaining six pastry cases.

Prepare the apple filling by cutting two of the halves into tiny dice; sprinkle the dice with half of the lemon juice. Slice the other two halves into paper-thin slices and sprinkle with the remaining lemon juice. Mix the diced apple with the peach jam and the lemon rind. Fill the cases lined with breadcrumbs with the diced apple and arrange the slices in a pinwheel pattern on top. Sprinkle with the remaining sugar.

Put the tartlets on a baking sheet and bake them in an oven preheated to 190°C (375°F or Mark 5) for 25 minutes or until the edges are golden-brown. At the same time, blind-bake the other six pastry cases, also for 25 minutes.

While the tartlets are cooking, prepare the glazes. In two separate saucepans and over a low heat, melt the redcurrant jelly with the framboise and the apricot jam with the cognac, brandy or sherry. Sieve the glazes separately into small bowls and allow them to cool a little.

Remove the tartlets from the oven. Put the apple tartlets under a hot grill for a moment just to singe the edges of the sliced apple. Brush them with the apricot jam glaze and let them cool in their moulds.

When the blind-baked cases are partially cooled, sprinkle the remaining breadcrumb mixture into the cases. Fill them with strawberries, standing the berries hulled ends down. Brush the strawberries with the redcurrant jelly glaze and sprinkle icing sugar around the edges.

DIONE LUCAS AND MARION GORMAN
THE DIONE LUCAS BOOK OF FRENCH COOKING

Pear Upside-Down Tart

Tarte aux Poires Renversée

The receptacle chosen to serve as a pie dish should be of a heavy material and able to support direct heat. It should be fairly deep in order to contain a sufficient quantity of wine during the first part of the cooking process. A frying pan is perfect if your oven is large enough to take the handle; a round enamelled ironware gratin dish will serve equally well.

The dessert may be served hot, tepid, or cold but should, in any case, be unmoulded only just before serving to prevent the pastry being soaked in the cooking juices.

To make one 25 cm (10 inch) tart

7	firm, slightly underripe eating pears, halved, cored and peeled	7
100 g	sugar	3½ oz
½ tsp	ground cinnamon	½ tsp
60 cl	red wine	1 pint
250 g	shortcrust dough (*page 165*)	8 oz

Arrange pear halves in the pan, cored surface facing upwards, the wide end of each pressed against the side of the pan, the elongated tips pointing in toward the centre of the pan so that the ungarnished areas form a fairly symmetrical star shape. Split the remaining pear halves and fill the empty spaces, slender tips pointing out, wide ends meeting in the centre so that, when unmoulded, the body of pears will form a neat geometric pattern.

Sprinkle over the sugar and cinnamon, pour over red wine

to cover, bring to the boil, and cook, covered, at a simmer, for from 1 hour to 1 hour and 10 minutes, or until the pears are tender, lending no resistance to the tip of a sharp knife, but still firmly intact. Drain all of the liquid into a saucepan, holding the lid firmly against the pears' surface so as not to displace them. Reduce the cooking liquid over a high heat, stirring from time to time, until only about 12.5 cl (4 fl oz) of syrupy liquid remains. Dribble the syrup regularly over the pears' surface.

Roll out a round of dough to the exact dimensions of the pan or slightly larger; prick the dough four or five times with a knife tip; roll up the edges and crimp them either with the floured side of your thumb or with fork prongs and lay the dough gently upside down over the pears. Bake in an oven preheated to 190° to 200°C (375° to 400°F or Mark 5 to 6) for about 40 minutes, or until golden and crisp.

Unmould with care—if you have used a frying pan, the handle will prevent the tart being unmoulded on to the centre of the plate: place the plate upside down over the pan, its edge pressed to the handle's point of attachment, turn everything over at once and ease the tart into the middle of the plate. The pears often spread slightly in the unmoulding—push them gently into place, pressing all round the outside with the back of a tablespoon or a spatula.

RICHARD OLNEY
SIMPLE FRENCH FOOD

Pear Cream Pie

Picanchagne

To make one 22 cm (9 inch) pie

750 g	pears, peeled, cored, and sliced	1½ lb
100 g	sugar	3½ oz
½ litre	double cream	18 fl oz
¼ tsp	freshly ground pepper (optional)	¼ tsp
1	egg yolk, lightly beaten	1
500 g	shortcrust dough (page 165)	1 lb

Roll out the dough to a thickness of 3 mm (⅛ inch) and use two-thirds of it to line a pie dish. Mix the pear slices with the sugar and cream, and add the pepper if desired. Fill the pie with this mixture and cover with the remaining dough rolled out thinly. Glaze with the egg yolk, and make a small hole in the middle for the steam to escape during cooking. Bake in an oven preheated to 180°C (350°F or Mark 4) for about 50 minutes or until the top is browned.

LES DESSERTS DE NOS PROVINCES

Cranberry Pie

To make one 20 cm (8 inch) pie

350 g	cranberries	12 oz
200 g	sugar	7 oz
350 g	shortcrust dough (page 165)	12 oz

Wash the cranberries in cold water, put them in an earthenware casserole with 15 cl (¼ pint) of water, bring them to the boil and simmer for 20 minutes, crushing the berries to extract the juice. Stir in the sugar and simmer over a low heat for 10 to 15 minutes longer. Put the berries in a basin, but do not strain them. Line a pie plate with three-quarters of the dough. Bake it blind in an oven preheated to 230°C (450°F or Mark 8) for 10 minutes. When the cranberries are cold, put them into the pastry case. Decorate the pie with strips of dough and bake for 20 minutes or until the strips of pastry are a delicate golden colour.

COUNTESS MORPHY
SWEETS AND PUDDINGS

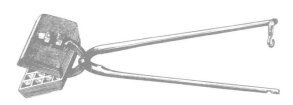

Kumquat Tart

Tarte aux Kumquats

The mirabelle called for in this recipe is a colourless brandy distilled from small yellow plums.

To make one 25 cm (10 inch) tart

300 g	kumquats, halved lengthwise	10 oz
170 g	castor sugar	6 oz
5	eggs	5
30 cl	double cream	½ pint
2 to 3 tbsp	mirabelle	2 to 3 tbsp
1	blind-baked pastry case made with rich shortcrust pastry (page 165)	1

Place the kumquats in a dish with 100 g (3½ oz) of the castor sugar, and leave to macerate for 2 hours. Arrange the kumquats in the pastry case.

Mix the eggs, cream, the remaining sugar and the mirabelle in a bowl. Pour this mixture over the kumquats. Bake in an oven preheated to 190°C (375°F or Mark 5) for 15 minutes, or until the cream is set at the centre of the tart. Serve the tart either warm or cold.

LA REYNIÈRE
200 RECETTES DES MEILLEURES CUISINIÈRES DE FRANCE

Quince Tarts

The original version of this 14th-century recipe reads, "Make amends coffyrs of paaste and take quynces and pare and take out the core and take sugar ynough (or ellse take hony in stede if thou maest more sugar) and if thou takest honey put thereto poudre, pepor and ginger and fill the quynces and bake them ynugh."

Dorothy Hartley, who reprinted the recipe, says that "coffyrs of paaste" were small tartlet cases, and that the quinces were cooked before being put in the cases for baking.

To make twelve 6 cm (2½ inch) tartlets

6	quinces, peeled and cored	6
90 g	sugar or honey	3 oz
	pepper	
	ground ginger	
	mixed spice	
500 g	shortcrust dough (page 165)	1 lb

Put the quinces in a baking dish and fill them with sugar or honey and a little pepper, ginger and mixed spice. Bake in an oven preheated to 180°C (350°F or Mark 4) for 45 minutes or until the quinces are soft but still hold their shape. Leave to cool and halve them.

Roll out the dough, cut it into rounds, and use it to line small tartlet tins. Place a quince half in each tin and bake at 200°C (400°F or Mark 6) for 20 minutes or until the edges of the pastry are lightly browned. Serve hot or cold.

DOROTHY HARTLEY
FOOD IN ENGLAND

Quince Custard Tart

Torta de Marmelos

To make one 25 cm (10 inch) tart

900 g	unripe quinces, quartered and scalded in boiling water	2 lb
1 kg	sugar	2 to 2½ lb
2 or 3	cloves	2 or 3
1	stick cinnamon	1
12	egg yolks	12
350 g	shortcrust dough (page 165)	12 oz

Over a medium heat cook the quinces with 600 g (1¼ lb) of the sugar, the cloves and the cinnamon stick until the mixture is thick and syrupy, about 30 minutes. Allow to cool.

Beat the egg yolks with the remaining sugar, and stir over a very low heat, or over a pan of hot water, until the mixture is lightly thickened. Cool, stirring occasionally.

Roll out the dough and use to line a tart tin. Put in the quince mixture, removing the cloves and cinnamon stick. Cover with the egg mixture.

Bake in an oven preheated to 180°C (350°F or Mark 4) for 30 minutes or until the pastry is lightly browned and the egg topping puffed and golden. Serve warm.

ANTONIO DE MACEDO MENGO
COPA E COZINHA

Cherry and Strawberry Tart

Tarte Nouvelle

To make one 22 cm (9 inch) tart

250 g	cherries, stoned	8 oz
250 g	strawberries	8 oz
60 g	sugar	2 oz
12.5 cl	water	4 fl oz
4 tbsp	kirsch	4 tbsp
45 cl	pastry cream (page 166)	¾ pint
12.5 cl	raspberry jelly, melted	4 fl oz
1	blind-baked pastry case (page 165) made with rich shortcrust pastry	1

Dissolve the sugar in the water, bring this syrup to the simmer, and gently poach the cherries in it for about 10 minutes. Drain them. Sprinkle the strawberries with the kirsch and allow them to macerate for about 30 minutes.

Fill the pastry case with the pastry cream. Cover the cream with alternating rings of cherries and strawberries. Glaze the tart with the melted raspberry jelly.

MADAME ELISABETH
500 NOUVELLES RECETTES DE CUISINE DE MADAME ELISABETH

Orange Tart

La Tarte à L'Orange

To make one 25 cm (10 inch) tart

4	oranges, thinly sliced but not peeled, pips removed	4
250 g	apricot jam, melted	8 oz
60 g	castor sugar (optional)	2 oz
2	egg whites, stiffly beaten (optional)	2
250 g	shortcrust dough (page 165)	8 oz

Butter a tart tin and line it with the dough. With a brush, cover the dough with a coating of jam. Arrange the orange slices in the tin, overlapping them. Spread them with the remaining jam. Bake in an oven preheated to 220°C (425°F or Mark 7) for 20 to 25 minutes or until the edges of the pastry have turned golden-brown.

If you wish, you may cover the tart with meringue: sprinkle the sugar on to the egg whites, and beat again until they are very stiff and glossy. Spread this meringue on the tart, and return it to a 170°C (325°F or Mark 3) oven until puffed and lightly browned, about 10 minutes.

JOSEPHINE BESSON
LA MÈRE BESSON "MA CUISINE PROVENÇALE"

Melon Marmalade Tart

Tourte de Melon en Marmellade

The pastry shell for this tart may be baked blind before the filling is added (page 72).

To make one 20 cm (8 inch) tart

One 1 kg	canteloupe, ogen or other orange-fleshed variety melon, quartered, seeded, flesh cut up	One 2 to 2½ lb
20 cl	white wine	7 fl oz
2	macaroons	2
60 g	sugar	2 oz
½ tsp	ground cinnamon	½ tsp
	castor sugar	
	orange flower water (optional)	
250 g	shortcrust dough (*page 165*)	8 oz

Boil the melon with the wine, stirring often, until the mixture has reduced to a purée and thickened. Pound together the macaroons, sugar and cinnamon, and add the melon purée.

Line a tart tin with the dough, and pour in the melon mixture. Bake in an oven preheated to 190°C (375°F or Mark 5) for 30 to 35 minutes, until the pastry is crisp and golden. Sprinkle the top with castor sugar and orange flower water before serving, or sprinkle with sugar and return to a hot oven or beneath the grill for 1 to 2 minutes to glaze the top.

PIERRE DE LUNE
LE NOUVEAU CUISINIER

Melon Tart

Tarte au Melon

To make one 20 cm (8 inch) tart

Three 600 g	charentais melons, one halved, two quartered, seeds removed	Three 1¼ lb
1 tbsp	lemon juice	1 tbsp
30 g	leaf gelatine, soaked in cold water	1 oz
25 g	castor sugar	1 oz
1	blind-baked pastry case (*page 165*)	1

With a melon baller, scoop 24 balls out of the halved melon and set them aside for decoration. Spoon out the remaining flesh, without shaving too close to the skin, and press it through a fine sieve into a bowl. Stir in the lemon juice, and refrigerate the mixture.

With a spoon, scoop out the flesh from the quartered melons and place it in a saucepan with the sugar; cook, stirring, for about 10 minutes to evaporate the excess moisture. Drain the gelatine, add it to the melon, and stir until it is thoroughly dissolved. Remove the pan from the heat. Cool, then add the refrigerated sieved melon.

Fill the pastry case with the mixture, and refrigerate for 2 hours or until the filling is set. Decorate the tart with the reserved melon balls, and serve very cold.

JEAN ET PIERRE TROISGROS
CUISINIERS À ROANNE

Two-Crust Fresh Pineapple Pie

To make one 20 cm (8 inch) pie

300 g	peeled and cored ripe pineapple, diced	10 oz
250 g	sugar	8 oz
40 g	flour	1½ oz
	salt	
2	eggs, lightly beaten	2
1 tbsp	strained fresh lemon juice	1 tbsp
15 g	butter	½ oz
500 g	shortcrust dough (*page 165*)	1 lb

Combine the sugar, flour and a pinch of salt, then add the eggs. Mix the pineapple with the lemon juice and add the pineapple to the egg mixture. Line a pie plate with two-thirds of the dough and pour the pineapple filling into the dough case. Dot the top of the filling with the butter. Cover with the remaining dough. Bake in an oven preheated to 230°C (450°F or Mark 8) for 10 minutes, then at 180°C (350°F or Mark 4) for 35 minutes or until the pastry is brown.

HAWAII STATE SOCIETY OF WASHINGTON
HAWAIIAN CUISINE

Apricot Tart

Tourte d'Abricots

To make one 20 cm (8 inch) tart

500 g	apricots, halved, stones split, kernels halved	1 lb
60 g	castor sugar	2 oz
60 g	candied lemon peel, finely chopped	2 oz
250 g	puff dough *(page 167)*	8 oz

If the apricots are not quite ripe, plunge them into boiling water, return the water to the boil, then drain, halve and stone them. Line a tart tin with puff dough, sprinkle 30 g (1 oz) of the castor sugar over the base, then sprinkle on the lemon peel. Arrange the apricots in the case, topping each half with half a kernel. Dust with the remaining sugar and bake in an oven preheated to 220°C (425°F or Mark 7) for 15 minutes, reducing the heat to 190°C (375°F or Mark 5) for 20 to 30 minutes or until the pastry is puffed and golden-brown.

MENON
LES SOUPERS DE LA COUR

Rhubarb Tart

Tarte à la Rhubarbe

To make one 22 cm (9 inch) tart

500 g	young rhubarb, halved lengthwise and cut into 10 cm (4 inch) lengths	1 lb
100 g	butter	3½ oz
100 g	sugar	3½ oz
2	eggs	2
1 tbsp	grated lemon rind	1 tbsp
1 tbsp	lemon juice	1 tbsp
100 g	wholemeal flour	3½ oz
	salt	
	breadcrumbs	
	castor sugar	

To make the dough, cream together the butter and sugar. Beat in the eggs, one by one, then add the lemon rind and juice. Finally blend in the flour and a small pinch of salt.

Butter a tart tin, sprinkle it with breadcrumbs, and line it with the dough. Arrange the rhubarb pieces on the dough, radiating fanwise from the centre. Bake in an oven preheated to 180°C (350°F or Mark 4) for 45 minutes or until the edges of the tart are browned. When the tart is cooked, sprinkle it with castor sugar while still hot. Eat hot or cold.

MME. F. NIETLISPACH
TOURTES TARTES, PÂTISSERIES METS SUCRÉS

Rhubarb Pie

Tarte à la Rhubarbe

To make one 20 cm (8 inch) pie

500 g	rhubarb, peeled if necessary, cut in pieces	1 lb
30 g	sugar	1 oz
30 g	demerara sugar	1 oz
	ground cinnamon	
3 tbsp	cold water	3 tbsp
1	egg, lightly beaten	1
250 g	puff dough *(page 167)* or shortcrust dough *(page 165)*	8 oz

Arrange the rhubarb in a deep pie dish. Sprinkle with both kinds of sugar and with a pinch of cinnamon. Moisten with the water. Roll out the dough to the shape of the dish. Cover the pie with the dough, sealing the edges well. Trim off excess dough with a knife. Paint the top with the beaten egg, using a pastry brush. Prick it all over with a fork. Bake in a preheated 190°C (375°F or Mark 5) oven for about 45 minutes or until the top is golden-brown.

PHILÉAS GILBERT
LA CUISINE DE TOUS LES MOIS

Prune Tart with Cream

La Tarte aux Pruneaux à la Crème

To make one 30 cm (12 inch) tart

500 g	prunes	1 lb
125 g	sugar	4 oz
1	vanilla pod	1
60 cl	pastry cream *(page 166)*	1 pint
90 g	almonds, blanched and halved	3 oz
500 g	rich shortcrust dough *(page 165)*	1 lb

Roll out the dough and use it to line a flan ring set on a baking sheet. Fill the case with lentils and bake it in an oven preheated to 180°C (350°F or Mark 4) for about 30 minutes. Remove the lentils, and allow the case to cool completely.

Make a syrup by boiling the sugar and the vanilla pod in 30 cl (½ pint) of water for about 5 minutes. Poach the prunes in this syrup for 30 minutes, over a low heat, until they are plump and tender. Drain and stone the prunes. Remove the vanilla pod from the syrup and cook the syrup until it is thick and reduced by at least half.

Fill the pastry case with the pastry cream. Arrange the prunes on the cream, and put an almond half on top of each prune. Glaze the tart with the reduced syrup.

ÉDOUARD NIGNON
LES PLAISIRS DE LA TABLE

Prune Tart from Wisch

Aleanentorte aus Wisch

To make one 22 cm (9 inch) tart

750 g	stoned dried prunes	1½ lb
½ litre	water	16 fl oz
½ litre	milk	16 fl oz
200 g	sugar	7 oz
9	eggs, yolks separated from whites, yolks lightly beaten, whites stiffly beaten	9
1	lemon, juice strained, rind grated	1
10 cl	double cream, whipped	3½ fl oz
	Dough	
250 g	flour	8 oz
125 g	butter	4 oz
60 g	sugar	2 oz
1	egg yolk	1
	salt	
1 tbsp	rum	1 tbsp

To make the dough, put the flour on to a board and make a well in the centre. Put the butter, sugar, egg yolk, a pinch of salt and the rum into the well. Blend the mixture together with your fingertips to make a smooth dough. Form the dough into a ball and leave it to rest in a cool place for 30 minutes.

Put the prunes into a saucepan with the water and simmer gently for 40 minutes or until they are soft. Leave them to cool. Meanwhile, roll out the dough mixture and fit it into a cake tin with a removable base; bake in an oven preheated to 180°C (350°F or Mark 4) for 40 minutes or until the pastry is golden. Strain the prunes, cut them into quarters and arrange them on the tart.

Bring the milk to the boil. Remove it from the heat and stir in the sugar. Allow to cool slightly and stir in the beaten egg yolks. Bring gently to the boil again, stirring continuously and taking care that the yolks do not curdle. Allow the mixture to cool and fold in the lemon juice and rind, and the egg whites.

Pour the mixture on to the prunes and bake at 200°C

(400°F or Mark 6) for 1 hour or until the topping is set and brown. Cool completely in the tin before lifting out. Before serving, decorate the top with whipped cream.

JUTTA KURTZ
DAS KOCHBUCH AUS SCHLESWIG-HOLSTEIN

Swiss Chard Pie

Tourte de Blettes

To make one 25 cm (10 inch) pie

1.5 kg	Swiss chard, ribs removed	3 lb
	salt	
100 g	raisins, soaked in 10 cl (3½ fl oz) milk	3½ oz
3	apples, cored, peeled and finely sliced	3
75 g	pine-nuts	2½ oz
2 tbsp	redcurrant jelly	2 tbsp
120 g	demerara or castor sugar	4 oz
50 g	Edam or Gruyère cheese, grated	2 oz
2	eggs, lightly beaten	2
1	lemon, rind grated	1
3 tbsp	rum	3 tbsp
	fine castor sugar (optional)	
	Dough	
400 g	flour	14 oz
80 g	butter	2½ oz
1	egg	1
75 g	sugar	2½ oz
17.5 cl	milk	6 fl oz
2 tsp	baking powder	2 tsp
	salt	

Work all of the dough ingredients together until the mixture is thoroughly blended.

Blanch the chard leaves for 15 minutes in boiling salted water. Drain the chard, squeeze it dry, and chop it fine. Simmer the raisins in the milk for abut 10 minutes or until plump; drain and rinse them.

Combine the chard, raisins, apples, pine-nuts, jelly, sugar, cheese, eggs, lemon rind and rum.

Oil a fairly deep pie plate, and line it with two-thirds of the dough. Spread the filling mixture on the base, and cover it with the remaining dough. Bake in an oven preheated to 220°C (425°F or Mark 7) for 30 minutes or until the pastry is golden-brown. The pie may be dusted with very fine sugar when it comes out of the oven. Serve hot.

RAYMOND ARMISEN AND ANDRÉ MARTIN
LES RECETTES DE LA TABLE NIÇOISE

Sorrel Tart

Tourte de Jus d'Oseille

To make one 20 cm (8 inch) tart

200 g	sorrel leaves	7 oz
100 g	sugar	3½ oz
1 tsp	ground cinnamon	1 tsp
3	macaroons, crumbled	3
30 g	butter	1 oz
3	egg yolks	3
1 tbsp	candied lemon peel, finely chopped	1 tbsp
1 tsp	orange flower water	1 tsp
1	blind-baked pastry case (*page 165*)	1
	castor sugar	

Pound the sorrel leaves in a mortar, then twist the purée in a towel to extract the juice. Mix the sorrel juice with the sugar, cinnamon, macaroons, butter, egg yolks, candied peel and orange flower water. Cook this mixture over a low heat, stirring constantly, until it thickens.

Fill the pastry case with the sorrel mixture, and bake in an oven preheated to 180°C (350°F or Mark 4) for 30 minutes or until lightly browned. Serve sprinkled with castor sugar.

PIERRE DE LUNE
LE NOUVEAU CUISINIER

Spinach Tart

A handful of raisins macerated in brandy, and a few pine-nuts, may be added to the filling.

To make one 22 cm (9 inch) tart

1 kg	spinach, stemmed and washed	2 to 2½ lb
30 g	butter	1 oz
3 or 4	eggs	3 or 4
35 cl	double cream	12 fl oz
100 g	sugar	3½ oz
	grated nutmeg	
	ground allspice	
1 tsp	grated lemon rind	1 tsp
1	egg yolk, beaten with 1 tbsp water	1
500 g	shortcrust dough (*page 165*)	1 lb

Plunge the spinach into a large pot of boiling water, parboil it for 1 minute, then drain it in a colander and run cold water over it. Squeeze out excess moisture with your hands. Chop the spinach and sauté it for about 2 minutes in the butter. Beat the eggs, cream and sugar together, stir in pinches of

nutmeg and allspice, and the lemon rind, and combine this mixture thoroughly with the spinach.

Line a tart tin with dough. Fill with the spinach mixture, and cover with a lattice made from strips of the remaining dough. Brush the lattice top and border with the egg yolk and water. Bake in an oven preheated to 170°C (325°F or Mark 3) for 50 minutes to 1 hour or until lightly browned.

The tart is best when eaten neither hot nor cold, but a bit warmer than tepid, 30 minutes out of the oven.

PETITS PROPOS CULINAIRES II

Lindy's Cheesecake

The United States has dozens of different cheesecake recipes, but none more famous than this one. It originated in Lindy's Restaurant, a New York establishment, that in its heyday was a favourite with stage, screen and radio stars and with the tourists who came to see them. The restaurant is gone but the cake survives in this recipe.

To make one 22 cm (9 inch) cake

	Biscuit dough	
125 g	flour, sifted	4 oz
60 g	sugar	2 oz
1 tsp	grated lemon rind	1 tsp
1	egg yolk	1
¼ tsp	vanilla extract	¼ tsp
125 g	butter, cut into small pieces	4 oz
	Cheese filling	
1 kg	cream cheese, at room temperature	2 to 2½ lb
400 g	sugar	14 oz
3 tbsp	flour	3 tbsp
1½ tsp	grated orange rind	1½ tsp
1½ tsp	grated lemon rind	1½ tsp
¼ tsp	vanilla extract	¼ tsp
5	eggs	5
2	egg yolks	2
6 tbsp	double cream	6 tbsp

Prepare the biscuit dough by first combining the flour, sugar and lemon rind in a small bowl. Make a well in the centre and place the egg yolk, vanilla extract and butter in it. Using your fingertips, mix the ingredients until the dough comes away from the sides of the bowl and forms a ball. Wrap the dough tightly in aluminium foil and refrigerate it for about 1 hour.

Preheat the oven to 200°C (400°F or Mark 6). Lightly grease the bottom of a spring-form tin. Place half of the dough on a lightly floured board and roll it out to 3 mm (⅛ inch) thick. Place the dough on the bottom of the tin and trim the edges. Add the trimmings to the rest of the dough in the refrigerator. Place the bottom crust on the middle shelf of the preheated oven and bake it for about 20 minutes, or until the crust is pale gold.

Remove the crust from the oven and place on a rack to cool. When the crust is cool, grease the sides of the tin, set it around the base and lock it. Roll the remaining dough into two strips about 3 mm ($\frac{1}{8}$ inch) thick and long enough to line the side of the tin. Fit the strips into the tin, pressing the ends together to seal. Trim and discard the excess dough. Preheat the oven to 230°C (450°F or Mark 8).

Beat the cream cheese with a wooden spoon. Blend in the sugar, flour, orange and lemon rind, and vanilla. Beat in the eggs one at a time, and then the egg yolks. Stir in the cream. Pour the mixture into the assembled crust and place it in the oven for 15 minutes. Reduce the temperature to 100°C (200°F or Mark $\frac{1}{4}$) and bake the cake for 1 hour more.

Remove the cheesecake from the oven and place it on a rack to cool. Let it cool for at least 2 hours before removing the sides of the spring-form tin.

THE WORLD ATLAS OF FOOD

Corsican Cheese Pie

Strenna Corse

This pie takes its name—Corsican gift—from a New Year's Day tradition in the Corsican town of Vico, where it is presented to relatives who have come to offer their good wishes for the coming year. It is made with the most famous of Corsican cheeses, brocciu *or* broccio, *a fresh curd cheese made from sheep's milk.*

To make one 25 cm (10 inch) pie

200 g	fresh *brocciu* cheese	7 oz
50 g	sugar	2 oz
3	eggs, 1 egg lightly beaten	3
1	orange or lemon, rind grated	1
	Dough	
250 g	flour	8 oz
1	egg	1
15 g	lard, softened	$\frac{1}{2}$ oz
12.5 cl	milk	4 fl oz
2 tsp	sugar	2 tsp

Prepare the dough by working all of the ingredients together with the fingers until a smooth dough is formed. Roll out the dough about 5 mm ($\frac{1}{4}$ inch) thick. Cut out two large circles. Use one to line a pie plate.

Place the cheese in a bowl and beat in the sugar, two of the eggs, and the grated rind. Put the cheese mixture into the pie case, and cover with the second circle of dough. Moisten the edges and seal them together, forming a crimped edge. Brush the top with the beaten egg, and bake in an oven preheated to 220°C (425°F or Mark 7) for 35 minutes or until golden.

NICOLE VIELFAURE AND CHRISTINE BEAUVIALA
FÊTES, COUTUMES ET GÂTEAUX

Sweet Cheese Pie

Erbazzone Dolce

To make one 20 cm (8 inch) pie

500 g	ricotta	1 lb
500 g	sugar	1 lb
100 g	beetroot leaves, boiled, finely chopped and squeezed dry	3$\frac{1}{2}$ oz
100 g	sweet almonds, blanched and chopped	3$\frac{1}{2}$ oz
10 g	bitter almonds, blanched and chopped	$\frac{1}{2}$ oz
6 tbsp	rum	6 tbsp
4	eggs, 1 lightly beaten	4
1	lemon, rind grated	1
500 g	shortcrust dough (*page 165*)	1 lb

Combine the *ricotta* with the sugar, beetroot leaves, almonds, rum, three of the eggs and the lemon rind.

Roll out the dough and line a greased tart tin with most of it, reserving the trimmings. Pour in the *ricotta* filling. Use the remaining dough to form a lattice top, and brush the top with the remaining, lightly beaten egg. Bake in an oven preheated to 180°C (350°F or Mark 4) for about 1 hour. If the top browns too much, cover it with a sheet of greased paper. The pie is done when the filling is set.

GIORGIO CAVAZZUTI (EDITOR)
IL MANGIARFUORI: ALMANACCO
DELLA CUCINA MODENESE

139

Cream Cheese and Honey Pie

To make one 20 cm (8 inch) pie

175 g	cream cheese	6 oz
15 cl	milk or single cream	¼ pint
4 tbsp	sugar	4 tbsp
1 tsp	grated lemon rind	1 tsp
1 tsp	ground cinnamon	1 tsp
4 tsp	honey, warmed if stiff	4 tsp
2	eggs, lightly beaten	2
250 g	shortcrust dough (*page 165*)	8 oz

Roll the dough into a ball, then spread it into a removable-base flan or tart tin, patting it into place with your fingers.

To make the filling, beat the cream cheese until smooth. Add the milk or cream gradually. Then stir in the sugar, lemon rind, cinnamon, honey and lastly the beaten eggs.

Pour this filling mixture into the pastry case, stand the flan or tart tin on a baking sheet and cook in the centre of a preheated moderately hot oven—190°C (375°F or Mark 5)—for about 45 minutes or until the filling is set. After the first 15 to 20 minutes, look to see if the top is browning too fast. If so, cover with a round of buttered greaseproof paper which should be ready prepared.

ELIZABETH DAVID
SPICES, SALT AND AROMATICS IN THE ENGLISH KITCHEN

Bishop Auckland Cheese Cakes

These were called cheese cakes because the potato-based filling resembled one made with curd cheese.

To make eight tartlets

175 g	mashed, boiled potatoes	6 oz
60 g	butter, melted	2 oz
125 g	castor sugar	4 oz
1	egg, lightly beaten	1
30 g	finely grated lemon rind	1 oz
¼ tsp	lemon extract	¼ tsp
125 g	currants	4 oz
	rum	
250 g	shortcrust dough (*page 165*)	8 oz

Put the potatoes in a bowl and beat in the butter, sugar, egg, and lemon rind and extract. Fold in the currants. Line eight tartlet tins with the dough, then fill with the mixture and bake in an oven preheated to 180°C (350°F or Mark 4) for 30 minutes or until the filling is lightly browned. When cooked, put a few drops of rum on to each tartlet. Serve hot or cold.

PEGGY HUTCHINSON
OLD ENGLISH COOKERY

Maids of Honour Cakes

These cakes are said to derive their name from Queen Elizabeth I of England's maids of honour when she lived at Richmond Palace in Surrey. The recipe is taken from a 16th-century cooking manuscript.

To make approximately 12 individual tarts

30 cl	milk	½ pint
2 tbsp	fresh white breadcrumbs	2 tbsp
125 g	butter, in small pieces	4 oz
30 g	sugar	1 oz
60 g	ground almonds	2 oz
1	lemon, rind grated	1
3	eggs	3
250 g	puff dough (*page 167*)	8 oz

Boil the milk with the breadcrumbs and let the mixture stand for a few minutes, then add the butter, sugar, almonds and lemon rind. Beat in the eggs, one at a time; line some tartlet tins with the puff dough and spoon the mixture into them. Bake in an oven preheated to 220°C (425°F or Mark 7) for 20 minutes or until the tarts are golden-brown.

BERNARD DARWIN
RECEIPTS AND RELISHES

Maple Macadamia Pie

Most macadamia nuts are sold in airtight jars, and they are usually whole. The best way to prepare the nuts for this pie is to place them on a chopping block and cut each nut in half. Macadamias are tender and may break into more than two pieces as you are cutting them, but don't fret about that.

To make one 20 to 22 cm (8 to 9 inch) pie

¼ litre	maple syrup	8 fl oz
125 g	macadamia nuts, chopped or halved	4 oz
90 g	coconut, shredded	3 oz
3	eggs, lightly beaten	3
4 tbsp	sugar	4 tbsp
¼ tsp	salt	¼ tsp
90 g	butter, melted and cooled	3 oz
250 g	shortcrust dough (*page 165*)	8 oz

Line a 20 to 22 cm (8 to 9 inch) pie plate with the dough, making a raised, crimped edge. Arrange the macadamias in one layer over the unbaked pie case, covering as much of the dough as you can. Sprinkle the shredded coconut over the nuts, and refrigerate the pie case.

In a large bowl, add to the beaten eggs the sugar, maple syrup, salt and butter. Mix well, and pour into the pie case.

Bake the pie in an oven preheated to 200°C (400°F or Mark 6) for 15 minutes. Lower the heat to 180°C (350°F or Mark 4), and bake for an additional 20 to 25 minutes, until the filling is custard-like. (If the top browns too quickly, cover it with a sheet of foil.) Insert a knife to test for doneness. The filling will rise substantially, but it will fall to the level of the pie plate as it cools. This pie is best served lukewarm with a dollop of ice-cold whipped cream.

JOE FAMULARO AND LOUISE IMPERIALE
THE FESTIVE FAMULARO KITCHEN

Frangipane Pie

Tourte de Frangipane

A 16th-century cook named Frangipani is said to have created the almond filling that gives this pie its name. La Varenne, on the other hand, can take full credit for the unusual puff pastry that surrounds the almond cream. His idea of rolling out thin sheets of dough and layering them in a pie plate has been abandoned today by French cooks, whose method of making puff pastry is more complicated—although not superior, in this case, to the technique developed by La Varenne three centuries ago.

To make one 22 cm (9 inch) pie

6 tbsp	flour	6 tbsp
½ litre	milk	16 fl oz
60 g	shelled pistachio nuts, blanched	2 oz
60 g	shelled almonds, blanched	2 oz
	orange flower water (optional)	
75 g	sugar	2½ oz
	salt	
5	egg yolks	5
	Dough	
225 g	flour	7½ oz
5	egg whites	5
250 g	butter, softened	8 oz

For the almond cream, mix the flour with several teaspoons of the milk. Place the remaining milk in a saucepan. Add the flour mixture. Cook for 10 minutes over a low heat, stirring constantly. Remove from the heat and cool.

Pound the pistachio nuts and almonds in a mortar until a fine paste is formed. (A few drops of orange flower water can be sprinkled on the nuts to prevent them from losing their oil.) Mix the pounded nuts with the sugar and salt. Stir the egg yolks, one by one, into the cool flour and milk mixture. Stir in the nut mixture until thoroughly blended.

For the dough, place the flour in a bowl. Mix with the egg whites until the dough is smooth and can be formed into a ball.

Leave the dough in the bowl, and cover it with a cloth. Let stand for 2 hours before using.

Butter a pie plate with 1 tablespoon of the butter. Divide the dough into two equal parts. Take the first part, and divide it into six pieces. Take one of these small pieces, and with the hands or a rolling pin, flatten it until it is paper-thin (almost transparent) and the size of the plate. Place it on the plate.

Divide the remaining butter into 11 equal parts. Spread one part of the butter over the dough on the plate. Flatten another small piece of dough, and place it over the first. Spread with another part of the butter. Repeat this operation until you have six layers of dough. Spread the almond cream over the sixth layer of dough.

Make six more layers with the second half of the dough. Place these over the almond cream, separating each layer by a layer of butter. Butter the top of the pie.

Bake in an oven preheated to 200°C (400°F or Mark 6) for 35 minutes or until golden-brown. Serve warm or cold.

CÉLINE VENCE AND ROBERT COURTINE
THE GRAND MASTERS OF FRENCH CUISINE

Almond Tart

Tarte aux Amandes

To make one 18 cm (7 inch) tart

90 g	ground almonds	3 oz
2	eggs	2
100 g	sugar	3½ oz
8 cl	milk	3 fl oz
	cream (optional)	
	Dough	
125 g	flour, sifted	4 oz
125 g	butter	4 oz
30 g	sugar	1 oz
	milk	

Prepare the dough by mixing the flour, butter and sugar with two knives or with your fingertips until the mixture is crumbly. Add just enough milk to make a dough that adheres. Roll out the dough and use to line a greased tart tin.

Beat together the ground almonds, eggs, 90 g (3 oz) of the sugar and the milk until the mixture is smooth and the consistency of thick cream.

Prick the bottom of the dough lining with a fork, pour in the almond filling, and bake in an oven preheated to 190°C (375°F or Mark 5) for about 15 minutes or until the filling is set. Two minutes before the end sprinkle the tart with the remaining sugar. Serve hot, with cream, or cold.

X. M. BOULESTIN
THE FINER COOKING

Linzer Tart with Almonds

Linzer Torte (mit Mandeln)

As an alternative to the lattice pattern, make a pattern on top of the dough with four semi-circles, and make a pattern on the edge with the end of a spoon. Or, form different designs of diamonds, hearts, etc., and place these on top of the tart.

To make one 28 cm (11½ inch) tart

250 g	almonds, blanched and chopped	8 oz
250 g	flour	8 oz
250 g	butter, softened and cut in pieces	8 oz
2	egg yolks	2
250 g	sugar	8 oz
2 tsp	cherry schnaps	2 tsp
¼ tsp	ground cloves	¼ tsp
2 tsp	ground cinnamon	2 tsp
½	lemon, rind grated	½
1 tbsp	cocoa powder	1 tbsp
100 g	raspberry or strawberry jam	3½ oz
1	egg, lightly beaten	1

Put the flour and pieces of butter on to a board. Put the rest of the ingredients, apart from the jam and beaten egg, on top, and work the mixture with your fingertips to form it into a smooth dough. Leave it to stand for 1 hour.

Roll out two-thirds of the dough and use it to line a baking tin. Spread it with the jam. Roll out the rest of the dough, cut into strips and decorate the edges and the top of the tart with a lattice pattern. Brush the edge of the pastry and lattice pattern with the beaten egg, and bake in an oven preheated to 180°C (350°F or Mark 4) for 35 minutes or until the pastry is light brown. Serve hot or cold.

HERMINE KIEHNLE AND MARIA HÄDECKE
DAS NEUE KIEHNLE-KOCHBUCH

Walnut and Honey Pie

La Bonissima

To make one 20 cm (8 inch) pie

250 g	shelled walnuts, chopped	8 oz
200 g	honey	7 oz
4 tbsp	rum	4 tbsp
125 g	plain chocolate, melted over hot water, or heavy sugar syrup	4 oz

Shortcrust dough

400 g	flour	14 oz
150 g	sugar	5 oz
150 g	butter	5 oz
1	egg	1
½ tsp	grated lemon rind	½ tsp
15 g	vanilla extract	½ oz

Mix together the honey, walnuts and rum.

For the dough, mix the flour and sugar and work in all the remaining ingredients with your fingers. Roll out the dough and use half of it to line a tart tin. Pour in the nut mixture and cover it with the remaining dough, sealing the edges well. Bake in an oven preheated to 180°C (350°F or Mark 4) for about 30 minutes or until lightly browned.

Allow the pie to cool, then cover it with melted chocolate or sugar syrup. Let the topping set and harden before serving.

GIORGIO CAVAZZUTI (EDITOR)
IL MANGIARFUORI: ALMANACCO
DELLA CUCINA MODENESE

Vanilla Cream Tarts

Babeczki Śmietankowe

To make 12 tartlets

12.5 cl	double cream	4 fl oz
3	egg yolks	3
150 g	castor sugar	5 oz
½	vanilla pod, split lengthwise, seeds scraped out	½

Dough

200 g	unsalted butter	7 oz
400 g	flour	14 oz
½ tsp	bicarbonate of soda	½ tsp
120 g	castor sugar	4 oz
1	egg	1
4	egg yolks, 2 hard-boiled and sieved	4

To make the dough, cut the butter into the flour, then add the remaining ingredients and knead briefly but thoroughly. Wrap or cover the dough to prevent drying and allow to rest, refrigerated, for at least 1 hour.

For the filling, put the egg yolks in a saucepan and stir in the sugar, cream and vanilla pod. Cook over a low heat, stirring continuously with a wooden spoon, until the mixture thickens. Remove from the heat and put the saucepan in a shallow pan of cold water to stop the cooking. Cool the custard, stirring occasionally.

Roll out the dough and line buttered tartlet moulds with it.

Fill the cases with the custard, and cover with rounds of the dough. Crimp the edges together to seal, and bake the tartlets in an oven preheated to 180°C (350°F or Mark 4) for 30 minutes or until lightly browned. Cool before unmoulding.

I. PLUCINSKA
KSIAZKA KUCHARSKA

Sweetmeat Pudding

This recipe is from the 17th-century cookery book written by Hannah Glasse, who signed it "By a Lady".

To make one 25 cm (10 inch) tart

30 g each	candied lemon peel, candied orange peel, and citron, thinly sliced	1 oz each
8	egg yolks	8
2	egg whites	2
250 g	sugar	8 oz
250 g	butter, melted	8 oz
350 g	puff dough (*page 167*), rolled out thinly	12 oz

Put a thin puff-paste all over your dish; then lay the thinly sliced sweetmeats all over the bottom of your dish. Beat the egg yolks and whites with the sugar and melted butter. Beat all well together; when the oven is ready, pour the mixture on your sweetmeats. An hour or less will bake it, in an oven preheated to 180°C (350°F or Mark 4). The filling should be set and the top brown. Serve warm.

THE ART OF COOKERY, MADE PLAIN AND EASY

A Tender Tart

To make one 18 cm (7 inch) pie

140 g	butter	4½ oz
165 g	flour	5½ oz
1	egg yolk	1
2	eggs	2
250 g	sugar	8 oz
1 tsp	vanilla extract	1 tsp
140 g	hazelnuts, finely chopped	5 oz

Blend the butter, flour and egg yolk with knives. Add only enough water to hold the dough together, knead lightly, then refrigerate the dough for 15 minutes.

Stir the eggs and sugar together. Do not beat. Add the vanilla extract and hazelnuts. Roll out a little more than half of the dough; place it in a deep pie plate with a detachable bottom, fill this case with the egg and nut mixture. Roll out

the remaining dough and cover the pie, press the edges together so that the bottom and top crusts adhere. Bake for 40 minutes, or until the top is brown, in an oven preheated to 180°C (350°F or Mark 4).

ALICE B. TOKLAS
THE ALICE B. TOKLAS COOK BOOK

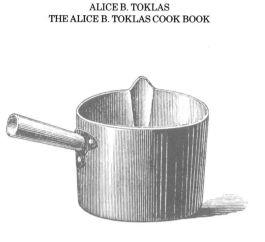

Christmas Tart

Tarte de Natal

To make one 22 cm (9 inch) tart

300 g	dried figs, minced	10 oz
100 g	Malaga raisins, seeded	3½ oz
10 cl	vermouth	3½ fl oz
6	apples, peeled, cored and sliced	6
150 g	almonds, blanched and ground	5 oz
2	eggs, beaten	2
	sugar	
	ground cinnamon	
350 g	shortcrust dough (*page 165*), made with 2 tbsp sugar and 1 tsp ground cinnamon	12 oz

Marinate the figs and raisins in the vermouth for 1 hour. Line a flan ring, or a tart tin with a removable base, with the dough. Bake it blind for 20 minutes in an oven preheated to 190°C (375°F or Mark 5).

Combine the apples, the vermouth mixture, the almonds and the eggs. Fill the baked case with this mixture, and sprinkle the top with sugar and cinnamon. Return the tart to a 180°C (350°F or Mark 4) oven for 30 minutes or until the filling is set.

Remove the tart from the tin and serve hot or cold.

ETELVINA LOPES DE ALMEIDA
ABC DA CULINÁRIA

Lemon Meringue Pie

To make one 25 cm (10 inch) pie

	Crumb mixture	
2 tbsp	sugar	2 tbsp
2 tbsp	dry breadcrumbs	2 tbsp
¼ tsp	ground cardamom seed	¼ tsp
	Lemon curd filling	
2	lemons, rind grated, juice strained	2
200 g	sugar	7 oz
3	eggs, well beaten	3
250 g	unsalted butter	8 oz
	Meringue	
6	egg whites, stiffly beaten	6
225 g	sugar	7½ oz
	castor sugar	
	Dough	
250 g	flour	8 oz
½ tsp	salt	½ tsp
175 g	unsalted butter at room temperature	6 oz
1	lemon, rind grated	1
2 tbsp	sugar	2 tbsp
3 tbsp each	iced lemon juice and iced water	3 tbsp each
	unsalted butter, melted and cooled	

To make the dough, put the flour and salt in a bowl and rub in the butter with your fingertips until the texture resembles coarse cornmeal. Add the lemon rind and sugar. Pour in the lemon juice and water and quickly work the mixture up to a firm dough. Set a flan ring on a baking sheet. Turn the dough out on a lightly floured board and roll it out a little larger than the flan ring. Carefully lift the dough, lay it over the flan ring and line the ring firmly. Trim off the edges and, with your fingers, shape a slightly thicker rim round the top. Trim the rim with a pastry wheel, prick all over the bottom of the shell with a fork, brush the dough with cool melted butter.

Bake the pastry case blind in an oven preheated to 190°C (375°F or Mark 5) for 30 minutes. Remove the flan ring and return the case on the baking sheet to the oven to bake for 10 minutes more. Remove the shell from the oven.

In a little bowl mix the sugar, breadcrumbs and cardamom for the crumb mixture and dust it over the bottom of the pastry shell while the shell is still warm.

To make the lemon curd, in the top of a double saucepan put the lemon rind and juice, sugar, eggs and butter. Set over hot, not boiling water. Stir with a wooden spoon over a low heat until the mixture is the consistency of thick cream sauce. Pour it into a shallow 22 cm (9 inch) cake tin and put it into the freezer to set for about 15 minutes.

When the lemon curd is firmly set, put it into the pastry case. Use a rubber scraper to scrape it out of the pan and pat it evenly into the case.

Slowly beat the sugar into the egg whites. Continue beating until the whites are stiff. Fill a piping bag, fitted with a number 8 or 9 star tube, with the meringue. Pipe out large scallop shapes to cover the lemon curd completely. Sprinkle the meringue with castor sugar and bake the pie for 10 to 15 minutes or until the meringue is a delicate golden-brown. Cool the pie, then place it in the refrigerator to chill for an hour before serving.

DIONE LUCAS AND MARION GORMAN
THE DIONE LUCAS BOOK OF FRENCH COOKING

The Perfect Lemon Meringue Pie

To make one 22 cm (9 inch) pie

	Lemon filling	
7	eggs, yolks separated from whites	7
250 g	sugar	8 oz
5 to 6 tbsp	lemon juice	5 to 6 tbsp
	Flaky dough	
100 g	flour	3½ oz
3 tbsp	icing sugar	3 tbsp
100 g	very cold butter	3½ oz
1	large egg	1
1 tbsp	iced water	1 tbsp

To prepare the dough, place the flour and sugar in a bowl. Cut the butter into small bits and add these to the flour-sugar mixture. Using a pastry cutter or two knives, cut the butter into the flour until the mixture is the texture of meal. Break the egg into the mixture and beat it well in using a fork. Add a tablespoon of iced water, if necessary, to make the dough more manageable. Form the dough into a ball and knead lightly until it is quite smooth. Wrap the dough in greaseproof paper and refrigerate it for about 1 hour.

Preheat the oven to 180°C (350°F or Mark 4). Roll out the

pastry to 3 mm (⅛ inch) thickness and use it to line a pie plate. Trim the excess dough round the edges, leaving a 5 mm (¼ inch) overhang. Press or pinch the overhang decoratively. Line the pastry case with foil, fill the foil with dried beans and bake for 15 minutes or until the pastry is firm but not coloured. Remove the beans and foil, prick the bottom of the case with a fork, and bake for 10 minutes more, or until lightly coloured. Leave the pastry case to cool.

For the filling, beat the egg yolks with a whisk in a heatproof bowl or the top of a double saucepan, off the heat. Add 200 g (7 oz) of the sugar and the lemon juice and beat again briefly. Place over a container of simmering water and cook, stirring constantly, until the mixture is quite thick. Remove from the heat and cool.

Beat the egg whites until they hold soft peaks. Using a spatula, fold about one-third of the egg whites into the yolk and lemon mixture. Pour the filling into the baked crust. Gradually add the remaining sugar to the remaining egg whites, beating constantly. When the egg whites are glossy but not overly stiff, pile them on to the lemon filling, covering it completely. You can do this by using a large spoon to scoop up the egg whites and drop them on to the filling. The meringue should look fluffy, like puffy clouds. Place the pie in the oven at the same temperature for no more than 10 minutes, or until the meringue is very lightly browned.

DORIS TOBIAS AND MARY MERRIS
THE GOLDEN LEMON

Lemon Pudding

Naples biscuits are a variety of hard macaroon flavoured with rose water. If you must substitute amaretti *or other maca-roons, add a teaspoonful of rose water to the filling mixture.*

To make one 25 cm (10 inch) tart

2	lemons, rind grated	2
2	Naples biscuits, grated	2
350 g	castor sugar	12 oz
12	egg yolks, lightly beaten	12
6	egg whites, stiffly beaten	6
350 g	butter, melted	12 oz
30 cl	double cream	½ pint
250 g	shortcrust dough (*page 165*)	8 oz

Mix the grated rind and biscuits with the sugar. Stir in the egg yolks, the whites, the butter and the cream. Mix well. Line a tart tin with the pastry, and pour in the filling. Bake at 190°C (375°F or Mark 5) for about an hour, or until the filling is set.

J. STEVENS COX (EDITOR)
GUERNSEY DISHES OF BYGONE DAYS

Pumpkin Pie

Some cooks vary the ordinary taste of pumpkin pie by adding a little cider, good brandy or sherry to the custard.

To make one 22 cm (9 inch) pie

45 cl	sieved baked pumpkin	16 fl oz
4	eggs, yolks separated from whites, yolks beaten until lemon coloured, whites stiffly beaten	4
250 g	brown sugar	8 oz
½ tsp each	ground cinnamon, nutmeg and allspice	½ tsp each
5 tbsp	double cream	5 tbsp
60 g	butter, melted	2 oz
1 tbsp	cornflour	1 tbsp
4 tbsp	clear honey, slightly melted (optional)	4 tbsp
60 g	pecans, finely chopped (optional)	2 oz
250 g	shortcrust dough (*page 165*)	8 oz

Line a pie plate with the dough. Set aside in a cool place. Combine the beaten egg yolks with the sugar and spices, and blend until the sugar is thoroughly dissolved.

Mix the pumpkin with the cream and melted butter until thoroughly blended. Stir into the yolk mixture. Sprinkle the cornflour on to the beaten egg whites, then fold the whites into the pumpkin mixture.

Pour the pumpkin filling into the prepared unbaked pastry case and bake for 10 minutes in an oven preheated to 230°C (450°F or Mark 8) to set the crust, then reduce the heat to 180°C (350°F or Mark 4) and continue baking for a further 20 to 25 minutes, or until a knife blade comes out clean when inserted.

To give added flavour, when the pie is thoroughly cold, mix the honey with the chopped pecans and pour the mixture over the surface of the tart.

LOUIS P. DE GOUY
THE GOLD COOK BOOK

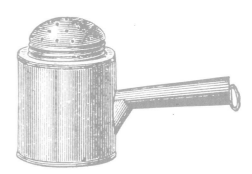

Chestnut Tart

To purée fresh chestnuts, slit the nuts down one side, parboil them for 1 to 2 minutes, shell and peel them. Cook the chestnuts for about 20 minutes in simmering water until they are tender enough to force through a sieve after draining.

To make one 25 cm (10 inch) tart

500 g	chestnuts, puréed, or 250 g (8 oz) tinned unsweetened chestnut purée	1 lb
125 g	castor sugar	4 oz
15 cl	double cream	¼ pint
1 tbsp	orange juice	1 tbsp
1 tbsp	sweet sherry	1 tbsp
2	egg yolks, well beaten	2
60 g	butter, cut into small pieces	2 oz
1	partially blind-baked pastry case, made with puff dough (*page 167*) or shortcrust dough (*page 165*)	1

Mix the chestnut purée with the sugar, cream, orange juice, sherry and egg yolks. Allow the pastry case to cool for 5 minutes after baking, then pour in the chestnut mixture. Do not allow it to overflow. If any filling is left over, make up some small tartlets. Dot the filling all over with the butter. Bake in an oven preheated to 150°C (300°F or Mark 2) for 20 minutes or until just firm. Sprinkle the top with more sugar while it is still hot. Serve cold with whipped cream.

ELISABETH AYRTON
THE COOKERY OF ENGLAND

Sweet Pumpkin Tart

La Tarte de Courge Sucrée

To make one 22 cm (9 inch) tart

1 kg	pumpkin, peeled, seeded and diced	2 to 2½ lb
60 g	butter	2 oz
30 g	flour	1 oz
1 tsp	orange flower water	1 tsp
1	orange, rind grated	1
1	lemon, rind grated	1
100 g	castor sugar	3½ oz
2 or 3	eggs, lightly beaten	2 or 3
4 tbsp	rum	4 tbsp
	icing sugar	
500 g	shortcrust dough (*page 165*)	1 lb

Cook the pumpkin in the butter over a low heat, covered, until it is soft enough to be puréed with a potato masher or put through a sieve. Sprinkle the puréed pumpkin with the flour, then stir in the orange flower water, grated rinds, castor sugar, beaten eggs and rum.

Line a tart tin with dough and fill with the pumpkin mixture. Cover with a lattice of dough strips cut with a serrated pastry wheel. Bake in an oven preheated to 190°C (375°F or Mark 5) for 30 to 35 minutes.

Immediately on removing from the oven, sprinkle the tart with icing sugar. Serve warm or cold.

JOSEPHINE BESSON
LA MÈRE BESSON "MA CUISINE PROVENÇALE"

Bacon and Rose Water Tart

Tourte au Lard

This recipe is from a cookbook published in 1606; the author was Joseph du Chesne, sieur de la Violette, physician to King Henry IV of France.

To make one 20 cm (8 inch) tart

40 g	green bacon, very finely chopped	1½ oz
	rose water	
12	almonds, blanched	12
2 or 3	egg yolks	2 or 3
½ tsp	ground cinnamon	½ tsp
100 g	sugar	3½ oz
250 g	shortcrust dough (*page 165*)	8 oz

Pound the chopped bacon in a mortar with a few drops of rose water until a perfectly smooth paste is formed. Pound the almonds separately, then add them to the bacon and pound the mixture together, adding a few more drops of rose water if necessary to achieve a creamy consistency. Add to this mixture the egg yolks, cinnamon and sugar to taste. Mix all the ingredients together well.

Roll out the dough and line a tart tin. Spread the filling mixture in the case, and bake in an oven preheated to 180°C (350°F or Mark 4) for 30 minutes or until the top is golden and the filling is set.

JOSEPH DU CHESNE
LE POURTRAICT DE LA SANTÉ

Beef Marrow Pie

Tarte à la Moelle

Raw marrow may be extracted from a large beef bone with the help of a small sharp knife. The bone should first be cut into sections by the butcher.

To make one 22 cm (9 inch) pie

125 g	beef marrow, diced	4 oz
1	bread roll, soaked in water and squeezed dry	1
2	eggs, beaten	2
100 g	sugar	3½ oz
4 tbsp	rum or kirsch	4 tbsp
1 tsp	ground cinnamon	1 tsp
60 g	blanched almonds, chopped or slivered	2 oz
1	egg yolk, lightly beaten	1
500 g	shortcrust or rich shortcrust dough (*page 165*)	1 lb

Mix together the marrow, soaked bread, eggs, sugar, rum, cinnamon and almonds to form a smooth mixture.

Roll out the dough and use two-thirds of it to line a pie plate. Fill with the marrow mixture, and cover with the remaining pastry. Seal the edges, brush the top with the egg yolk, and make three slits in the top. Bake in an oven preheated to 200°C (400°F or Mark 6) for 25 minutes or until the crust is browned and the filling set. Serve hot.

HUGUETTE COUFFIGNAL
LA CUISINE RUSTIQUE

Carrot Pudding

To make one 25 by 15 cm (10 by 6 inch) tart

100 g	grated carrot	3½ oz
60 g	breadcrumbs	2 oz
60 cl	hot milk	1 pint
1	lemon, rind grated, juice strained	1
60 g	raisins	2 oz
½ tsp	mixed spice	½ tsp
2	eggs, well beaten	2
125 g	sugar	4 oz
250 g	shortcrust dough (*page 165*)	8 oz

Butter a pie dish and line it with the dough. Mix together the carrots and breadcrumbs then pour on the hot milk. Leave to cool and add the grated lemon rind, raisins, mixed spice and beaten eggs. Stir in the sugar and lemon juice, blending well before pouring into the dough-lined dish. Bake for 1½ hours or until set in an oven preheated to 170°C (325°F or Mark 3).

JOAN POULSON
OLD THAMES VALLEY RECIPES

Sweet Lamb Pie from Westmorland

Make up this pie on a pie plate, the kind that is much used in the north of England. The best ones are tin, but the enamelled kind do quite well. Put any filling left over into a jam jar, cover it and use it up for small mince pies.

To make one 25 cm (10 inch) pie

175 g	boned lean lamb	6 oz
90 g	lamb fat, trimmed from chops, etc.	3 oz
175 g	grated peeled raw apple	6 oz
125 g	currants	4 oz
125 g	raisins	4 oz
125 g	sultanas	4 oz
60 g	candied mixed peel, chopped	2 oz
1	orange, juice strained	1
½	lemon, juice strained	½
60 g	blanched almonds, chopped	2 oz
4 tbsp	rum	4 tbsp
	salt and freshly ground pepper	
½ tsp	ground mace	½ tsp
½ tsp	ground cinnamon	½ tsp
¼	nutmeg, grated	¼
500 g	shortcrust dough (*page 165*)	1 lb
	1 egg, beaten, or top of milk (optional)	

Mince the meat, both lean and fat. Put it into a basin and mix in the remaining filling ingredients, making sure that everything is well distributed. Add a little more spice if you like.

Roll out half of the dough and line a pie plate. Turn enough of the filling into the dough to mound up over the level of the rim. Roll out the remaining dough and cover the pie, brushing the rim of the bottom crust first with beaten egg or top of the milk. Press down and crimp the edge, make a central hole, and brush the lid over with egg or top of the milk. Bake for 30 minutes in an oven preheated to 200°C (400°F or Mark 6). The pie is done when the top is golden-brown. Serve hot or cold.

JANE GRIGSON
ENGLISH FOOD

Cream of Artichoke Tart

Tourte de Crème d'Artichaux au Sucre

If desired, the pastry case can be baked blind (see page 72) before adding the artichoke filling.

To make one 20 cm (8 inch) tart

3	artichoke bottoms, cooked, pounded and puréed through a nylon sieve	3
30 g	butter, melted and cooled	1 oz
2	egg yolks	2
10 cl	double cream	3½ fl oz
1	macaroon, crumbled	1
	salt	
About 50 g	sugar	About 2 oz
15 g	candied lemon peel, finely chopped	½ oz
	orange flower water	
250 g	shortcrust dough (*page 165*)	8 oz

Blend the artichoke purée thoroughly with the butter, egg yolks, cream and macaroon crumbs. Season the mixure to taste with salt and sugar, and add the lemon peel.

Roll out the dough and line a tart tin. Pour in the artichoke cream mixture. Bake in an oven preheated to 180°C (350°F or Mark 4) for 30 minutes or until the cream is set. Sprinkle with sugar and glaze beneath a grill or in a hot oven. Sprinkle with orange flower water before serving.

L'ESCOLE PARFAITE DES OFFICIERS DE BOUCHE

Beetroot Tart

Tourte de Betteraves

To make one 20 cm (8 inch) tart

2	beetroots, baked until tender	2
20 cl	white wine	7 fl oz
2	sugar lumps	2
	salt	
15 g	candied lemon peel, finely chopped	½ oz
30 g	butter	1 oz
	sugar	
	orange flower water	
250 g	shortcrust dough or 1 blind-baked pastry case (*page 165*)	8 oz

Peel and cut up the beetroots, and cook them with the white wine until all of the wine is absorbed, about 20 minutes. Pound the mixture in a mortar with the sugar lumps and a pinch of salt, until it forms a smooth purée. Blend in the chopped candied lemon peel and butter.

Use the baked case or roll out the dough and use it to line a tart tin. Put in the beetroot mixture, and bake the tart in an oven preheated to 180°C (350°F or Mark 4) for 30 minutes—20 minutes if using the pre-baked case—until the filling is lightly browned. Sprinkle with sugar and orange flower water before serving.

L'ESCOLE PARFAITE DES OFFICIERS DE BOUCHE

Red Wine Tart

Tourte de Vin Vermeil

If desired, before adding the wine mixture, the pastry case can be baked blind (see page 72). The redcurrant juice is obtained by putting redcurrants through a sieve or vegetable mill.

To make one 20 cm (8 inch) tart

12.5 cl	port or red wine	4 fl oz
12.5 cl	redcurrant juice	4 fl oz
2	macaroons, crumbled	2
4	egg yolks, lightly beaten	4
	salt	
About 50 g	sugar	About 2 oz
15 g	candied lemon peel, finely chopped	½ oz
15 g	butter, softened	½ oz
	orange flower water	
250 g	shortcrust dough (*page 165*)	8 oz

In a saucepan, mix the wine and redcurrant juice with the macaroons, egg yolks, salt and sugar to taste. Stirring constantly, cook over a very low heat until the mixture is lightly thickened. Off the heat, stir in the candied lemon peel and the butter. Line a tart tin with the dough, and pour in the wine mixture. Bake the tart in an oven preheated to 180°C (350°F or Mark 4) or until the filling is set. Sprinkle with orange flower water before serving.

L'ESCOLE PARFAITE DES OFFICIERS DE BOUCHE

Pastries

Puff Pastry Slices with Whipped Cream

Mille-Feuille à la Crème Légère

Puff pastry tends to shrink in the oven. To avoid this, cut out the rectangles the day before you bake them and let them rest overnight in the refrigerator, protected by plastic film.

When strawberries and raspberries are in season, you can add 250 g (8 oz) of one or a mixture of both to the whipped cream when you fold the two creams together. Keep a few berries to one side for decorating the top. You can also make a criss-cross, or *quadrillage*, pattern of caramel in the icing sugar coating by laying a thin steel skewer, heated to white hot in a fire or gas flame, on the sugar.

	To make one 20 by 16 cm (8 by 6 inch) pastry	
¼ litre	pastry cream (*page 166*)	8 fl oz
10 cl	double cream, chilled	3½ fl oz
40 g	icing sugar	1½ oz
350 g	puff dough (*page 167*)	12 oz

Preheat the oven to 220°C (425°F or Mark 7). Lightly flour the worktop and roll out the dough into a 20 by 45 cm (8 by 18 inch) rectangle and about 2 mm (¹/₁₀ inch) thick. Using a heavy knife, cut the dough cleanly into three 15 by 20 cm (6 by 8 inch) strips.

Brush a large baking sheet with water, lay the three strips of dough on it and prick all over with a fork to stop the pastry from puffing too much during the cooking.

Bake the pastry for 20 minutes or until puffed and browned. Remove the pastry from the baking sheet and allow it to cool on a wire rack; the pastry should be a beautiful hazelnut brown.

While the pastry is baking, make the pastry cream and cool it rapidly, stirring and aerating it well with a whisk.

Combine the double cream and 10 g (½ oz) icing sugar in a chilled bowl, and beat with a small wire whisk for 1 minute, then beat more rapidly for a further 5 minutes until the cream is the consistency of egg whites whipped until they form soft peaks. Add the pastry cream to the whipped cream and fold the two together carefully with a wooden spatula, using an upwards motion to aerate the mixture and retain its light texture.

With a metal spatula, spread half of the resulting cream on one of the strips of pastry. Place the second pastry strip on top, spread with the rest of the cream, and cover it with the last pastry rectangle, smooth side up.

Sprinkle the confection lavishly with the remaining icing sugar to give it an even white coating. Then place it on a serving dish and slice it carefully with a serrated knife in front of your guests.

MICHEL GUÉRARD
MICHEL GUÉRARD'S CUISINE GOURMANDE

Pithiviers

Gâteau d'Amandes, dit Pithiviers

The almond cream in this recipe produces twice the quantity needed for one pastry. You can either use it to make two pastries at the same time, or save half of the cream for up to a week under refrigeration, for fruit tarts or cake fillings.

	To make one 20 cm (8 inch) pastry	
1	egg, beaten	1
	icing sugar	
200 g	puff dough (*page 167*)	7 oz
	Almond cream	
100 g	blanched almonds	3½ oz
100 g	sugar	3½ oz
2	egg yolks	2
40 g	butter	1½ oz
4 tbsp	rum	4 tbsp

For the cream, pound the almonds in a mortar with the sugar until they are finely ground. Add the egg yolks, then the butter, and finally the rum, working all of the ingredients together with a spatula to form a smooth cream.

Roll out one-third of the puff dough into a circle 3 to 4 mm (⅙ inch) thick. Place this round on a baking sheet and spread it with half of the almond cream to within 2.5 cm (1 inch) of the edge. Moisten the border with a pastry brush dipped in water. Roll out the remaining dough into a round of the same diameter but twice as thick; place this over the first round, and seal the edges by pressing with your fingers.

With a knife, draw lines radiating outwards from the centre of the dough, and notch the edges decoratively without cutting through the dough. Prick right through the dough to the baking sheet in five or six places. With a brush, glaze the top with the beaten egg.

Bake in an oven preheated to 200°C (400°F or Mark 6) for 20 to 30 minutes or until the pastry is well risen and golden-brown. Five minutes before the end of the cooking time, sprinkle the top of the pastry with icing sugar and return to the oven. The sugar will caramelize and give a shiny glaze to the pastry.

HENRI-PAUL PELLAPRAT
LE NOUVEAU GUIDE CULINAIRE

Cream Horns

Cornets de Crème

The technique of forming cream horns is shown on page 80.

To make seven or eight horns

1	egg, beaten with 2 tbsp milk	1
125 g	raspberry jam	4 oz
15 cl	double cream, whipped and sweetened to taste, with ¼ tsp vanilla extract beaten in	¼ pint
30 g	pistachio nuts, chopped	1 oz
350 g	puff dough (*page 167*) or flaky dough (*page 166*), with ½ tsp lemon juice added	12 oz

Roll out the dough 3 mm (⅛ inch) thick and cut it into strips 1 by 30 to 35 cm (½ by 12 to 14 inches). Moisten the strips with water, and wind each one, overlapping slightly, round a cornet mould, from the pointed end upwards, keeping the moist surface on the outside. Finish the final overlap on the underside of the mould, and trim neatly. Allow the horns to stand for about 1 hour.

Place the horns on a greased baking sheet, brush them with the egg mixture, and bake in an oven preheated to 220°C (425°F or Mark 7) for 15 to 20 minutes, or until nicely browned and cooked through.

Remove the moulds from the horns and return the pastries to the oven to dry for a few minutes. Allow to cool. When cool, place a little jam in each horn, pipe a rosette of whipped cream on top and sprinkle with the nuts.

MRS. ISABELLA BEETON
MRS. BEETON'S EVERYDAY COOKERY

Strawberry Vol-au-Vent

Strawberry jam may be used instead of meringue to seal the layers of puff pastry together. The case may be filled with any fruit of your choice, cooked or uncooked.

To make one large pastry

	strawberries, sliced and sugared to taste	
75 g	sugar	2½ oz
2	egg whites, stiffly beaten	2
	double cream, whipped (optional)	
250 g	puff dough (*page 167*)	8 oz

Roll the dough into a thin sheet. Cut out an oval piece for a bottom, and three oval rims; prick with a fork, chill for 30 minutes, and bake in an oven preheated to 220°C (425°F or Mark 7) for 20 to 25 minutes.

Make a meringue by beating 60 g (2 oz) of the sugar into the egg whites until the mixture is stiff and glossy. Spread the edge of the pastry bottom with the meringue and press a rim upon it and so continue until the rims are used. Decorate the edges of the case with the remaining meringue mixture. Sprinkle with sugar and return the pastry to a 200°C (400°F or Mark 6) oven. The meringue will not take colour in less than 6 minutes.

When the meringue is delicately browned, remove the pastry case to a serving dish and fill with strawberries. Whipped cream may be added on top. The pastry may be kept several days after baking, reheating it before filling.

MAY BYRON
PUDDINGS, PASTRIES, AND SWEET DISHES

Cream Tart

Farce de Cresme

To make the free-form pastry case shown on page 82, the strips of dough may be arranged on the base to form several compartments. For certain fillings, such as whipped cream or fruits in syrup, the case should be pre-baked. The filling in this recipe is intended to be made in quantity and kept on hand; for one tart, the quantities of cream ingredients may be quartered.

To make one 25 cm (10 inch) tart

8	eggs	8
125 g	flour	4 oz
1 litre	milk	1¾ pints
125 g	butter	4 oz
	salt	
About 100 g	sugar	About 3½ oz
	rose water	
250 g	shortcrust dough (*page 165*) or puff dough (*page 167*)	8 oz

Mix four of the eggs into the flour. When they are thoroughly incorporated, beat in the remaining four eggs, one by one. Heat the milk to boiling point, and pour it gradually into the flour and eggs, stirring constantly. Add the butter and a pinch of salt. Stirring constantly with a wooden spatula, cook the mixture for 6 to 7 minutes or until thick. Pour the thickened cream into a bowl and allow it to cool before covering and refrigerating it. It will keep for about 1 week.

To use the cream, cut about a quarter of it from the mass and work in about 50 g (2 oz) of sugar with a wooden spatula. Roll out the dough to any shape desired, and press strips of dough on the edges to form borders. Spread the surface with the cream filling, sprinkle with sugar, and bake in an oven preheated to 190°C (375°F or Mark 5) for about 30 minutes or until lightly browned. When it is baked, sprinkle the tart again with sugar and with a few drops of rose water.

NICOLAS DE BONNEFONS
LES DELICES DE LA CAMPAGNE

Almond Cream Turnovers

Chaussons à la Crème d'Amandes

The almonds and sugar for the cream filling may be ground in an electric blender and granulated sugar substituted for the cubes. The result, however, will be grainier and less creamy than if the almonds were pounded in a mortar.

To make one large or six individual turnovers

1	egg, beaten with 4 tbsp water	1
	castor sugar	
500 g	puff dough (*page 167*)	1 lb
	Almond cream	
250 g	almonds, blanched (including a few bitter almonds if possible)	8 oz
250 g	sugar cubes	8 oz
6	eggs	6
150 g	butter, softened	5 oz
1 tbsp	orange flower water	1 tbsp

To make the cream, pound the almonds and sugar cubes in a mortar and pass the mixture through a fine sieve; return to the mortar for more pounding whatever will not go through the sieve. Return the mixture to the mortar and add the eggs, one by one, then the butter and orange flower water.

Roll out the dough into a rectangle 20 by 25 cm (8 by 10 inches). Place the cream mixture on one half of the dough and fold the other half over to enclose the cream completely. Brush the edges with a little water, and pinch them to seal in the filling. If desired, the dough can be cut into six rounds which can be filled and sealed in the same way.

Place the turnover on a baking sheet and brush the top with the beaten egg. Bake in an oven preheated to 230°C (450°F or Mark 8) for 15 to 18 minutes for small turnovers, 25 to 30 minutes for a large one, or until the pastry is well puffed and golden-brown. A minute before removing from the oven, sprinkle the top with sugar to make a shiny glaze.

J. B. REBOUL
LA CUISINIÈRE PROVENÇALE

Latticed Cream Tart

Jalousie à la Crème

To make one 15 by 30 cm (6 by 12 inch) pastry

20 cl	pastry cream (*page 166*) or jam	7 fl oz
1	egg, beaten	1
500 g	puff dough (*page 167*)	1 lb

On a lightly floured board, roll out just under half of the dough 3 mm (⅛ inch) thick. Cut into a rectangle 15 cm (6 inches) wide and 30 cm (12 inches) long and put it on a baking sheet moistened with water. Garnish the centre of the rectangle with pastry cream or jam, leaving a 1 cm (½ inch) wide border of dough all round.

Roll out the remaining dough to 5 cm (¼ inch) thick and cut a second rectangle of the same dimensions as the first. Fold the dough in half lengthwise and slash it along the fold at 2.5 cm (1 inch) intervals. The slashes should be 5 cm (2 inches) long, so that when the band of dough is opened they will be 10 cm (4 inches) long. Moisten the edge of the first band and cover it with the decorative band, brush the top with the beaten egg, and bake in an oven preheated to 230°C (450°F or Mark 8) for 20 minutes or until golden-brown. When cool, cut the pastry crosswise into 2.5 cm (1 inch) wide slices.

ANN SERANNE
THE COMPLETE BOOK OF DESSERTS

Crazy Paving

Opus Incertum

To make one 15 by 30 cm (6 by 12 inch) pastry

80 g	castor sugar	2½ oz
10 g	icing sugar	½ oz
200 g	puff dough (*page 167*), turned four times	7 oz

Dust a working surface with 30 g (1 oz) of castor sugar; roll out the dough and fold it in thirds, thus giving it a fifth turn. Sprinkle another 30 g (1 oz) of sugar on the board; roll and turn the dough for the sixth time. Refrigerate for 20 minutes.

Dust the board with the remaining castor sugar and roll out the dough into a rectangle 15 cm (6 inches) wide. Slice the rectangle into three lengthwise, so that you have three strips 5 cm (2 inches) wide. Brush the strips with water and place them one on top of the other. Press lightly with the rolling pin to seal them together. Put the strips on a plate and place them in the freezer for 15 minutes.

Cover a baking sheet with greaseproof paper, dust it with icing sugar, and sprinkle it lightly with water. Cut the dough strip crosswise into slices 5 mm (¼ inch) thick. Place these cut side down on the baking sheet, arranging them at right angles to each other in zig-zag fashion, leaving a space of 2 to 4 cm (¾ to 1½ inches) between them.

Place the baking sheet in an oven preheated to 150°C (300°F or Mark 2). Turn off the oven when you put in the pastry; turn it on again after 10 minutes, and bake for 10 minutes more. The pastry expands as it bakes and the sugar caramelizes, forming the pieces into a single block reminiscent of crazy paving. Cool the pastry on the baking sheet for 30 minutes.

To serve, carefully turn the pastry upside-down on a plate covered with a napkin, and peel off the paper. The guests can then serve themselves by breaking off pieces of the pastry with their fingers.

JEAN AND PIERRE TROISGROS
CUISINIERS À ROANNE

Layered Cheese Pastry

Domashna Banitza

This dish is prepared with dough sheets rolled paper-thin around a long thin rolling pin on a large pastry board or perfectly flat table-top. You can substitute a smooth, unfinished broom handle for the rolling pin.

To make one 20 by 30 cm (8 by 12 inch) pastry

150 g	*feta*, Lancashire or Cheshire cheese	5 oz
3	eggs, lightly beaten	3
100 g	butter, melted	3½ oz
	Dough	
250 g	strong plain flour	8 oz
1 tbsp	wine vinegar	1 tbsp
2 tbsp	oil	2 tbsp
½ tsp	salt	½ tsp

To make the dough, sieve 225 g (7 oz) of the flour into a large bowl. Make a well in the centre and pour into it about 8 cl (3 fl oz) tepid water, the vinegar and oil and the salt. Stir with a round-bladed knife in a circular motion, drawing in the flour from the sides and adding a little more water if necessary to make a rather stiff, not sticky, dough. Knead the dough for about 10 minutes, until smooth. Brush the dough with oil, cover it and leave it in a warm place for about 30 minutes.

Cut the dough into six pieces. Roll out each piece with a thin rolling pin or broom handle, using the remaining flour to keep the dough from sticking. When the circle of dough is as large as a dinner plate, start stretching it sideways with your hands as you roll it around the pin. It will form a very large thin, almost transparent sheet. Place the dough sheets on a cloth to dry slightly, for no longer than 15 minutes.

Brush a roasting tin with melted butter. Crumble the cheese into a bowl, and mix in most of the beaten egg. Place a dough sheet in the tin, crumpling it into folds until it fits. Sprinkle the sheet with melted butter and with some of the filling. Continue until all of the dough and filling are used up, ending with a layer of dough. Brush the top sheet with butter and then with the remaining egg.

Put the pastry into an oven preheated to 200°C (400°F or Mark 6), on the shelf above the centre, and lower the heat immediately to 180°C (350°F or Mark 4). Bake for about 50 minutes, the last 10 minutes at 170°C (325°F or Mark 3). The pastry is done when it is browned on top. Remove it from the oven. Sprinkle it with 1 tablespoon of water, and cover with a lid or foil for 15 minutes or until the top crust has softened.

Serve warm or cold, cut into rectangular pieces, with tea or—Bulgarian-style—with home-made plain yogurt.

DR. GEORGI SHISHKOV AND STOIL VUCHKOV
BULGARSKI NAZIONALNI YASTIYA

Nut-Filled Pastry Bathed in Fragrant Syrup

Baklava

The baklava recipe that follows is made with walnuts and a syrup flavoured with cloves and lemon. If you wish to substitute chopped almonds or pecans for the walnuts, flavour the syrup with 2 teaspoons rose water and 2 tablespoons brandy or with two cinnamon sticks and two pieces of orange rind.

Makes 30 to 36 small pastries

2 kg	shelled walnuts, finely chopped or coarsely ground	4 lb
1 tsp	ground cinnamon	1 tsp
¼ tsp	ground cloves	¼ tsp
1.15 kg	sugar	2½ lb
500 g	unsalted butter, melted and kept warm	1 lb
45 cl	cold water	¾ pint
1	thin lemon slice with rind	1
2 tbsp	lemon juice	2 tbsp
2	whole cloves	2
12.5 cl	clear honey	4 fl oz
750 g	phyllo pastry, at room temperature (*page 166*)	1½ lb

Place the chopped or ground walnuts in a large mixing bowl. Add the cinnamon, ground cloves, and 250 g (8 oz) of the sugar. Mix well with your hands, and set aside.

Brush melted butter over the sides, corners and bottom of a large rectangular baking tin measuring about 50 by 36 by 5 cm (20 by 14 by 2 inches).

Drape a slightly dampened paper towel over a portion of phyllo to prevent it from drying out while you work with it. Refrigerate the rest until ready to use. Peel off one sheet and lay it flat on the bottom of the tin. Brush with melted butter. When you have stacked 10 sheets of buttered phyllo on top of one another, you have the bottom crust for the baklava.

Sprinkle the tenth sheet lightly with some of the nut mixture. Continue adding buttered phyllo sheets; sprinkle every second sheet with the nut mixture until it is used up.

Preheat the oven to 170°C (325°F or Mark 3). Make the top crust of the baklava with the remaining sheets of individually buttered phyllo, including those you had refrigerated. When you have finished, roll down any buttered edges and tuck them inside the tin.

Brush the top of the baklava liberally with warm melted butter and sprinkle with about 10 drops of cold water. This prevents the phyllo from curling up when baking. Using a sharp-pointed knife, cut only the top layer of phyllo into small diamond or triangle-shaped pieces. Bake for 1½ hours, or until golden-brown.

Make the syrup while the baklava is baking. Combine the

remaining sugar, water, lemon slice, lemon juice and whole cloves in a saucepan and bring to a fast boil. Reduce heat and boil gently for 20 minutes. Remove the saucepan from the heat and discard the lemon slice and cloves. Stir in the honey and set the syrup aside to cool.

When the baklava is done remove from the oven and pour half the syrup slowly all over it. Twenty minutes later slowly dribble the rest of the syrup all over the pastry. Allow the pastry to rest in the tin for 4 hours or overnight before cutting and serving. Do not refrigerate.

When ready to remove the pieces from the tin, remember you cut through only the top layers of the pastry before baking. You must now cut through the entire pastry, including the bottom crust. Using a sharp knife, cut deeply and at least twice, so that the pieces come out cleanly and easily.

ANNE THEOHAROUS
COOKING THE GREEK WAY

Cottage Cheese Strudel
Túrós Töltelék

To fill 350 g (12 oz) strudel dough or two strudel strips approximately 40 cm (16 inches) long

500 g	cottage cheese, sieved	1 lb
3	eggs, yolks separated from whites, whites stiffly beaten	3
60 g	butter, softened	2 oz
175 g	vanilla sugar	6 oz
12.5 cl	soured cream	4 fl oz
1 tbsp	flour	1 tbsp
40 g	raisins	1½ oz
½	lemon, rind grated	½
	salt	
1 tbsp	coarsely ground semolina	1 lb
350 g	strudel dough (*page 166*)	12 oz

Beat the egg yolks with the butter and the sugar, until the mixture is foamy. Slowly beat in the soured cream, flour, raisins, lemon rind and a pinch of salt. Let the mixture stand for 15 minutes. Fold the cottage cheese into the beaten egg whites. Mix this with the yolk and soured cream mixture.

Sprinkle the semolina on the section of the prepared sheet of strudel dough where you plan to put the cottage cheese filling. Spread the filling on top of the semolina. Roll up the strudel, and bake in an oven preheated to 200°C (400°F or Mark 6) for about 40 minutes or until the strudel is crisp and brown. Serve while still warm, cut into short lengths.

GEORGE LANG
THE CUISINE OF HUNGARY

Poppy Seed Strudel
Mákos Töltelék

Although many traditional recipes mix poppy seeds with apricot jam, you will find grated apple a wonderful taste addition. For yet another variation, reduce the quantity of poppy seeds to 125 g (4 oz) and, instead of the apple, use 500 g (1 lb) of pumpkin, diced and cooked. The poppy seeds are cooked before baking so that they do not become hardened during the baking process.

To fill 350 g (12 oz) strudel dough or two strudel strips approximately 40 cm (16 inches) long

250 g	poppy seeds, ground with a pestle and mortar	8 oz
175 g	vanilla sugar	6 oz
2	eggs, yolks separated from whites, whites stiffly beaten	2
1 tbsp	flour	1 tbsp
½	lemon, rind grated	½
90 g	unsalted butter, softened	3 oz
¼ litre	milk, heated	8 fl oz
40 g	raisins	1½ oz
1	apple, peeled, cored and grated	1
350 g	strudel dough (*page 166*)	12 oz

In a bowl, beat the vanilla sugar with the egg yolks until the mixture is smooth and light coloured. Beat the flour, lemon rind, butter and finally hot milk into the egg and sugar mixture. Put the resulting mixture into a saucepan. Bring it gently to a simmer and mix in the ground poppy seeds. When the mixture starts simmering again, remove the saucepan from the heat. Let the mixture cool.

When the mixture has cooled, mix in the raisins, grated apple and stiffly beaten egg whites. If this filling is too thick to spread, add a little cold water.

Spread the filling on the prepared sheet of strudel dough, roll up the strudel and bake in an oven preheated to 200°C (400°F or Mark 6) for about 40 minutes or until crisp and brown. Serve while still warm, cut into short lengths.

GEORGE LANG
THE CUISINE OF HUNGARY

Turkish Strudel

Türkenstrudel

For instructions on rolling a strudel, see page 85.

To make one 45 cm (18 inch) strudel

140 g	unsalted butter	5 oz
110 g	castor sugar	4 oz
5	eggs, yolks separated from whites, whites stiffly beaten	5
1 tsp	finely grated lemon rind	1 tsp
1 tsp	ground cinnamon	1 tsp
70 g	candied mixed peel, finely chopped	2½ oz
70 g	seedless raisins, chopped	2½ oz
70 g	dried figs, chopped	2½ oz
70 g	dates, chopped	2½ oz
150 g	shelled walnuts, chopped	5 oz
	melted butter	
	icing sugar	
350 g	strudel dough (*page 166*)	12 oz

Cream the butter, the castor sugar and the egg yolks until light and fluffy. Add the lemon rind, ginger, candied peel, raisins, figs, dates and walnuts, and mix them together. Then fold in the egg whites.

Roll out the strudel dough to make a large thin sheet, pulling it out until it is transparent. Spread the filling evenly over the sheet, leaving a wide border. Fold three sides of the border over the filling, and roll up the dough, enclosing the filling completely. Place the strudel on a greased baking tray, curving the strudel if necessary to fit, and brush the top with melted butter. Bake in an oven preheated to 190°C (375°F or Mark 5) for about 40 minutes or until golden-brown and crisp. Serve warm or cold, sprinkled with icing sugar.

EVA BAKOS
MEHLSPEISEN AUS ÖSTERREICH

Baklava

To make 25 small cakes

500 g	butter, melted	1 lb
250 g	shelled walnuts, chopped	8 oz
350 g	honey	12 oz
¼ litre	water	8 fl oz
20	sheets phyllo pastry (*page 166*)	20

Spread out five sheets of pastry, one on top of the other. Place a large square tin in the centre of these and cut around it, through all of the sheets. Place the sheets in the tin, one at a time, brushing each generously with melted butter. Sprinkle

with all of the trimmings and brush the trimmings with butter. Repeat with five more sheets of pastry.

Spread the walnuts evenly in the tin and continue adding layers of pastry until all of the sheets have been used, adding the last trimmings beneath the last sheet.

With a sharp knife, score the top of the pastry diagonally into five sections in each direction, making 25 diamond-shaped cakes. Allow to rest for 2 hours.

Preheat the oven to 230°C (450°F or Mark 8), then reduce the temperature to 180°C (350°F or Mark 4). Pour one-third of the remaining butter over the pastry and bake for 7 minutes. Pour over another third of the remaining butter, reduce the oven temperature to 170°C (325°F or Mark 3), and bake for 20 minutes longer. Remove the baklava from the oven.

Drain off all excess butter and return the pastry to the oven to bake and crisp for 5 minutes. Again drain off any excess butter and bake for 5 minutes longer.

In a saucepan, combine the honey and water and boil to a thick syrup. Pour the hot syrup around the edge of the tin and over the pastry. Let the baklava cool and cut it into diamonds so that the pieces can absorb the syrup before serving.

ANN SERANNE
THE COMPLETE BOOK OF DESSERTS

Apple Strudel

Apfelstrudel

For instructions on rolling and stretching strudel dough, see the demonstration on page 58.

To make three 40 cm (16 inch) strudels

2 kg	apples, peeled, cored and thinly sliced	4 lb
200 g	butter, melted	7 oz
150 g	breadcrumbs, browned in 60 g (2 oz) butter	5 oz
125 g	shelled walnuts, chopped	4 oz
70 g	raisins	2½ oz
150 g	sugar	5 oz
¼ tsp each	ground cinnamon and cloves	¼ tsp each
½	lemon, juice strained	½
1 tbsp	rum	1 tbsp
12.5 cl	double cream, whipped	4 fl oz
	icing sugar	
500 g	strudel dough (*page 166*)	1 lb

Roll out the dough on a large floured board or cloth, and stretch it with your hands until it is almost transparent. Sprinkle with half of the melted butter. Then, leaving a 2.5 cm (1 inch) border, cover half of the dough with the apples, mixed with the browned breadcrumbs, walnuts, raisins, sugar, cinnamon, cloves, lemon juice and rum. Pour over a little more of the melted butter, then spread with the cream.

Roll up the strudel, starting with the side covered by the filling, so that the filling is completely enclosed in the pastry. Brush off any excess flour. Cut the strudel into three long sections, and place them on greased baking trays. Bake in an oven preheated to 180°C (350°F or Mark 4) for 30 to 40 minutes, basting occasionally with the remaining melted butter. The strudel is done when it is golden-brown. Sprinkle thickly with icing sugar and serve hot or cold.

HANS KARL ADAM
DAS KOCHBUCH AUS SCHWABEN

Chocolate Strudel

Schokoladestrudel

To make one 70 cm (28 inch) strudel

100 g	plain chocolate, grated	3½ oz
4	eggs, yolks separated from whites	4
70 g	icing sugar	2½ oz
70 g	unsalted butter	2½ oz
70 g	ground almonds	2½ oz
70 g	sponge finger crumbs	2½ oz
70 g	seedless raisins	2½ oz
12.5 cl	double cream	4 fl oz
2 tbsp	vanilla sugar	2 tbsp
¼ litre	milk, heated to boiling	8 fl oz
350 g	strudel dough (*page 166*)	12 oz

Cream the egg yolks, icing sugar and butter until the mixture is light and fluffy. Add the almonds, sponge finger crumbs, chocolate, raisins and cream, and mix thoroughly. Whisk the egg whites with the vanilla sugar until stiff, and fold them into the chocolate mixture.

Roll out the dough very thinly on a floured cloth and then stretch the dough until it is almost transparent. Trim the edges. Spread the filling evenly over the pastry sheet, leaving a 5 cm (2 inch) border on three sides, and a 10 cm (4 inch) border on the side furthest away from you. Fold the three narrow dough edges over the filling and roll up the strudel, gradually lifting the cloth underneath to help.

With the join underneath, slide the strudel on to a greased baking tray, curving the strudel to fit the tray if necessary. Bake in an oven preheated to 190°C (375°F or Mark 5) for about 30 minutes or until nicely browned and crisp. Pour the hot milk over the strudel and leave it in the oven for a few more minutes for the milk to be absorbed. Serve warm or cold, sprinkled with icing sugar.

EVA BAKOS
MEHLSPEISEN AUS ÖSTERREICH

Éclairs

Éclairs au Café ou au Chocolat

To make 12 éclairs

35 cl	pastry cream (*page 166*), flavoured with coffee or chocolate	12 fl oz
15 cl	fondant icing (*page 92*) or glacé icing (*page 94*), flavoured with coffee or chocolate	¼ pint
150 g	choux dough (*page 166*)	5 oz

With a piping bag, pipe on to a baking sheet strips of choux dough about 8 to 9 cm (3¼ to 3½ inches) long and as thick as your little finger. Bake in an oven preheated to 200°C (400°F or Mark 6) for 20 minutes or until puffed and golden-brown. Allow to cool. Slit the éclairs along one side, and fill them with the pastry cream. Glaze them with an icing of the same flavour as the cream.

HENRI-PAUL PELLAPRAT
LE NOUVEAU GUIDE CULINAIRE

Croquembouche

Pièce-montée ou Croquembouche

A demonstration of how to assemble a croquembouche is shown on page 90.

To make one large choux ball pyramid

½ litre	pastry cream (*page 166*), flavoured with 2 tbsp rum	16 fl oz
250 g	sugar	8 oz
500 g	choux dough (*page 166*)	1 lb

On an ungreased baking sheet, make small balls of choux dough with a spoon. Bake them in an oven preheated to 200°C (400°F or Mark 6) for 20 minutes or until they are puffed and golden-brown. Allow them to cool completely.

When the choux balls are cold, fill them with the pastry cream, using a piping bag or slitting the balls close to the base.

Dissolve the sugar over a medium heat with 2 tablespoons of water, and boil until the syrup is a light golden, caramel colour. Remove from the heat. Dip the top of each filled choux ball in turn into the hot caramel, and arrange the balls on a serving dish, forming tiers of decreasing size. The caramel will harden and hold the pyramid together.

NICOLE VIELFAURE AND A. CHRISTINE BEAUVIALA
FÊTES, COUTUMES ET GÂTEAUX

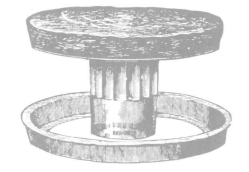

Choux Cake with Almond Cream and Strawberries

To make one 22 to 25 cm (9 to 10 inch) pastry

	Almond cream and strawberry filling	
90 g	almonds, toasted and ground	3 oz
500 g	strawberries, sliced	1 lb
¼ litre	milk	8 fl oz
1½ tbsp	cornflour	1½ tbsp
125 g	light brown sugar	4 oz
1	egg, lightly beaten with 1 egg yolk	1
1 tsp	vanilla extract	1 tsp
1¼ litre	whipping or double cream	8 fl oz
1 tbsp	almond liqueur (optional)	1 tbsp
	Choux dough	
¼ litre	water	8 fl oz
6 tbsp	unsalted butter	6 tbsp
	salt	
About 5 tbsp	sugar	About 5 tbsp
1	lemon, rind grated	1
125 g	flour	4 oz
5	large eggs	5

To make the dough, combine the water, butter, a pinch of salt, 1 tablespoon of the sugar and the lemon rind in a heavy saucepan. Bring to a rolling boil over a medium heat and pour in all the flour at once. Keeping the pan over heat, stir vigorously with a wooden spoon until the ingredients merge into a smooth, pasty ball. Keep spreading and stirring until the mixture firms and dries. A covering film of paste on the bottom of the pan will indicate that the dough is dry enough.

Remove from the heat, let cool a moment, then stir in the five eggs, one at a time. Each egg added will cause the mass to break apart but vigorous stirring will return it to cohesion.

Oil or butter a soufflé dish or metal tin with straight sides. Spoon in the paste and bake in an oven preheated to 200°C (400°F or Mark 6) for 50 minutes. Remove from the oven and turn out the pastry cake. Carefully slice off the top of

the pastry cake and remove all of the soft undercooked dough from both the top and the base. Place the cut-out lid on a sheet of greaseproof paper and return both sections of the cake to the oven for 10 minutes. Brush the top of the cake lid with a little water and sprinkle the remaining sugar over it. Place it briefly under the grill, to crystallize the sugar. Cool to room temperature before filling.

To make the almond cream filling, scald the milk and pour it over the combined cornflour and brown sugar. Whisk the milk mixture into the beaten egg, then return this custard to a gentle heat and continue whisking without boiling until it thickens.

Add the vanilla and the ground almonds. Chill. When the custard is cool, whip the whipping or double cream and fold it into the custard along with the optional liqueur.

Fill the bottom of the cake with the almond cream, heap on the sliced strawberries, and replace the lid on the top.

JUDITH OLNEY
SUMMER FOOD

Choux Tart

Gâteau St. Honoré

This tart is named after the seventh-century bishop of Amiens, Honoré, now the patron saint of pastrycooks.

The filling of pastry cream with beaten egg whites is known as *crème St. Honoré*. Whipped cream may be used as a filling instead, and pastry cream as the filling for the choux balls. Also, the small balls may be decorated with candied cherries.

To make one 25 cm (10 inch) tart

1	egg, beaten with 2 tbsp milk	1
30 cl	double cream, whipped	½ pint
290 g	sugar	9½ oz
1 tbsp	powdered gelatine	1 tbsp
¾ litre	pastry cream (*page 166*)	1¼ pints
6	egg whites	6
	glacé cherries (optional)	
250 g	rich shortcrust dough (*page 165*)	8 oz
500 g	choux dough (*page 166*)	1 lb

Roll out the rich shortcrust dough 5 mm (¼ inch) thick and cut it in a circle, using a 25 cm (10 inch) plate as a guide. Form an edge of choux dough about the thickness of a thumb all around the circle. Brush the top of the choux dough ring with the egg and milk mixture.

Bake this in an oven preheated to 200° to 220°C (400° to 425°F or Mark 6 to 7) for 25 to 30 minutes or until the choux circle has puffed up and the whole tart is brown.

Next make some small choux balls. Drop walnut-sized balls of the choux dough on to a dampened baking sheet, leaving a space of about 5 cm (2 inches) between them. Brush the tops with the egg and milk mixture and bake them in an oven preheated to 200°C (400°F or Mark 6) for 20 minutes, or until the balls are puffed, brown and crisp. Cool on a wire rack. When the choux balls are cold, fill them with pastry cream or with the whipped cream.

Make some caramel by mixing 250 g (8 oz) of the sugar with 10 cl (3½ fl oz) of water in a heavy saucepan. Let the sugar dissolve over a medium heat, and boil the syrup over a high heat until it thickens and turns golden. Dip the filled choux balls into the caramel and arrange them on the choux pastry edge, sticking them with the caramel.

Make the pastry cream. Soften the gelatine in 2 tablespoons of cold water and add it to the pastry cream while it is still hot. Beat the egg whites until stiff, adding the remaining sugar during the last few minutes of beating. Fold them into the pastry cream. Fill the centre of the tart with this, putting a small amount into a pastry bag with a fancy tube to decorate the top. Glacé cherries can be used to decorate the tops of the small balls if wished.

LOUIS DIAT
FRENCH COOKING FOR AMERICANS

Choux Balls with Chocolate Sauce
Profiteroles au Chocolat

As an alternative to the chocolate sauce, these choux balls can be used to make "religieuses", as in the demonstration on page 89. Two choux balls are filled with sweetened whipped cream. They are stacked and iced with coffee-flavoured fondant (page 92) or glacé icing (page 94). For serving with chocolate sauce, the balls may instead be filled with ice cream.

To make 12 choux balls

35 cl	pastry cream (*page 166*) or sweetened whipped cream	12 fl oz
125 g	choux dough (*page 166*)	4 oz
	Hot chocolate sauce	
150 g	plain chocolate	5 oz
10 cl	water	3½ fl oz
1 tsp	cornflour, dissolved in 1 tsp water	1 tsp
30 g	butter	1 oz

On a baking sheet, form 12 small balls of the choux dough. Bake in an oven preheated to 200°C (400°F or Mark 6) for 20 minutes or until well puffed and browned. Allow the balls to cool. Slit them close to the base, and with a spoon or a piping bag, fill them with the pastry cream.

Melt the chocolate with the water in a bowl over hot water. When it is melted and syrupy, stir in the dissolved cornflour and allow the sauce to thicken for a minute or two. Stir in the butter until it is melted.

Arrange the filled choux balls on a serving dish or on individual plates. Cover them with the hot chocolate sauce and serve immediately.

HENRI-PAUL PELLAPRAT
LE NOUVEAU GUIDE CULINAIRE

Spanish Fritters
Churos

These delicious and very special fritters are usually eaten for breakfast in Spain—breakfast consisting merely of a cup of chocolate or coffee, in which the Spaniard dips his *churos*. The *churos* are suitable as a light luncheon sweet, and their peculiar shape makes them both attractive and novel.

To make about six fritters

30 cl	water	½ pint
60 g	butter, cut into small pieces	2 oz
	salt	
150 g	flour	5 oz
3	large eggs, or 4 small ones, lightly beaten	3
½ tsp	vanilla extract or 2 tsp lemon juice, rum, or orange flower water	½ tsp
	oil for deep frying	
	sugar	

Put the water and the butter in a small saucepan with a pinch of salt. Stir until the butter melts. As soon as the liquid is boiling, remove the saucepan from the heat, add the flour and stir vigorously with a wooden spoon, until the mixture is a perfectly smooth paste. Now replace the pan on a low heat and stir till the paste no longer clings to the pan or to the spoon. Then add the eggs, one at a time, mixing thoroughly so that the paste absorbs them. Add the flavouring and, when the paste is sufficiently firm, put a little of it in a piping bag used for icing cakes, with a piping funnel about 1 cm (½ inch) wide.

Drop the mixture into a deep frying pan of hot oil in long lengths of about 30 cm (12 inches) and fry till a light golden colour. The *churos* will curl up as they are cooked, and swell out to about 2.5 cm (1 inch) in thickness. As soon as they are done, the *churos* should be removed from the oil and drained on a cloth in the oven. Serve hot, sprinkled with sugar.

COUNTESS MORPHY (EDITOR)
RECIPES OF ALL NATIONS

Yorkshire Mint Pasty

To make one large pasty

30 g	mint leaves, finely chopped	1 oz
100 g	currants	3½ oz
100 g	raisins	3½ oz
60 g	candied mixed peel, finely chopped	2 oz
60 g	brown sugar	2 oz
30 g	butter	1 oz
½ tsp	grated nutmeg or ground mixed spice	½ tsp
250 g	shortcrust dough (*page 165*)	8 oz

Roll out the dough about 5 mm (¼ inch) thick, and trim it into a large round. Put the rolled dough on to a baking sheet. On one half of the round, place a layer of half of the currants, raisins and candied peel. Sprinkle with the mint, then with the brown sugar. Make another layer of the remaining currants, raisins and peel. Dot with the butter and sprinkle on the grated nutmeg or ground mixed spice.

Wet the edges of the dough. Turn the plain half over to cover the fruit. Pinch the edges of the dough together. Bake in an oven preheated to 180°C (350°F or Mark 4) for about 30 minutes or until browned. Serve hot or cold.

FLORENCE WHITE (EDITOR)
GOOD THINGS IN ENGLAND

Frying Pan Pastry

Flarntårta

The pastry layers may be baked ahead of time. To retain their crispness, store them in an airtight container. If desired, serve the pastry with hot chocolate sauce (*made as in the demonstration on page 10*). Or spread each layer with melted chocolate before assembling.

To make one 25 cm (10 inch) three-layer pastry

125 g	butter	4 oz
125 g	hazelnuts or blanched almonds, finely chopped	4 oz
100 g	sugar	3½ oz
2 tbsp	milk	2 tbsp
2 tbsp	flour	2 tbsp
1 litre	vanilla ice cream or 30 cl (½ pint) double cream, whipped and flavoured with rum or cognac if desired	1¾ pints

Preheat the oven to 200°C (400°F or Mark 6), and butter a cast-iron frying pan.

In a small saucepan, melt the butter over a low heat. Add the nuts, sugar, milk and flour. Bring to the simmer, stirring constantly. Do not let the mixture boil. When it reaches the simmer, remove it from the heat.

Spread one-third of the batter in the buttered frying pan. Bake for about 10 minutes, or until the pastry layer is golden-brown. Cool the frying pan on a wire rack for a few minutes. Using a long, slender spatula, remove the layer when somewhat hardened but before it is too crisp. Bake two more layers the same way. Let them all cool completely.

Just before serving, assemble the pastry with ice cream or whipped cream between the layers.

GÖREL KRISTINA NÄSLUND
SWEDISH BAKING

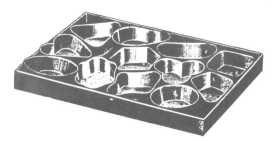

Almond Crumble

Sbrisolona

Though *sbrisolona* is a Mantuan dish, over the past ten years it has become a favourite throughout Italy. A successful *sbrisolona* should be soft and crumbly, for it is not cut with a knife, but broken into pieces. Some cooks prefer to leave the almonds whole and add a little aniseed.

To make one 25 cm (10 inch) pastry

200 g	almonds, blanched and chopped	7 oz
300 g	cornmeal	10 oz
100 g	flour	3½ oz
2	egg yolks	2
100 g	sugar	3½ oz
100 g	butter or lard, slightly softened	3½ oz
½ tsp	vanilla extract	½ tsp

Place the almonds, cornmeal, flour, egg yolks, sugar, butter and vanilla in a mixing bowl. Mix all of the ingredients together without blending them too much. The mixture needs only to hold together. Butter a pie dish, and pour in the mixture to a depth of about 2 cm (¾ inch). Watching over it carefully, bake the *sbrisolona* in an oven preheated to 200°C (400°F or Mark 6) for 1 to 1½ hours or until a skewer inserted into the centre comes out clean.

RENZO DALL'ARA AND EMILIO FANIN
MANGIAR MANTOVANO

Almond Pastry Cake

Kopenhághi

This rich pastry cake bears the name of the capital city of Denmark because it was created by the royal Greek baker to honour the Danish King George I upon his coronation as the King of Greece in 1863.

The pastry has a shortbread crust on the bottom, sponge cake with crushed almonds in the centre, and phyllo pastry sheets on top. After baking the entire pastry is bathed in a flavourful syrup. This is a time-consuming and expensive, but truly exquisite, dessert. It easily serves 30 people and can be made ahead of time for a party.

To make one 36 by 25 cm (14 by 10 inch) cake

325 g	almonds, blanched, toasted and finely chopped	11 oz
8	eggs, yolks separated from whites, at room temperature	8
125 g	sugar	4 oz
1 tsp	baking powder	1 tsp
1 tsp	ground cinnamon	1 tsp
1 tsp	almond extract	1 tsp
1 tbsp	cognac	1 tbsp
125 g	unsalted butter, melted and kept warm	4 oz
225 g	phyllo pastry, (*page 166*) at room temperature	8 oz
	Syrup	
90 cl	water	1½ pints
700 g	sugar	1½ lb
1	stick cinnamon	1
8	cloves	8
4	thin slices orange with rind	4
4	thin slices lemon with rind	4
1 tsp	lemon juice	1 tsp
	Shortbread crust	
225 g	unsalted butter, at room temperature	8 oz
60 g	icing or castor sugar	2 oz
2	egg yolks, at room temperature	2
½	orange, rind grated	½
1 tbsp	cognac	1 tbsp
½ tsp	vanilla extract	½ tsp
175 g	flour	6 oz

To make the shortbread crust, cream the butter and the sugar in the bowl of an electric mixer at medium speed for several minutes or until light and fluffy. Beat in the egg yolks and continue beating for another 10 minutes. Add the grated orange rind, cognac and vanilla, and beat for 5 minutes.

Stir in the flour gradually, mixing with your hand, or the dough hook of the mixer, to make a very soft dough. Knead the dough for 10 minutes on a floured surface or for 4 minutes in the mixer bowl if you are using the dough hook.

Lay the soft pastry dough in a buttered baking tin. Pat evenly and smoothly. Prick well with a fork and bake in an oven preheated to 180°C (350°F or Mark 4) for 15 minutes or until lightly golden. Remove the tin from the oven and allow the crust to cool in the tin.

To make the sponge cake filling, beat the egg yolks in the large mixing bowl of an electric mixer for 5 minutes or until thick and creamy. Add the sugar and the baking powder and beat for 2 more minutes. Fold in the chopped almonds, cinnamon, almond extract and cognac.

In another bowl, beat the egg whites with clean beaters until stiff but not dry. Using a rubber spatula or your hands, gently fold the whites into the yolk and almond mixture.

Pour this cake mixture gently on top of the cooled baked shortbread crust. Lay the phyllo lightly on top of the cake mixture filling, a sheet at a time, brushing melted butter over each sheet. Work quickly and with a light hand so that the cake filling does not lose the air beaten into it. If the sheets of phyllo are larger than the tin and stick up over the edges, butter these edges as well and fold or push them gently down around the mixture to retain the filling before laying on the next pastry sheet (never trim phyllo the way you would a pie crust). This will give your pastry a neat look when baked. Brush the last top sheet of phyllo and the pushed-down edges of the pastry with the remaining melted butter.

Using a sharp pointed knife, cut three slits each about 7.5 cm (3 inches) long through the phyllo, but not into the filling. Sprinkle the surface with 10 drops warm water to prevent the phyllo from curling up while it is baking. Bake in an oven preheated to 180°C (350°F or Mark 4) for 45 minutes.

At the end of that time, insert a thin sharp knife into the centre of the cake right down to the filling. If the knife comes out clean, remove the tin from the oven. If the knife is not clean, bake for 10 to 15 minutes longer. The top of the pastry should be a deep, burnished gold colour. Remove the tin from the oven and set the pastry aside to cool to room temperature.

To make the syrup, combine the ingredients in a large pan and bring them to the boil. Turn the heat down and simmer for 30 minutes. Strain the syrup over the cooled cake slowly and evenly; this will take you 15 minutes or longer. If the cake seems to be swimming in syrup, stop the straining and wait for the syrup to be absorbed. Allow the cake to cool for 4 hours before cutting it into diamond, square or triangle-shaped pieces. Serve at room temperature.

ANNE THEOHAROUS
COOKING THE GREEK WAY

Stuffed Monkey

To make one 20 cm (8 inch) pastry

40 g	butter	1½ oz
60 g	mixed candied peel, chopped	2 oz
30 g	castor sugar	1 oz
60 g	ground almonds	2 oz
1	egg yolk	1
	Dough	
175 g	flour	6 oz
½ tsp	ground cinnamon	½ tsp
125 g	butter	4 oz
1	egg, yolk separated from white	1
125 g	soft brown sugar	4 oz

Sieve the flour and cinnamon into a bowl, rub in the butter, add the yolk of the egg and then the sugar, and knead to a pliable dough. For the filling, melt the butter and mix in the remaining ingredients.

Grease a deep sandwich tin. Roll out the dough into two rounds. Put one round into the tin, spread with the filling, and cover with the other half of the dough. Brush with egg white and bake in an oven preheated to 180°C (350°F or Mark 4) for about 30 minutes or until lightly browned. Cool in the tin.

FLORENCE GREENBERG
JEWISH COOKERY

Saucer Cake (Saucy Kate)

Coconut meat may be removed from the shell and grated, or scraped out into flakes with a spoon.

To make one 20 cm (8 inch) pastry

200 g	butter	7 oz
500 g	flour, sifted	1 lb
90 g	castor sugar	3 oz
	salt	
About 20 cl	milk	About 7 fl oz
	Coconut filling	
2	coconuts, grated or flaked	2
250 g	sugar	8 oz
1 tbsp	slivered almonds	1 tbsp
2 tbsp each	sultanas and currants	2 tbsp each
6	cardamom pods, seeds removed and pounded	6

Melt 90 g (3 oz) of the butter. Mix together the flour, sugar, a little salt, and the melted butter; add enough milk to make it into a pastry dough. Mix the grated coconut with the sugar, almonds, sultanas, currants and pounded cardamom seeds. Roll the pastry dough very thin, put a layer in a tin plate, sprinkle some of the coconut sweetmeat over the dough, repeat the process, dough and sweetmeat alternately, until there are seven layers. With a knife cut the paste in cross lines, 5 cm (2 inches) apart, not quite through. Put the remaining butter, in lumps, all over the surface. Bake a light brown in an oven preheated to 200°C (400°F or Mark 6)—about 30 minutes.

MRS. J. BARTLEY
INDIAN COOKERY GENERAL FOR YOUNG HOUSE-KEEPERS

Open-Faced Apple Slices

Peaches, plums or cherries can be substituted for apples; these need not be soaked in lemon juice. For darker-coloured fruits, omit the currants, and use redcurrant glaze, substituting redcurrant jelly for the apricot jam.

To make about twelve
9 by 5 cm (3½ by 2 inch) slices

2	large apples, peeled, cored and thinly sliced	2
2	lemons, juice strained, rind grated	2
1 tsp	vanilla extract	1 tsp
1	egg, beaten with 1 tbsp milk	1
75 g	currants	2½ oz
75 g	almonds, blanched and sliced	2½ oz
4 tbsp	sugar, mixed with a pinch of ground cinnamon	4 tbsp
250 g	apricot jam, sieved	8 oz
2 to 4 tbsp	cognac, kirsch, applejack, or calvados (optional)	2 to 4 tbsp
500 g	puff dough (*page 167*)	1 lb

Roll out the dough 5 mm (¼ inch) thick. Trim the edges. Cut the pastry into strips, and place them on an ungreased baking sheet. Chill in the refrigerator.

While the dough is chilling, soak the sliced apples in the lemon juice mixed with the vanilla. Brush the pastry strips with the egg mixture. Drain the apples, and arrange the slices down the centre of each strip, overlapping the slices slightly. Sprinkle with the currants, almonds, 1 teaspoon lemon rind and cinnamon sugar. Bake in an oven preheated to 180°C (350°F or Mark 4) for about 35 minutes, or until the strips have turned golden-brown.

Meanwhile, bring the sieved jam to the boil and stir in the liqueur of your choice. Brush the apples with the jam while both are still hot.

PAULA PECK
THE ART OF FINE BAKING

Cherry Turnover

Pirogui aux Cerises Anglaises

Pirogui are large circular or rectangular pastries, formed by placing the centre of a large circle of dough in a buttered pie plate. The centre is covered with the filling, and the sides are then folded to the centre, forming a symmetrical shape.

To make one 20 cm (8 inch) pastry		
500 to 600 g	sour cherries, stoned	1 to 1¼ lb
20 cl	double cream	7 fl oz
125 g	castor sugar	4 oz
500 g	rich shortcrust dough (*page 165*), made with the grated rind of 1 lemon	1 lb

Roll out the dough and place it in a buttered pie plate, allowing the sides of the dough to hang over the edge. Fill the lined plate with the cherries. Pour on the cream, then sprinkle with the sugar. Fold the edges of the dough over the filling, sealing them where they meet in the centre and trimming them to make a neat regular shape. Prick the pastry top in several places with a knife tip or fork.

Bake in an oven preheated to 180°C (350°F or Mark 4) for 30 minutes or until the pastry is lightly browned.

H. WITWICKA AND S. SOSKINE
LA CUISINE RUSSE CLASSIQUE

Almond and Pastry-Strip Tart

Torta di Mandorle e Tagliatelle

To make one 20 cm (8 inch) square pastry		
300 g	almonds	10 oz
300 g	sugar	10 oz
300 g	butter	10 oz
250 g	rich shortcrust dough (*page 165*), using 1 egg yolk	8 oz

Roll out the dough and cut it into very thin strips or *tagliatelle*. Blanch the almonds in a pan of boiling water for at least 5 minutes, peel them and chop them fine. Mix them with the sugar. Butter a square baking tin and place a thin layer of the *tagliatelle* in it, then a layer of almonds. Dot with butter. Continue to make these layers until the ingredients are used up, ending with a layer of *tagliatelle* dotted with butter.

Place in an oven preheated to 180°C (350°F or Mark 4) and bake for about 45 minutes, or until the top layer of *tagliatelle* has become slightly pink. Cool the pastry for about 2 hours, then place the tin over a low heat to warm the base slightly and make it easier to remove the pastry from the tin. Turn out upside-down on a plate, then repeat on to another plate so that the pastry is right-side up.

RENZO DALL'ARA AND EMILIO FANIN
MANGIAR MANTOVANO

Sautéed Apple Cake

To make one 20 cm (8 inch) square pastry		
2	egg whites lightly beaten with 2 tsp water	2
60 g	granulated sugar	2 oz
About 30 g	blanched almonds, sliced	About 1 oz
500 g	puff dough (*page 167*)	1 lb
	Apple filling	
2 kg	apples, peeled, cored and sliced or coarsely chopped	4 lb
125 g	butter	4 oz
3 tbsp	sugar	3 tbsp
1 tsp	grated lemon rind	1 tsp

Roll out the puff dough slightly less than 3 mm (⅛ inch) thick. Trim the edges. Divide the dough into two 20 cm (8 inch) squares and four strips 1 cm (½ inch) wide. Place the squares on a baking sheet. Brush one of them with some of the egg white mixture. Arrange the dough strips along the edges to make a border. Chill both squares. Just before baking, brush the plain square with egg white mixture. Sprinkle it with the sugar and the almonds. Bake both squares in an oven preheated to 180°C (350°F or Mark 4) for about 40 minutes or until the pastry is golden-brown.

To make the apple filling, using a large skillet, sauté chopped apples over a medium heat in approximately 125 g (4 oz) of butter, adding more butter if necessary. Sprinkle the apples with the sugar and lemon rind as they cook. Turn them with a spatula occasionally so the apples brown lightly on all sides. Do not stir, or the apples will become mushy. When the apples are tender and lightly browned, remove them from the heat and cool. Pile the apple filling on to the baked, unsugared case. Fit the sugared pastry square on top, sugared side up. Place in an oven preheated to 150°C (300°F or Mark 2) for 15 minutes before serving to let the filling heat through. The pastry may be served hot with whipped cream.

PAULA PECK
THE ART OF FINE BAKING

Irish Baked Apples

Apple Niamh Chinn Oir

To make six pastries

6	apples, peeled and cored	6
125 g	butter	4 oz
4 tbsp	liqueur Irish whiskey	4 tbsp
1 tbsp	honey	1 tbsp
1	lemon, rind grated	1
1 tbsp	sugar	1 tbsp
500 g	puff dough (*page 167*)	1 lb

Mash the butter with the whiskey, honey, lemon rind and sugar. Fill the cored apples with this mixture. Roll out the dough and cut it into six pieces. Place an apple on each piece of dough and wrap the dough around the apple. Place the apples on a baking sheet, and bake them in an oven preheated to 180°C (350°F or Mark 4) for 20 to 25 minutes or until the pastry is golden-brown. Serve hot.

IRISH RECIPES TRADITIONAL AND MODERN

Pumpkin Pasty

Citrouillat

To make one large pasty

	Pumpkin filling	
750 g to 1 kg	ripe pumpkin (depending on thickness of skin), peeled and diced	1½ to 2½ lb
2 tbsp	sugar	2 tbsp
1 tbsp	double cream	1 tbsp
2 tbsp	vanilla sugar	2 tbsp
1 tbsp	milk or lightly beaten egg yolk	1 tbsp
	Cream dough	
500 g	flour	1 lb
½ tsp	salt	½ tsp
1 tbsp	sugar	1 tbsp
1	egg	1
2 to 3 tbsp	double cream	2 to 3 tbsp
10 cl	milk	3½ fl oz

To make the dough, sift the flour on to a pastry board and make a well in the centre. Put in the salt, sugar, egg, cream and milk. Blend all of the ingredients together rapidly with your fingers, and knead the dough for a minute or two to make it smooth. If necessary, add a little more milk or some water. Roll out the dough to about 5 mm (¼ inch) thick and place it on a floured or lightly oiled baking sheet.

Bring a large pan of water to the boil and add the pumpkin pieces. Return the pot to the boil, and immediately remove and drain the pumpkin.

Arrange the pumpkin pieces in rows down the middle of the dough. Sprinkle on the sugar, cream and vanilla sugar. Fold the dough over the pumpkin like a parcel, first the sides, then the ends. Moisten with water or milk to make the edges adhere. Brush the top with milk or egg yolk and place in a hot oven, preheated to 200°C (400°F or Mark 6), for 45 minutes or until the top is golden-brown. Serve warm.

LES DESSERTS DE NOS PROVINCES

Pears in Pastry Cases

Douillons à la Paysanne

To make four pastries

4	pears, peeled and cored, stems left attached	4
200 g	butter, cut into pieces	7 oz
10 cl	white wine, warmed	3½ fl oz
	salt	
3 tbsp	sugar	3 tbsp
300 g	flour	10 oz
	ground cinnamon	
1	egg yolk, beaten with 1 tbsp water	1
10 cl	double cream	3½ fl oz

Add the butter, piece by piece, to the wine, and beat the mixture with a whisk until it becomes creamy. Beat in a pinch of salt, 1 tablespoon of the sugar, and all of the flour, spoonful by spoonful. You will obtain a dough that can be rolled into a ball; leave to rest under a cloth in a cool place for 2 hours.

Mix the remaining sugar with the cinnamon. Roll the pears in this mixture. Roll out the dough 5 mm (¼ inch) thick and cut it into four squares large enough to wrap around the pears. Wrap each pear in a case of dough, leaving the stems sticking out. Brush the pastries with the egg yolk.

Put the pears on a floured baking sheet. Bake them in an oven preheated to 220°C (425°F or Mark 7) for 25 minutes, or until the pastry is golden and the pears are tender. Serve hot with cream.

MARIE BISSON
LA CUISINE NORMANDE

Apple or Fruit Turnovers

To make six turnovers

150 g	stewed apples or other fruit, or fruit jam	5 oz
3 tbsp	castor sugar	3 tbsp
300 g	shortcrust dough (*page 165*), puff dough (*page 167*), or flaky dough (*page 166*)	10 oz

Roll out the dough thinly and cut it into 10 cm (4 inch) rounds. Place the rounds on a floured baking sheet. Put a little of the fruit or jam in the centre of each round. Carefully fold in three sides of the dough so that they meet in the centre to form a triangle. Moisten the edges of the dough and pinch them tightly together to seal them. Brush the top of each pastry with a little water, then sprinkle with castor sugar. Bake in an oven preheated to 180°C (350°F or Mark 4) for about 35 minutes or until lightly browned.

COUNTESS MORPHY
SWEETS AND PUDDINGS

Apple Turnover

Feuilleté aux Pommes

To make one 20 by 15 cm (8 by 6 inch) pastry

6	apples (reinettes or pippins), peeled, quartered, cored and sprinkled with lemon juice	6
30 g	sugar	1 oz
80 g	butter	3 oz
30 cl	pastry cream (*page 166*)	½ pint
1	egg, beaten	1
	icing sugar	
¼ litre	double cream, slightly sweetened	8 fl oz
500 g	puff dough (*page 167*)	1 lb

Place the apples in a pie dish with the sugar and butter. Bake in an oven preheated to 220°C (425°F or Mark 7) for 15 minutes (the sugar should caramelize slightly).

Roll out the dough as thinly as possible. Spread the pastry cream over half of it, and arrange the apples on top of the pastry cream. Fold over the other half of the dough and seal the edges. Decorate with scraps of dough if desired, and glaze with the beaten egg. Bake for 20 minutes or until puffed and golden-brown, sprinkling with icing sugar towards the end of the baking time.

Serve very hot, accompanied by cold, thick cream.

LA REYNIÈRE
200 RECETTES DES MEILLEURES CUISINIÈRES DE FRANCE

Apricot Torte

Tort Morelowy Krakowski

This is an excellent "dry" torte, that gets better as it waits. It can be prepared three or four days ahead of time.

To make one 4-layer 20 cm (8 inch) pastry

300 g	apricot jam, melted	10 oz
5	egg whites, stiffly beaten	5
5 tbsp	sugar	5 tbsp
50 g	blanched almonds, halved or chopped (optional)	2 oz
	Apricot glaze (optional)	
120 g	apricot jam, sieved	4 oz
200 g	castor sugar	7 oz
1 tbsp	lemon juice	1 tbsp
	Dough	
250 g	flour	8 oz
200 g	butter	7 oz
100 g	castor sugar	3½ oz
3	egg yolks	3
1 tbsp	vinegar	1 tbsp

To make the dough, sift the flour and cut in the butter until the mixture is crumbly. Add the sugar, egg yolks and vinegar. Work the mixture on a board quickly, and when it forms a smooth dough, wrap or cover it and refrigerate for 2 hours.

Divide the dough into four parts, roll out each part very thinly, and bake the rounds, one at a time, in a flan ring or sandwich tin, in an oven preheated to 180°C (350°F or Mark 4) for 20 minutes or until golden-brown. Cool.

For the filling, gradually beat the sugar and then the warmed jam into the beaten egg whites. Continue beating until the mixture is stiff and fluffy. Spread this filling between the rounds of pastry.

Decorate the top with the halved or chopped almonds. Alternatively, mix all of the glaze ingredients until smoothly blended, and ice the pastry with this mixture.

Z. ZAWISTOWSKA
Z. NASZEJ KUCHNI

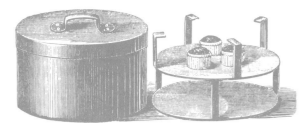

Prune Pastry
Galette Béarnaise
To make one 25 cm (10 inch) pastry

250 g	prunes	8 oz
½ litre	water	16 fl oz
125 g	sugar	4 oz
30 g	butter	1 oz

Orange flower dough

250 g	flour	8 oz
1	egg	1
½ tsp	salt	½ tsp
1 tsp	cognac or fruit brandy	1 tsp
2 tsp	orange flower water	2 tsp
150 g	butter, cut into small pieces	5 oz

Put the prunes in a saucepan with the cold water and 75 g (2½ oz) of the sugar. Bring slowly to the boil and cook over a low heat for 20 to 25 minutes or until the prunes are very tender. Drain the prunes, cut them in half and stone them.

To make the dough, pour the flour on to a pastry board and make a well in the centre. Put in the egg, salt, cognac, orange flower water and butter. Work the ingredients together with your hands to form a smooth dough. Roll out the dough, fold it in quarters, and roll it out again as thinly as possible.

Cut a round of dough just big enough to line the bottom and sides of a tart tin. Butter the tin and line it with the dough. Arrange a layer of prune halves on the dough, and cover the prunes with another thin round of dough. Continue alternating layers of prunes and dough until the tin is full.

Finish with a layer of dough, and seal it to the bottom crust by moistening the edges. Sprinkle with the remaining sugar, dot with the butter, and bake in an oven preheated to 170°C (325°F or Mark 3) for 1 hour or until golden-brown.

LES DESSERTS DE NOS PROVINCES

Country Doughnuts
Ciambelle Campagnole
To make twelve 6 cm (2½ inch) doughnuts

250 g	flour	8 oz
100 g	castor sugar	3½ oz
10 cl	red wine	3½ fl oz
10 cl	olive oil	3½ fl oz

Put the flour and sugar into a bowl and gradually mix in the wine and oil to make a firm dough. Turn it out on a board and knead until smooth. Form it into a ball, wrap it up in a cloth and rest it for 30 minutes.

Grease a baking sheet, unwrap the dough, break off a piece and roll it into a cylinder, joining the ends to form a ring. Repeat until no dough remains. Place the doughnuts on the baking sheet and bake in an oven preheated to 220°C (425°F or Mark 7) for approximately 20 minutes or until they are golden-brown. Eat them hot.

LUIGI VOLPICELLI AND SECONDINO FREDA
L'ANTIARTUSI: 1,000 RICETTE

Lavardin Cakes

Lavardin cakes have nothing at all to do with Lavardin, in the Loire Valley. They came from the south-west of France, via an old pastrycook in Normandy who had specialized, against the dominant French tradition, in cakes which keep. And these do. They are also very much to English taste. Lavardins show off well the flavour and texture of walnuts.

If time is short, there is no reason why you should not make two or three large lavardins, instead of the 20 or 30 small ones. Use a French flan ring, a tart tin with a removable base, or a straight-sided tart tin.

To make twenty to thirty 7.5 to 10 cm (3 to 4 inch) cakes

300 g	shelled walnuts, roughly chopped	10 oz
300 g	sugar	10 oz
3 tbsp	water	3 tbsp
17.5 cl	evaporated milk	6 fl oz
60 g	unsalted butter, cut into small pieces	2 oz
4 tbsp	double cream	4 tbsp
	bicarbonate of soda	

Sweet pastry dough

500 g	flour	1 lb
250 g	castor sugar	8 oz
250 g	butter	8 oz
3	eggs	3

Icing

2	egg whites	2
125 g	icing sugar	4 oz

First make the filling: put the sugar and water into a saucepan, bring to the boil over a brisk heat, and cook, stirring with a wooden spoon from time to time until the syrup reaches the hard crack stage. Remove from heat and quickly stir in the evaporated milk, butter, cream and bicarbonate of soda. Stir until the mixture forms a soft ball, add the walnuts and pour the mixture out on to a marble slab or a sheet of greased paper. It will cool to a soft nut toffee.

While the filling cools, make the dough. Put the flour on to a board and scatter the sugar over it. Make a well in the centre and put in the butter and eggs. Pound the ingredients together with your fingertips until you have a smooth dough. Roll it out thinly and line 20 to 30 small flan rings or smooth-sided tart tins laid on a greased baking sheet leaving a little frill of dough overlapping each edge. Fill each tart slightly over half-full with the walnut mixture. Brush the dough edges with water and fit in lids of dough, which have been pricked half a dozen times with a fork. Take off the surplus dough by running a rolling pin across the tins.

Bake in an oven preheated to 180°C (350°F or Mark 4) for about 15 minutes or until the pastry is cooked but not brown. As with mince pies, the point is to bake these little cakes so that the pastry cooks without the filling bursting through. Remove the lavardins from their rings or tins and cool upside down on a wire rack.

For the icing, set a pudding basin over a pan of boiling water, put in the egg whites and icing sugar, and whisk until they blow up to a fairly stiff meringue, which feels hot but not uncomfortably so. Spread the meringue thinly over the top and sides of the inverted cakes with a palette knife, leaving the pricked surface exposed. Dry overnight in a cool place, or refrigerator, and store in an airtight tin.

JANE GRIGSON
GOOD THINGS

"Drunkards"
(Pastries Soaked in Wine)

Borrachos

To make 10 pastries

3	eggs, yolks separated from whites, whites stiffly beaten	3
250 g	sugar	8 oz
125 g	flour	4 oz
15 cl	sweet white wine	5 fl oz
10 cl	dry sherry	3½ fl oz
4 tbsp	water	4 tbsp
	ground cinnamon	

Beat the egg yolks with 50 g (2 oz) of sugar until the mixture is pale and forms a ribbon. Add the flour and egg whites, and mix thoroughly. Line a shallow baking tin, about 20 by 30 cm (8 by 12 inches), with greaseproof paper, and oil the paper. Pour the mixture into the tin and bake in an oven preheated to 180°C (350°F or Mark 4) for 20 minutes or until the mixture is firm and beginning to brown.

Meanwhile, make a syrup by combining the remaining sugar with the wine, sherry and water. Stir to dissolve the sugar, then bring the mixture to the boil. Allow it to cool.

When the pastry is baked, cool it in the tin and cut it into squares. Pour on the syrup, sprinkle with cinnamon, and leave in the tin until they have absorbed all of the syrup.

MARIA DEL CARMEN CASCANTE
150 RECETAS DE DULCES DE FACIL PREPARACION

Standard Preparations

Basic Shortcrust Dough

To pre-bake or "blind bake" a pastry case, roll out the dough to a thickness of 3 to 5 mm (⅛ to ¼ inch) and use it to line a tart tin or flan ring. Cut a piece of greaseproof paper or aluminium foil slightly larger than the tin, and press it into the tin against the pastry. Fill the lining with dried peas, beans or rice. Bake in an oven preheated to 180°C (350°F or Mark 4) for about 15 minutes or until the edges of the pastry are pale gold. Remove the paper and beans, and continue to bake for 5 minutes for a partially pre-baked case or for 15 minutes for a totally pre-baked case.

To make 750 g (1½ lb) dough

500 g	flour	1 lb
2 tsp	salt	2 tsp
250 g	butter, cubed	8 oz
8 to 12 cl	iced water	3 to 4 fl oz

Sift the flour and salt together into a large mixing bowl. Add the cubes of butter. Rub the butter and flour together with your fingertips, or cut the butter into the flour with two knives, until the mixture has a coarse mealy texture.

Stirring lightly with a knife, sprinkle water over the dough until it just begins to cohere. Gather the dough into a ball, pressing it together with your hands. Wrap the dough in plastic film, greaseproof paper or aluminium foil and chill it for about 15 minutes before using.

Rich Shortcrust Dough

To make 1 kg (2 lb) dough

500 g	flour	1 lb
2 tbsp	castor sugar or icing sugar	2 tbsp
2 tsp	salt	2 tsp
300 g	unsalted butter, softened	10 oz
2	whole eggs or 4 yolks	2

Sieve the dry ingredients together on to a marble slab or pastry board. Make a well in the centre, and put in the butter and egg yolks. Using the fingers of one hand, pinch the butter and eggs together until they are lightly blended. With a spatula, cut the flour gradually into the butter mixture, chopping and blending until the dough is crumbly. If necessary, add a little water drop by drop, to make the dough cling together. Form the dough into a ball, pressing it together with your hands, and wrap it in plastic film or foil. Chill the dough in the refrigerator for at least 30 minutes before rolling it out.

Flaky Dough

This is a type of rough-puff dough.

To make 1 kg (2 lb) dough		
500 g	flour	1 lb
2 tsp	salt	2 tsp
300 g	butter	10 oz
About 20 cl	water	About 7 fl oz

Sift the flour and salt into a mixing bowl. Add a quarter of the butter, and rub it into the flour with your fingertips—or cut it in with two knives—for about a minute or until the mixture looks like breadcrumbs. Add just enough cold water to make the dough cohere. Continue to work the dough until it comes cleanly away from the sides of the bowl. Shape the dough into a ball, wrap it in plastic film or aluminium foil, and refrigerate for about 30 minutes.

On a floured board roll the dough into a rectangle about three times as long as it is wide. Dot two-thirds of the length of the rectangle with a quarter of the butter. Fold the unbuttered third of the rectangle over the centre, then fold over the remaining buttered third. Wrap and chill for 30 minutes. Repeat the rolling, buttering and folding twice more, then roll the dough to make the final folds cohere. Chill before using.

Strudel Dough

This dough can be used in any recipe that calls for phyllo pastry. To make phyllo sheets, the dough may be rolled out in small batches, or cut to size after rolling and stretching.

To make 500 g (1 lb) dough		
300 g	flour	10 oz
1 tsp	salt	1 tsp
17.5 cl	water	6 fl oz
1	egg	1
60 g	butter, melted	2 oz
	vinegar or lemon juice (optional)	

Sift the flour and salt on to a board or into a large bowl. Make a well in the centre. Lightly beat together half the melted butter, the water and egg, and pour this mixture into the well adding, if needed, a dash of vinegar or lemon juice. Stir until all the flour is incorporated and you have a smooth dough,

adding a little more flour or more water as necessary. On a flour-sprinkled board, knead the dough thoroughly for at least 10 minutes, or until smooth, shiny and blistered on the surface. Cover with a warm, inverted bowl and allow to rest for 30 minutes.

Cover a table top completely with a floured cloth. Place the dough in the centre and spread it with a little of the remaining melted butter. Working in all directions, roll the dough out as thinly as possible. Spread with a little more butter, and stretch it with your hands, working carefully all around the table to avoid tearing the dough, until it is very thin and almost transparent. As you stretch, brush with more butter as necessary. Cut off any thick edges before filling and rolling.

Choux Dough

To form choux balls, place teaspoonfuls of this dough on an ungreased baking sheet. The uncooked balls should be about 4 cm (1½ inch) in diameter. For éclairs, fill a piping bag with the dough, and pipe 10 cm (4 inch) strips on to the baking sheet. Bake choux balls or éclairs in a preheated 190°C (375°F or Mark 5) oven for 20 minutes or until the pastry is puffed and lightly browned. Cool on a rack.

To make fifteen 7.5 cm (3 inch) choux balls or 10 éclairs		
12.5 cl	water	4 fl oz
60 g	unsalted butter	2 oz
75 g	flour	2½ oz
½ tsp	salt	½ tsp
2	eggs	2

Put the water in a heavy saucepan over a low heat. Add the butter. Sift the flour and salt on to greaseproof paper.

When the butter has melted, increase the heat to bring the water to the boil. Turn off the heat, and slide all of the flour off the paper into the water. Stir the mixture until thoroughly combined, then stir over a medium heat until the mixture forms a solid mass that comes away cleanly from the sides of the pan. Remove the pan from the heat and cool the mixture for a few minutes.

Break one egg into a bowl and add it to the contents of the pan, beating with a spoon to incorporate the egg thoroughly. Repeat with the other egg. Continue beating until the ingredients are smoothly blended.

Pastry Cream
Crème Pâtissière

This cream may be lightened by the addition of stiffly beaten egg whites or whipped cream. To make chocolate pastry cream, substitute 125 g (4 oz) of plain chocolate for the vanilla bean; to make coffee pastry cream, substitute 2 tablespoons of crushed coffee beans and strain the milk after it has boiled.

	To make about ½ litre (16 fl oz) pastry cream	
125 g	sugar	4 oz
5 or 6	egg yolks	5 or 6
40 g	flour	1½ oz
	salt	
½ litre	milk	16 fl oz
5 cm	piece vanilla pod	2 inch

Mix the sugar and egg yolks together with a spoon, beating until the mixture is thick and cream-coloured. Gradually work in the flour, and season with a pinch of salt.

Heat the milk with the vanilla pod to boiling point. Stirring constantly, pour the hot milk into the egg mixture in a thin stream. Turn the pastry cream mixture into a saucepan and, stirring vigorously, cook over a medium heat until the mixture comes to boiling point. Lower the heat and continue to stir for about 2 minutes, until thick and smooth. Strain the pastry cream and allow it to cool, stirring occasionally to prevent a skin from forming. The cream may be stored, covered, in a refrigerator for 2 days.

Puff Dough

	To make 1 kg (2 lb) dough	
500 g	flour	1 lb
2 tsp	salt	2 tsp
500 g	butter	1 lb
15 to 20 cl	water	5 to 7 fl oz

Sift the flour and salt into a bowl. Cut a quarter of the butter into small pieces and add them to the bowl. Rub the butter into the flour with your fingertips. Add just enough cold water to bind the ingredients, and work them into a ball. Wrap it in floured plastic film and refrigerate for 30 minutes.

Place the remaining butter between two sheets of greaseproof paper and, with a rolling pin, flatten it into a slab about 15 cm (6 inch) square and 1 cm (½ inch) thick. Chill the butter in the refrigerator for about 30 minutes.

Place the dough on a lightly floured board, and roll it into a 30 cm (12 inch) square. Place the square of butter diagonally in the centre of the dough, and fold the corners of dough over the butter so that they meet in the centre. Roll the dough into a rectangle 30 by 45 cm (12 by 18 inches).

Fold the dough in thirds, and give it a quarter turn. Roll the dough again into a rectangle, and fold it again into thirds. Wrap and chill the dough for about 30 minutes. Roll and turn the dough twice more, refrigerate and repeat, giving it six turns in all. After a final refrigeration, it is ready to use.

Whole Egg Sponge Cake

	To make one 20 cm (8 inch) cake	
6	eggs	6
175 g	sugar	6 oz
150 g	flour	5 oz
90 g	butter, melted and cooled (optional)	3 oz

In a bowl, whisk the eggs and sugar lightly together. Place the bowl over a pan of simmering water, the bowl should fit snugly but not touch the water. Over a low heat, whisk the eggs and sugar with a hand whisk or electric mixer until the mixture is lukewarm, about 5 to 10 minutes. Remove the pan from the heat, and without removing the bowl, continue to whisk the mixture until it triples in bulk and falls from the whisk in a thick ribbon, about 20 minutes by hand or 10 by electric mixer. Sieve the flour into the egg mixture in two or three stages, adding it alternately with the butter if using. Fold the flour in gently just until blended.

Pour the batter into a buttered and floured deep cake tin, or into two sandwich tins. Bake in an oven preheated to 180°C (350°F or Mark 4) for 35 to 40 minutes for a deep cake, 20 to 25 minutes for shallow layers. The cake is done when the top is springy and the edges have begun to shrink from the sides of the tin.

Place the tin on a wire rack for 5 minutes, then unmould the cake on to the rack to cool completely.

Separated Egg Sponge Cake

	To make one 20 cm (8 inch) cake	
6	eggs, yolks separated from whites, whites stiffly beaten	6
175 g	sugar	6 oz
150 g	flour, sifted	5 oz
90 g	butter, melted and cooled (optional)	3 oz

In a bowl, whisk the egg yolks with the sugar until the mixture is pale and falls in a thick ribbon from the whisk. Fold in the flour in two or three additions, alternating with additions of egg whites and of butter if using.

Pour the mixture into a buttered and floured deep cake tin, or into two sandwich tins. Bake in an oven preheated to 180°C (350°F or Mark 4) for 35 to 40 minutes for a deep cake, 20 to 25 minutes for shallow layers. The sponge cake is done when the top is springy and the edges have begun to shrink from the sides of the tin.

Place the tin on a wire rack for 5 minutes, then unmould the cake on to the rack to cool completely.

Recipe Index

English recipe titles are listed by categories such as "Almond", "Chocolate", "Filling", "Puff Pastry", "Tart" and "Rolled Sponge", and within those categories alphabetically. Foreign recipe titles are listed alphabetically without regard to category.

General Index/Glossary

Included in this index are definitions of many of the culinary terms used in this book: definitions are in italics. The recipes in the Anthology are listed in the Recipe Index on page 168.

Recipe Credits

The sources for the recipes in this volume are shown below. Page references in brackets indicate where the recipes appear in the Anthology.

Adam, Hans Karl, *Das Kochbuch aus Schwaben*. © Copyright 1976 by Verlagsteam Wolfgang Hölker. Published by Verlag Wolfgang Hölker, Münster. Translated by permission of Verlag Wolfgang Hölker (*pages 107, 155*).

Adams, Charlotte, *The Four Seasons Cookbook*. Copyright 1971 in all countries of the International Copyright Union by the Ridge Press, Inc. By permission of Crown Publishers, Inc., New York (*page 99*).

Almeida, Etelvina Lopes de, *ABC da Culinária*. © 1977 Publicações Europa-América, Lda. Published by Publicações Europa-América Lda. Translated by permission of Publicações Europa-América Lda (*page 143*).

Anderson, Beth, *Wild Rice for all Seasons Cookbook*. © 1977 Minnehaha Publishing. Published by Minnehaha Publishing, 1977. By permission of Beth Anderson, Minnesota (*page 122*).

Armisen, Raymond and Martin, André, *Les Recettes de la Table Niçoise*. © Librairie Istra 1972. Published by Librairie Istra, Strasbourg. Translated by permission of Librairie Istra (*page 137*).

Art of Cookery, Made Plain and Easy, The. By a Lady. The Sixth Edition, 1758 (*page 143*).

Ayrton, Elisabeth, *The Cookery of England*. © Copyright Elisabeth Ayrton, 1974. Published by Penguin Books Ltd., London. By permission of Penguin Books Ltd. (*pages 116, 146*).

Bakos, Eva, *Mehlspeisen aus Österreich*. © 1975 by Verlag Carl Ueberreuter, Wien-Heidelberg. Published by Carl Ueberreuter Verlag. Translated by permission of Carl Ueberreuter Verlag (*pages 154, 155*).

Barker, William, *The Modern Pâtissier*. © William Barker and Northwood Publications Ltd., 1974 and 1978. Published by Northwood Publications Ltd., London. By permission of Northwood Publications Ltd. (*page 93*).

Bartley, Mrs. J., *Indian Cookery General for Young House-Keepers*. Seventh Edition 1935. Eighth Edition 1946. Published by C. Murphy for Thacker & Co., Ltd., Bombay (*pages 126, 160*).

Bates, Margaret, *Talking about Cakes*. © Copyright 1964 Pergamon Press Ltd. Published by Pergamon Press Ltd. By permission of Pergamon Press Ltd. (*page 106*).

Beard, James, *James Beard's American Cookery*. © Copyright 1972 by James A. Beard. Published by Hart-Davis, MacGibbon Ltd. Granada Publishing Ltd., Hertfordshire and Little, Brown and Co., Boston. Reproduced with the permission of Granada Publishing Ltd., and Little, Brown and Co. (*page 124*).

Beck, Simone and James, Michael, *New Menus from Simca's Cuisine*. © Copyright 1979 by Simone Beck and Michael James. First published in Great Britain 1980 by John Murray, London. By permission of John Murray (Publishers) Ltd. (*pages 98, 111*).

Beeton, Mrs. Isabella, *Mrs. Beeton's Everyday Cookery*. © Ward Lock Limited 1963. Published by Ward Lock Limited, London. By permission of Ward Lock Limited (*pages 92, 94 and 150*).

Benoit, Felix and Jouve, Henry Clos, *La Cuisine Lyonnaise*. © Solar, 1975. Published by Solar, Paris. Translated by permission of Solar (*page 130*).

Bergeron, Victor J., *Trader Vic's Rum Cookery and Drinkery*. © Copyright 1974 by Victor J. Bergeron. Published by Doubleday and Company, Inc., New York, 1974. Reprinted by permission of the Harold Matson Company Inc., New York (*page 125*).

Besson, Josephine, *La Mère Besson "Ma Cuisine Provençale"*. © Éditions Albin Michel, 1977, Paris. Published by Éditions Albin Michel, Paris. Translated by permission of Éditions Albin Michel (*pages 135, 146*).

Bisson, Marie, *La Cuisine Normande*. © Solar, 1978. Published by Solar, Paris. Translated by permission of Solar (*pages 130, 162*).

Bonnefons, Nicolas de, *Les Delices de la Campagne*. 1655 (*page 150*).

Booth, Letha (Editor), *The Williamsburg Cookbook*. (With commentary by Joan Parry Dutton.) © 1971, 1975 by The Colonial Williamsburg Foundation. Published by The Colonial Williamsburg Foundation, Virginia. By permission of The Colonial Williamsburg Foundation and Holt, Rinehart and Winston, Inc., New York (*page 129*).

Borer, Eva Maria, *Tante Heidi's Swiss Kitchen*. English text copyright © 1965 by Nicholas Kaye Ltd. Published by Kaye and Ward Ltd., London. First published as "Die Echte Schweizer Küche" by Mary Hahns Kochbuchverlag, Berlin W., 1963. By permission of Kaye and Ward Ltd. (*pages 106, 128*).

Boulestin, X. Marcel, *Simple French Cooking for English Homes*. Published by William Heinemann, Ltd., London 1923. By permission of A. D. Peters and Co., Ltd., Writers' Agents (*page 112*).

Boulestin, X. Marcel, *The Finer Cooking*. Published by Cassel and Company Limited, London, 1937. By permission of A. D. Peters and Co., Ltd., Writers' Agents (*page 141*).

Bozzi, Ottorina Perna, *Vecchia Milano in Cucina*. © 1975 by Aldo Martello-Giunti Editore, S.p.A. Published by Aldo Martello-Giunti Editore, S.p.A. Translated by permission of Giunti Publishing Group, Florence (*page 121*).

British Columbia Women's Institutes, *Adventures in Cooking*. Published by British Columbia Women's Institutes, British Columbia, 1958. By permission of British Columbia Women's Institutes (*pages 116, 118 and 121*).

Brown, Marion, *The Southern Cook Book*. Copyright 1951, by The University of North Carolina Press. Published by The University of North Carolina Press, Chapel Hill. Reprinted by permission of The University of North Carolina Press (*pages 104, 123*).

Buckeye Cookbook: Traditional American Recipes, The. As published by the Buckeye Publishing Co., 1883. Published by Dover Publications, Inc., New York, 1975 (*page 94*).

Byron, May, *May Byron's Cake Book*. Published by Hodder and Stoughton Ltd., London. By permission of Hodder and Stoughton Ltd. (*pages 105, 119*).

Byron, May, *Puddings, Pastries and Sweet Dishes*. Published by Hodder and Stoughton Ltd., London, 1929. By permission of Hodder and Stoughton Ltd. (*pages 131, 150*).

Carnacina, Luigi and Buonassisi, Vincenzo, *Il Libro Della Polenta*. © Di Aldo Martello Editore, Milano. Published by Aldo Martello Editore, Milan, 1967. Translated by permission of Giunti Publishing Group, Florence (*page 127*).

Cascante, Maria del Carmen, *150 Recetas de Dulces de Fácil Preparación*. © Editorial De Vecchi S.A., 1975. Published by Editorial De Vecchi, S.A. Translated by permission of Editorial De Vecchi, S.A. (*pages 99, 165*).

Cavazzuti, Giorgio (Editor), *Il Mangiarfuori: Almanacco della Cucina Modenese*. Published by Camera di Commercio di Moderna, 1965. Translated by permission of Camera di Commercio Industria Artigianato e Agricolture Modena (*pages 139, 142*).

Chesne, Joseph du, *Le Pourtraict de la Santé*. Published in Paris, 1606 (*page 117*).

Comelade, Éliane Thibaut, *La Cuisine Catalane*. © Éditions CLT J. Lanore. Published by Éditions Jacques Lanore, Paris, 1978. Translated by permission of Éditions Jacques Lanore (*page 100*).

Costa, Margaret, *Margaret Costa's Four Seasons Cookery Book*. © Copyright Margaret Costa. First published in Great Britain by Thomas Nelson & Sons Ltd., 1970, also by Sphere Books Ltd., London, 1972, 1976. By permission of Margaret Costa (*pages 102, 109*).

Couffignal, Huguette, *La Cuisine Rustique*. © 1970 Robert Morel Éditeur. Published by Robert Morel Éditeur, 84400 Apt., France. Translated by permission of Robert Morel Éditeur (*page 147*).

Cox, J. Stevens (Editor), *Guernsey Dishes of Bygone Days*. © James and Gregory Stevens Cox, Toucan Press, Guernsey, 1974. Published by The Toucan Press, Guernsey. By permission of Gregory Stevens Cox, The Toucan Press (*page 145*).

Craig, Elizabeth, *The Scottish Cookery Book*. © Elizabeth Craig, 1956. Published by André Deutsch Ltd., London, 1956. By permission of André Deutsch Ltd. (*page 119*).

Curnonsky, *Recettes des Provinces de France*. Published by Les Productions de Paris, Paris (*page 130*).

Dall'Ara, Renzo and Fanin, Emilio, *Mangiar Mantovano*. Consultant: Giulio "Baffo" Ghidetti. © Copyright by Renzo Dall'Ara ed Emilio Fanin, 1976. Published by Litografica Cannetese di Attilio e Giorgio Mussini, Mantova. Translated by permission of Renzo Dall'Ara, Milan (*pages 158, 161*).

Dannenbaum, Julie, *Julie Dannenbaum's Creative Cooking School*. © Copyright 1971 by Julie Dannenbaum. Published by E. P. Dutton & Co., Inc., New York. Also published by The McCall Publishing Company, New York. By permission of John Schaffner, Literary Agent (*page 96*).

Dannenbaum, Julie, *Menus for All Occasions*. © Copyright 1974 by Julie Dannenbaum. Published by Saturday Review Press/E. P. Dutton & Co., Inc., New York. By permission of John Schaffner, Literary Agent, New York (*pages 96, 97*).

Darwin, Bernard, *Receipts and Relishes*. Published by Whitbread & Co., Ltd., London, 1950 (*page 140*).

David, Elizabeth, *Spices, Salt and Aromatics in the English Kitchen*. © Copyright Elizabeth David, 1970. Published by Penguin Books Ltd., London. By permission of Penguin Books Ltd. (*page 140*).

Desserts de Nos Provinces, Les. © Librairie Hachette, 1974. Published by Librairie Hachette, Paris. Translated by permission of Librairie Hachette (*pages 133, 162 and 164*).

Deutrom, Hilda, (Editor), *Ceylon Daily News Cookery Book*. Published by Lake House Investments Limited, Publishers, Sri Lanka. By permission of Lake House Investments Limited, Publishers (*page 126*).

Diat, Louis, *French Cooking for Americans*. Copyright 1941, 1946 by Louis Diat. © Copyright renewed 1969, by Mrs. Louis D. Diat. Published by J. B. Lippincott Company, Philadelphia and New York. By permission of Harper and Row Publishers, Inc., New York (*page 157*).

Dmochmowska-Gorska, J., *Domowe Ciasta i Desery*. Copyright by the author. Originally published by Wydawnictwo "Watra", Warsaw, 1976. Translated by permission of Agencja Autorska, Warsaw, for the author (*page 108*).

Dubois, Urbain, *Cuisine de Tous les Pays*. 4th Edition 1882 (*page 93*).

Duckitt, Hildagonda J., *Hilda's "Where is it?" of Recipes*. Published by Chapman and Hall Ltd., London, 1903. By permission of Associated Books Publishers Ltd., London (*page 100*).

Elisabeth, Madame, *500 Nouvelles Recettes de Cuisine de Madame Elisabeth*. Published by Éditions Baudinière, Paris (*page 134*).

Elliot, Rose, *Beanfeast, Natural Foods Cook Book*. © Copyright Rose Elliot September 1975. Published by The White Eagle Publishing Trust, New Lands, Liss, Hampshire, 1975. By permission of The Eagle Publishing Trust (*page 108*).

Escole Parfaite des Officiers de Bouche, L'. Published by Jean Ribou, Paris, 1662 (*page 148*).

Famularo, Joe and Imperiale, Louise, *The Festive Famularo Kitchen*. © Copyright 1977 by Joe Famularo and Louise Imperiale. Published by Atheneum Publishers, New York, 1977. By permission of Atheneum Publishers (*page 140*).

Fernie, W. T., *Kitchen Physic: At Hand for the Doctor, and Helpful for Homely Cures*. Published by John Wright and Co., Bristol, 1901. By permission of John Wright and Sons Ltd., Bristol (*page 117*).

Gilbert, Philéas, *La Cuisine de Tous les Mois*. Published by Abel Goubaud, Éditeur, Paris, 1893 (*page 136*).

Gouy, Louis P. De, *The Gold Cook Book* (revised edition). Copyright 1948, 1964 by the author. Published by Chilton

Book Company, Radnor, Pennsylvania. Reprinted by permission of the publisher, Chilton Book Company (*page 145*).
Greenberg, Florence, *Jewish Cookery.* © Copyright Florence Greenberg, 1963. Published by Penguin Books Ltd., 1967. First published by Jewish Chronicle Publications, 1947. By permission of The Jewish Chronicle Ltd., London (*page 160*).
Grigson, Jane, *English Food.* © Copyright Jane Grigson 1974. First published by Macmillan, 1974. Published by Penguin Books Ltd., London, 1977. By permission of Macmillan, London and Basingstoke (*page 147*).
Grigson, Jane, *Good Things.* © Copyright Jane Grigson 1971. First published by Michael Joseph, 1971. Published by Penguin Books Ltd., 1973. By permission of David Higham Associates Ltd., for the author (*page 164*).
Guérard, Michel, *Michel Guérard's Cuisine Gourmande.* © Macmillan London Ltd., 1977, 1978. Originally published in French as "La Cuisine Gourmande". © Éditions Robert Laffont S.A., Paris, 1978. Published by Macmillan London Ltd. By permission of Macmillan, London and Basingstoke (*page 149*).
Guinaudeau-Franc, Zette, *Les Secrets des Fermes en Périgord Noir.* © 1978, Éditions Serg, Paris. Published by Éditions Serg, Paris. Translated by permission of Madame Guinaudeau (*pages 95, 109*).
Hájková, Maria, *Múcniky.* © Maria Hájková 1974. Published by PRÁCA, Bratislava and Verlag für die Frau, Leipzig. German translation © 1974 by PRÁCA, Bratislava, CSSR and Verlag für die Frau, DDR-701, Leipzig. Translated by permission of PRÁCA, for the author (*page 110*).
Hartley, Dorothy, *Food in England.* © Copyright 1954 by Dorothy Hartley. Published by Macdonald and Jane's, London, 1954. By permission of Macdonald and Jane's Publishers Limited (*page 134*).
Hawaii State Society of Washington, D.C., *Hawaiian Cuisine.* Published by The Charles E. Tuttle Co., Inc. of Tokyo, Japan. By permission of The Charles E. Tuttle Co. Inc. (*page 135*).
Hutchinson, Peggy, *Old English Cookery.* © W. Foulsham & Co. Ltd. Published by W. Foulsham & Co. Ltd., London. By permission of W. Foulsham & Co. Ltd. (*page 140*).
Irish Recipes Traditional and Modern. Published by Mount Salus Press Limited, Dublin. By permission of Mount Salus Press Limited (*page 162*).
Kamman, Madeleine, *The Making of a Cook.* © Copyright 1971 by Madeleine Kamman. Published by Atheneum Publishers, New York, 1971. By permission of Atheneum Publishers (*page 100*).
Keller, Jean, *Les Pâtisseries et les Bonbons.* © Culture, Art, Loisirs 1979. Published by Culture, Art, Loisirs, Paris. Translated by permission of Culture, Art, Loisirs (*pages 92, 94, 95, 97*).
Kiehnle, Hermine, and Hädecke, Maria, *Das Neue Kiehnle-Kochbuch.* © Walter Hädecke Verlag, (vorm. Süddeutsches Verlagshaus) Weil der Stadt, 1960. Published by Walter Hädecke Verlag, Weil der Stadt. Translated by permission of Walter Hädecke Verlag (*pages 108, 111, 114 and 142*).
Kürtz, Jutta, *Das Kochbuch aus Schleswig-Holstein.* © Copyright, 1976 by Verlagsteam Wolfgang Hölker. Published by Verlag Wolfgang Hölker, Münster. Translated by permission of Verlag Wolfgang Hölker (*page 137*).
Ladies Auxiliary of the Lunenburg Hospital Society, The, *Dutch Oven.* Published by The Ladies Auxiliary of The Lunenburg Hospital Society, Nova Scotia, 1953. By permission of The Ladies Auxiliary of The Lunenburg Hospital Society (*page 106*).
Lang, George, *The Cuisine of Hungary.* © Copyright 1971 by George Lang. Published by Atheneum Publishers, New York. By permission of Atheneum Publishers (*page 153*).
Lemnis, M. and Vitry, H., *W Staropolskiej Kuchni i Przy Polskim Stole.* Copyright by Polska Agencja Interpress, Poland. Published by Wydawnictwo "Interpress", Warsaw. Translated by permission of Wydawnictwo "Interpress" (*page 118*).
Leyel, Mrs. C. F., *Cakes of England.* First published by George Routledge and Sons, Ltd., London, 1936. By permission of Routledge and Kegan Paul Ltd., London (*page 114*).
Lopez, Candido, *El Libro de Oro de la Gastronomía.* © 1979 by Candido Lopez. Published by Plaza & Janes S. A., Barcelona. Translated by permission of Plaza & Janes S. A. (*pages 102, 107 and 118*).
Lucas, Dione and Gorman, Marion, *The Dione Lucas Book of French Cooking.* Copyright 1947 by Dione Lucas. © Copyright 1973 by Mark Lucas and Marion F. Gorman. Published by Little, Brown and Company, Boston. By permission of Little, Brown and Company (*pages 132, 144*).
Lune, Pierre de, *Le Nouveau Cuisinier.* Paris, 1656 (*pages 135, 138*).
Mann, Gertrude, *A Book of Cakes.* © Gertrude Mann, 1957. Published 1957 by André Deutsch Limited, London. By permission of André Deutsch Limited (*pages 103, 104*).
Mardikian, George, *Dinner at Omar Khayyam's.* Copyright 1945 by George Mardikian. Copyright renewed. First published by The Viking Press, New York, 1944. By permission of McIntosh and Otis, Inc., New York (*page 119*).
Mathiot, Ginette, *Je Sais Faire la Pâtisserie.* © Albin Michel, 1938, 1966. Published by Éditions Albin Michel, Paris. Translated by permission of Éditions Albin Michel (*page 112*).
McNeill, F. Marian, *The Scots Kitchen.* First edition 1929. Second edition 1963. Published by Blackie and Son Limited, London. By permission of Blackie and Son Limited (*page 105*).
70 Médecins de France, *Le Trésor de la Cuisine du Bassin Méditerranéen.* Published by Les Laboratoires du Dr. Zizine (*page 127*).
Mengo, António de Macedo, *Copa e Cozinha.* © Celir/Apesar de Tudo. Published by Celir/Apesar de Tudo, Porto, 1977. Translated by permission of Celir/Apesar de Tudo (*page 134*).
Menon. *Les Soupers de la Cour,* Volume 3, 1755 (*page 136*).
Morphy, Countess, (Editor), *Recipes of All Nations.* First published by Herbert Joseph Limited, London, 1935. By permission of Herbert Joseph (*page 157*).
Morphy, Countess, *Sweets and Puddings.* The Kitchen Library, Volume 6. First published by Herbert Joseph Limited, London, 1936. By permission of Herbert Joseph (*pages 133, 163*).
Murray, Freda, *Lacock Tea Time Recipes.* Published by Freda Murray. Edited by Peter Murray (Ed. RIBA Journal). By permission of Freda Murray (*pages 101, 106*).
Murray, Janet, *With a Fine Feeling for Food.* © Copyright Janet Murray 1972. By permission of Janet Murray (*page 103*).
Näsland, Görel Kristina, *Swedish Baking.* © Copyright ICA-Förlaget 1973, Västeras, Sweden. Published by ICA-Förlaget Västeras. By permission of ICA-Förlaget AB (*pages 96, 107 and 158*).
Nietlispach, Madame F., *Tourtes Tartes, Pâtisseries Mets Sucrés.* Copyright 1931 by Otto Walter, Limited, Olten (Switzerland). Published by Édition Otto Walter S. A., Olten. Translated by permission of Walter Verlag AG, Amthausquai, Switzerland (*page 136*).
Nignon, Édouard, *Les Plaisirs de la Table.* Published by the author © 1920. Reprinted by Éditions Daniel Morcrette, B. P. 26, 95270 Luzarches, France, 1979. Translated by permission of Éditions Daniel Morcrette (*pages 130, 136*).
Norberg, Inga, *Good Food from Sweden.* First published by Chatto and Windus, London, 1935. By permission of Curtis Brown Ltd., London (*page 98*).
Nouveau Manuel de la Cuisinière Bourgeoise et Économique. Published by Bernardin-Béchet, Libraire, Paris, 1868 (*page 100*).
Olney, Judith, *Summer Food.* © Copyright 1978 by Judith Olney. Published by Atheneum Publishers, New York, 1978. By permission of Atheneum Publishers (*page 156*).
Olney, Richard, *Simple French Food.* © Copyright 1974 Richard Olney. Published by Jill Norman Books Ltd., London, 1980. By permission of Jill Norman (*pages 129, 132*).
Pascoe, Ann, *Cornish Recipes Old and New.* Published by Tor Mark Press, a Division of D. Bradford Barton Ltd., Truro. By permission of Tor Mark Press (*page 116*).
Peck, Paula, *The Art of Fine Baking.* © Copyright 1961 by Paula Peck. Published by Simon and Schuster, a Division of Gulf & Western Corporation, New York. By permission of John Schaffner Agency, Literary Agent, New York (*pages 124, 160 and 161*).
Pellaprat, Henri-Paul, *Le Nouveau Guide Culinaire.* © Copyright by René Kramer, Éditeur, Castagnola-Lugano, 1973. Published by René Kramer, Éditeur, CH 6976 Lugano-Castagnola. Translated by permission of René Kramer, Éditeur (*pages 149, 155 and 157*).
Pépin, Jacques, *La Technique.* © Copyright 1976 by Jacques Pépin. Published by Quadrangle/The New York Times Book Co., Inc., N. York. By permission of Times Books, a Division of Quadrangle/The New York Times Book Co., Inc. (*page 93*).
Petits Plats et les Grands, Les. © 1977 by Éditions Denoël, Paris. Published by Éditions Denoël Sarl, Paris. Translated by permission of Éditions Denoël Sarl (*page 113*).
Petits Propos Culinaires (Volume 1, February 1979). © Prospect Books 1979. Published by Prospect Books, London and Washington D.C. By permission of the publisher (*page 114*).
Petits Propos Culinaires (Volume 2, August 1979). © Prospect Books 1979. Published by Prospect Books, London and Washington D.C. By permission of the publisher (*page 138*).
Platt, June, *June Platt's New England Cook Book.* © 1971 by June Platt. Published by Atheneum Publishers, New York, 1971. By permission of Atheneum Publishers (*pages 112, 117 and 123*).
Plucińska, I, *Ksiazka Kucharska.* 1st Edition 1926. Published by Wydawnictwo Poznanskie, Poland, 1945. Translated by permission of Wydawnictwo Poznanskie (*page 142*).
Point, Fernand, *Ma Gastronomie.* Translated and adapted by Frank Kulla and Patricia Shannon Kulla. English language edition © 1974, Lyceum Books, Inc., Wilton, Ct., USA. Published by Lyceum Books, Inc., Wilton, Ct., USA. Translated by permission of Lyceum Books, Inc. (*pages 110, 120*).
Poulson, Joan, *Old Thames Valley Recipes.* Text © Joan Poulson 1977. Published by Hendon Publishing Co. Ltd., Nelson. By permission of Hendon Publishing Co. Ltd. (*page 147*).
Read, Miss, *Miss Read's Country Cooking.* © 1969 by Miss Read. Published by Michael Joseph Ltd., London, 1969. By permission of Michael Joseph Ltd., for the author (*page 101*).
Reboul, J. B., *La Cuisinière Provençale.* Published by Tacussel, Éditeur, Marseilles. Translated by permission of Tacussel, Éditeur (*pages 131, 151*).
Reynière, La, *200 Recettes des Meilleures Cuisinières de France.* © Albin Michel, 1978. Published by Éditions Albin Michel, Paris. Translated by permission of Éditions Albin Michel (*pages 133, 163*).
Savarin, Mme. Jeanne, (Editor), *La Cuisine des Familles* (Magazine), No 24, December 3, 1905 (*page 120*).
Schuler, Elizabeth, *Mein Kochbuch.* © Copyright 1948 by Schuler-Verlag, Stuttgart-N, Lenzhalde 28. Published by Schuler Verlagsgesellschaft, Stuttgart. Translated by permission of Schuler Verlagsgesellschaft mbH (*page 110*).
Seranne, Ann, *The Complete Book of Desserts.* © 1952, 1963 by Ann Seranne. Originally published 1964 by Faber and Faber Limited, London. Also published 1967 by Faber and Faber Limited for The Cookery Book Club, London. By permission of Faber and Faber Limited (*pages 151, 154*).
Shishkov, Dr. Georgi, and Vuchkov, Stoil, *Bulgarski Nazionalni Yastiya.* © by the authors 1978 c/o Jusautor, Sofia. First published by Profizdat, Sofia, 1959. Translated by permission of Jusautor Copyright Agency, Sofia (*page 152*).
Slater, Mary, *Caribbean Cooking for Pleasure.* © Copyright Mary Slater 1970. Published by The Hamlyn Publishing Group Limited, London. By permission of The Hamlyn Publishing Group Limited (*page 125*).
Société St. Thomas d'Aquin, La, *La Cuisine Acadienne (Acadian Cuisine).* Published by La Société St. Thomas d'Aquin, Succursale de Charlottetown, Île-du-Prince Edouard, Canada. Translated by permission of La Société St. Thomas d'Aquin (*page 101*).
Theoharous, Anne, *Cooking the Greek Way.* © Copyright 1977 by Anne Theoharous. Published in Great Britain 1979 by Methuen Paperbacks Ltd., London. First published as "Cooking and Baking the Greek Way" by Holt, Rinehart and Winston, Inc., New York. By permission of Methuen Paperbacks Ltd., and Holt, Rinehart and Winston, Inc. (*pages 128, 152 and 159*).
Tibbott, S. Minwel, *Welsh Fare.* © National Museum of Wales (Welsh Folk Museum). Published by the National Museum of Wales (Welsh Folk Museum) Cardiff, 1976. By permission of the National Museum of Wales (*page 115*).
Tita, Dona, *Receitas Experimentadas.* 8th Edition. Published by Editôra e Encadernadora Lumen Ltda., Sao Paulo. Translated by permission of Editôra Rideel Ltda., Sao Paulo (*page 122*).
Tobias, Doris and Merris, Mary, *The Golden Lemon.* © Copyright 1978 by Doris Tobias and Mary Merris. Published by Atheneum Publishers, New York, 1978. By permission of Atheneum Publishers (*page 144*).

Toklas, Alice B., *The Alice B. Toklas Cook Book*. Copyright, 1954, by Alice B. Toklas. Published by Harper and Row Publishers, Inc., New York. By permission of Harper and Row Publishers, Inc. (*page 143*).

Troisgros, Jean and Pierre, *Cuisiniers à Roanne*. © Éditions Robert Laffont, S.A., 1977. Published by Éditions Robert Laffont, Paris. Translated by permission of Macmillan, London and Basingstoke (*pages 135, 151*).

Tschirky, Oscar, *The Cookbook by "Oscar" of the Waldorf*. Copyright 1896 by Oscar Tschirky. Published by The Werner Company, New York (*page 117*).

Vence, Céline and Courtine, Robert, *The Grand Masters of French Cuisine*. © Copyright 1978 by G. P. Putnam's Sons, New York. Originally published in France as "Les Grands Maîtres de la Cuisine Française". © Copyright 1972 Éditions Bordas. Published by G. P. Putnam's Sons, New York. By permission of G. P. Putnam's Sons (*page 141*).

Vielfaure, Nicole and Beauviala, Christine, *Fêtes, Coutumes et Gâteaux*. © Christine Bonneton Éditeur. Published by Christine Bonneton Éditeur, 4300 Le Puy, France. Translated by permission of Christine Bonneton Éditeur (*pages 139, 155*).

Volpicelli, Luigi and Freda, Secondino, *L'Antiartusi: 1,000 Ricette*. © 1978 Pan Editrice, Milan. Published by Pan Editrice, Milan. Translated by permission of Pan Editrice (*pages 122, 127 and 164*).

Wales Gas Home Service, *A Welsh Welcome*. Published by the Wales Gas Board, 1966, Cardiff. By permission of the Wales Gas Board (*page 116*).

White, Florence, (Editor), *Good Things in England*. Published by arrangement with Jonathan Cape Ltd, 1968 by The Cookery Book Club, London. By permission of Jonathan Cape Ltd., London (*page 158*).

Willinsky, Grete, *Kulinarische Weltreise*. © by Mary Hahns Kochbuchverlag, Berlin W. Published by Büchergilde Gutenberg Frankfurt. Translated by permission of Mary Hahns Kochbuchverlag (*page 102*).

Witwicka, H. and Soskine, S., *La Cuisine Russe Classique*. © Éditions Albin Michel, 1968 and 1978. Published by Éditions Albin Michel, Paris. Translated by permission of Éditions Albin Michel (*page 161*).

World Atlas of Food, The. © Copyright Mitchell Beazley Publishers Limited 1974. Published by Mitchell Beazley Limited, London. By permission of Mitchell Beazley Publishers Limited (*page 138*).

Zawistowska, Z., *Z Naszej Kuchni*. Copyright by the author. Originally published by RSW Prasa-Ksiazka-Ruch, Warsaw. Translated by permission of Agencja Autorska, Warsaw, for the author (*page 163*).

Zobeltitz, Martha von, *Das Kasserol: Absonderliche Gaumenletzen aus aller Zeit*. © by Albert Langen-Georg Müller Verlag München. Published by Albert Langen-Georg Müller Verlag, Munich 1923. Translated by permission of Albert Langen-Georg Müller Verlag GmbH (*page 113*).

Zuliani, Mariù Salvatori de, *La Cucina di Versilia e Garfagnana*. © Copyright by Franco Angeli Editore, Milano. Published 1969 by Franco Angeli Editore, Milan. Translated by permission of Franco Angeli Editore (*page 122*).

Acknowledgements and Picture Credits

The Editors of this book are particularly indebted to Gail Duff of Maidstone, Kent; Ann O'Sullivan of Deya, Mallorca; and Jean Reynolds of London.

They also wish to thank the following: Julie Bailey, London; Caroline Baum, York, Yorkshire; Sarah Bunney, London; Dr. M. Burge and Wendy Godfrey, Tate & Lyle, London; Marisa Centis, London; Jennifer Davidson, London; Neyla Freeman, London; Maggie Heinz, London; Marion Hunter, Sutton, Surrey; Frederica L. Huxley, London; Brenda Jayes, London; Maria Johnson, Hatfield, Hertfordshire; Wanda Kemp-Welch, Nottingham; Dr. N. Knowles, British Egg Information Service, London; Mrs. B. Morrison, Ranks Hovis McDougall Ltd., London; Michael Moulds, London; Dilys Naylor, Kingston, Surrey; Jo Oxley, Morden, Surrey; Michael Schwab, London; Cynthia A. Sheppard, London; Dr. R. H. Smith, Aberdeen; Susan G. Smith, London; Anne Stephenson, London; Pat Tookey, London.

Colour separation by Gilchrist Ltd.—Leeds, England
Typesetting by Camden Typesetters—London, England
Printed and bound by Brepols S.A.—Turnhout, Belgium.

Photographers (in alphabetical order):

Tom Belshaw: 10—top and middle, 11—top right, middle right and bottom, 12—middle and bottom, 13—middle and bottom, 15—top right and centre and bottom right and centre, 16, 17—bottom left, 32—top right and bottom, 33, 41—top left and centre, 42—top right and bottom, 46, 47—bottom, 51—bottom, 55—top right and bottom right, 66, 67—top right, centre and bottom.

John Cook: 11—middle left and centre, 14, 15—bottom left, 34—top and bottom right, 35—top, 40—bottom, 41—top right and bottom.

Alan Duns: 4, 9—top, 11—top left and centre, 15—top left, 17—top, bottom right and centre, 18, 26, 27—top left and centre, 30—top, 31—top, 34—bottom left, 35—bottom, 38—top, 40—top, 42—top left and centre, 43, 47—top, 50—top, 62, 73 to 75, 76—bottom, 77—top right and bottom left, 82—bottom, 83—bottom, 88, 89—top and bottom left.

John Elliott: 8—bottom, 9—bottom left, 10—bottom, 20—top, 21—top, 22 to 23, 27—top right and bottom, 28 to 29, 30—bottom, 31—bottom, 32—top left, 38—bottom, 39, 44 to 45, 50—bottom, 51—top, 56 to 57, 60—top left and bottom, 64 to 65, 70, 72, 76—top left, 77—top centre, bottom right and centre, 80—top, 81—top, 82—top, 83—top, 84—bottom, 85—bottom.

Louis Klein: 2.

Bob Komar: Cover, 8—top, 9—bottom right, 12—top, 13—top, 20—bottom, 21—bottom, 24 to 25, 36, 48, 52 to 54, 55—top left and centre, bottom left and centre, 58 to 59, 60—top right, 61, 67—top left, 68 to 69, 71, 76—top right, 77—top left, 78, 80—bottom, 81—bottom, 84—top, 85—top, 86 to 87, 89—bottom right, 90.

All line cuts from Mary Evans Picture Library and private sources.

XXXXXXX

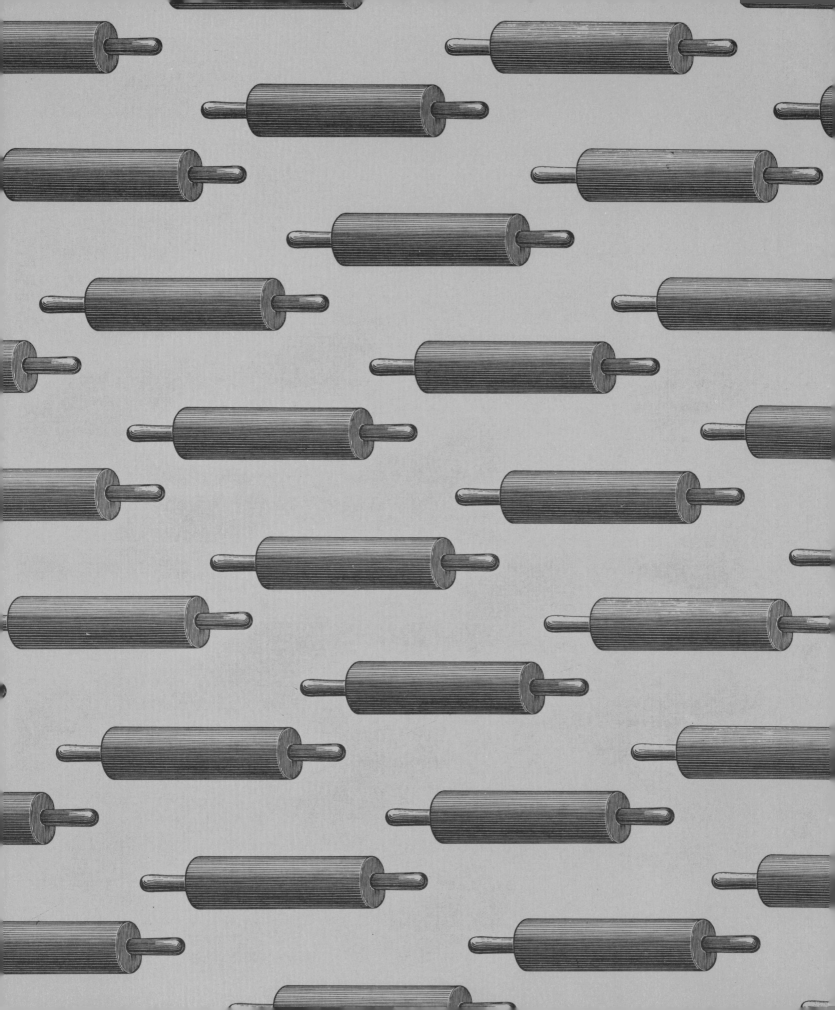